"*Make It Human is an essential read for HR leaders navigating the challenges of (re-)humanising the employee experience amidst technological advancements and productivity pressures. At last, we have a playbook for the future of work!*"

Adrian Seligman, member of the executive board, Top Employers Institute

"*Sarah McLellan challenges the organisations of today that are still operating with little focus on the humans that run them. We have reached a tipping point, as company cultures are cracking under the weight of disruption, and we need to find new ways to lead business by focusing on what we are good at: being human. Sarah explores practical models, new insights and tells personal stories to bring to life her guidance which will enable all of us to contribute to building happier and healthier human workplaces.*"

Liz Rider, organisational psychologist, leadership expert and LinkedIn Top Voice

# MAKE IT HUMAN

## A VISION FOR HAPPIER, HEALTHIER, MORE HUMAN WORKPLACES

### SARAH McLELLAN

\B^b\
**Biteback Publishing**

First published in Great Britain in 2024 by
Biteback Publishing Ltd, London
Copyright © Sarah McLellan 2024

The sketchnotes on pages 86, 149, 216 and 285 are reproduced by kind permission of Kacy Maxwell of Sketchwell.

Every reasonable effort has been made to trace copyright holders of material reproduced in this book, but if any have been inadvertently overlooked the publisher would be glad to hear from them.

ISBN 978-1-78590-875-0

10 9 8 7 6 5 4 3 2 1

A CIP catalogue record for this book is available from the British Library.

Set in Minion Pro, Freight Sans Pro and Skippy Sharp

Printed and bound in Great Britain by
CPI Group (UK) Ltd, Croydon CR0 4YY

*To Stephen, Georgia and Oscar who
make it human for me every day*

# CONTENTS

Preface: Journey to a Climate of Human Growth     ix

PART 1: HORRIBLE WORKPLACES     1

Chapter 1    Unhappy Humans     3
Chapter 2    Workplace Warfare     27
Chapter 3    Culture Is Cracking     51
Chapter 4    Happy Humans (Part 1)     83
Chapter 5    Happy Humans (Part 2)     113

PART 2: HOW TO MAKE IT HUMAN     145

Chapter 6    Body: Foundations for Growth     147
Chapter 7    Mind: Fuel the Organisation     175
Chapter 8    Heart and Soul: Spark Personal     205
              Meaning and Growth
Chapter 9    Get Better at Being Human     237
Chapter 10   How to Lead a Human Workplace     269
Chapter 11   A Climate for Human Growth     305

Resources     315
References     317
Acknowledgements     341
About the Author     343
Index     345

# PREFACE: JOURNEY TO A CLIMATE OF HUMAN GROWTH

Getting to happy, healthy, human workplaces is a destination many of us struggle to imagine, let alone understand how to reach. Our daily experiences of work can leave us feeling isolated, lost, burned-out and lacking in energy or clarity to create something more fulfilling…

- The conditions we're creating are holding us back
- We don't know which direction to take
- We're confused about what progress looks like
- We're failing to develop the skills, systems and tools to help us advance
- And we're stuck in an old model where leaders rule through ego, managers are crushed in the middle and people are an afterthought

We urgently and purposefully need to consider what we as humans need from our work so we can take steps to nurture more human workplaces. This is a destination eminently reachable in our lifetimes and on our planet, if we claim what is uniquely ours and choose to make it human.

To help in this journey, here are some useful resources for you to access and use alongside this book:

## MAKE IT HUMAN MODELS

Four new models are referenced throughout the book to help demonstrate the challenges we face and the opportunities we have to cultivate better experiences of work. There are some black and white illustrations linked to these models in this book. You can view the full, colour sketches of the models and complete a quick, free 'culture cracks' diagnostic (and receive personalised feedback on your culture) here:

The make it human model sketches have been illustrated by Kacy Maxwell of Sketchwell: https://www.sketchwell.co/

sketchnote by
KACY MAXWELL

## MAKE IT HUMAN IN YOUR TEAM AND WORKPLACE: JOIN THE MAKE IT HUMAN CLUB

Join a growing community of leaders, managers and individuals passionate about building better, brighter workplaces and receive FREE insights, stories, tools and exclusive offers to help make it human where you are.

Subscribe to receive free insights straight to your inbox, every two weeks (you can unsubscribe at any time):

For further information and consulting support, head to: https://make-it-human.com/

Together, let's make it human!

# PART I

# HORRIBLE
# WORKPLACES

# CHAPTER 1

# UNHAPPY HUMANS

My daughter is seven years old. She will likely enter the workplace in ten to fifteen years. Picture this...

The year is 2038. People rarely leave their houses to go into a workplace. 'Destinations' have shot up everywhere, turning old offices into on-demand spaces to meet, collaborate and socialise. The destinations look great! More digital tools and zones than you could ever wish for – virtual reality (VR) environments to meet with colleagues 'face to face'; live information streams across sectors and countries providing second-by-second accounts of events and company progress; and integrated work and 'work-out' stations enabling individuals to experience any environment they choose whilst joining virtual meetings and achieving their daily step target.

At home, most houses have similar technology. Individuals come into their work destination maybe once or twice a quarter to synch devices, download the latest software and upgrade systems and to have face time with leaders on the company's goals. The metaverse is fully operational, to the extent that individuals have very little need to physically meet with people outside their immediate families. Social meetups can be achieved virtually, meals out ordered in and experienced with VR restaurant backdrops, games of tennis, football and even swimming completed without leaving the living room.

People have moved out from cities to buy land where they can build extensive homes with space for advanced technology for all elements of life. Work and life are fully intertwined – the concept of a five-day working week has long gone. Teams and companies are more diverse and connected than we ever imagined, but jobs come and go rapidly. Growth cycles are much faster and companies appear and disappear constantly. Without the cost of expensive real estate to house workers every day, companies have generally shrunk in size, relying on flexible workforces to plug gaps when opportunities arise.

And so, individuals are increasingly working for themselves – touting their skills and experiences to multiple employers at once, as they balance contracts. In fact, many larger organisations have adopted talent-sharing programmes – rotating individuals between companies based on skill and organisational need. People are well versed in updating their own websites and skills profiles, asking for recommendations, advertising their capabilities and availability to enable a constant flow of work. On-demand learning and qualifications are freely available. People commonly blend paid-for work with self-driven studying to enable them to keep their profile sharp and relevant.

Autonomy has certainly increased, as people have more control over what they do, when and where. But the risks are intense. With layoffs a regular occurrence, families have gotten used to life without the security of a regular wage, and it is the norm for both partners to work for longer periods of time.

Flexibility is an option, but only for those who can afford to take it. For many, being available and willing to work whenever employers say jump is an everyday reality. Many are working longer hours and longer weeks. Virtual childcare services and surveillance apps to monitor children whilst parents and carers work in other parts of the home have taken off. Screentime is through the roof. There's barely a moment when we aren't connected, via technology, to another person or type of reality.

Fuelled by artificial intelligence (AI) advancements, the industries growing quickly are technology, healthcare (focusing on an ageing population, the rise of new viruses and prevalence of well-being challenges) and logistics and distribution (getting supplies to anyone, anywhere, at any time).

The fast manufacture of products required in smart technology are in high demand, as well as the distribution of convenience goods and fresh produce. Local providers of homegrown produce are popular and apprenticeships in running smallholdings, agriculture and sustainable food production have increased. Larger farms have sold off land to renewable energy providers, as the costs of farming at scale became untenable. Individual homes and families are rewarded financially by governments for living in sustainable ways (recycling, buying from sustainable sources, minimising carbon footprints, growing their own produce, producing their own renewable energy) and this has sparked a resurgence in older traditions and skills – e.g. crafts, cookery, horticulture. The contrast between individually driven actions and scaled automation is an interesting feature. At the other side of the spectrum, drones delivering packages to front doors is a common sight and most warehouses, production and distribution sites are entirely robot operated with minimal human supervision. Creative- and communication-focused jobs have increased, as comfort with using AI in knowledge-based work has grown, and the value humans bring has clearly shifted towards our 'human' skills.

Communication coaches are an emerging feature in organisations, as emphasis moves towards *how* we deliver messages rather than what they include (AI can help with that). Creativity permeates all industries and has been accelerated and democratised through AI – in design, art, writing, music, media creation and production. Today, with easily accessed help via AI tools, anyone could design an animation, create an artistic masterpiece, write a book or become a social media influencer – but the bar for success and impact is higher. Using AI to get *more* creative, produce work faster, diversify and build markets is the opportunity. Hospitality is big – but in new channels and destinations – and providers of education and skill development have grown significantly. As individuals become their own companies, lifelong learning in the flow of work is an everyday necessity.

As for my daughter, she's twenty-two. She completed several work placements as part of her studies in child development and has secured some freelance work providing teaching and tutoring for a global class of nine- and ten-year-olds. She delivers lessons and one-to-one tutoring for children whose parents have chosen, and pay for, additional educational support to accelerate their learning. It's very popular, and she can be online running classes and sessions at all hours. The flex means she can complete her own virtual learning and join remote exercise classes, catch up with friends in virtual spaces and earn a living.

She rarely meets anyone in person. Her work, socialising and fitness are all done through virtual channels. She has a cohort of new virtual academy teachers she shares experiences with online – they're dotted across the globe.

Her experience of starting work is night and day with mine. I went to a workplace most days. Met with people in real-life. Could ask questions about little things – what to wear, what not to say, how to complete processes. I bonded with colleagues through mistakes, funny moments and overcoming challenges. We experienced emotions together

– and, importantly, I could see the impact I had on others, and equally felt the impact people and situations had on me. We developed emotional intelligence, sensing when to adapt or use a different approach. I even made friends, many of whom I still have today, whom I can approach for advice and enjoy spending time with. I learned through observing others, getting feedback following meetings and presentations, joining group training sessions, overhearing conversations and interactions in an office environment.

In this vision of our working world, it would be difficult to capture these elements. There is, for some, more autonomy and flexibility. It might be easier to autonomously develop new skills and gain experiences across multiple companies. And perhaps technology has at last accelerated productivity through bringing together people and job opportunities without locations and time zones presenting barriers and through making tasks simpler and faster.

In this future world of work, feedback is mainly AI generated. Automated hints and tips shared through applications, advising on time spent talking, words overused, lack of questions etc. There are no chance encounters – bumping into someone new or in another team – interactions are carefully orchestrated or even avoided through virtual worlds and planned use of time. My daughter's reality is almost entirely virtual. Her milestones and accomplishments gamified through badges appearing on her virtual profile. She rarely sees, in real life, the impact she has on others. Emotions are muted; she has become almost desensitised, able to simply switch off the game-like version of work (and life) she plays.

In this vision, my daughter dips in and out of multiple virtual worlds with ease, juggling work and life (mainly from home), but is this the future we are looking for?

This might be an extreme view of what the future could hold, but it isn't too much of a stretch to imagine a world like this. Today, AI is advancing at such pace that many leaders are beginning to issue caution around the risks this poses to humankind and to take a step back. Children and teenagers mainly know a digital world. As they get older, so many of their experiences and connections are delivered via technology. Companies and employers are engaged in great debate over what the workplace should be for, how often people need to come in and the benefits of remote and in-person working.

A vision within reach, but is this a reality we want?

To answer that, let's first go back and consider where we are today and how we got here.

In today's world of work, we're far from succeeding. People are lonely, productivity continues to plateau, we face huge challenges through inequality and how we sustain resources and our planet remains a vital challenge.

We can travel to the moon, we use technology to mimic human interaction, we have developed new vaccines and made significant progress in treating diseases, we have designed robots, created virtual realities, made the car go faster for longer and yet... as a global population, we are more unhappy than we have ever been.

Since the Industrial Revolution, we have become pre-occupied with measuring things. How many hours? How many people? How fast? How much money? How can we go faster, make more money, do more with less? Yet, in our questions, we rarely consider the experience we create – how does this make people feel? Are our teams happy? Do they feel supported and able to be truly innovative? How are we contributing to society and the world around us? What more could we do to make a difference?

Today, we can spend over fifty years of our lives working. That's longer than most other roles and commitments in our lives. Generations to come could find themselves working for longer, say fifty-five to sixty years, as life expectancy increases and we must find ways to fund a longer life supporting younger and older dependants.

When the Industrial Revolution shaped the structure of work that we broadly recognise today, people were expected to live to about forty. Forty-five if they were lucky.

The mission was very different. Inextricably time-bound, individuals typically spent around twenty-five years employed and they were quite likely to literally die working. Work was predominantly manual, so measuring outputs to optimise inputs – hours worked, number of workers, equipment used – was logical. Families relied on one wage, typically the man's – because of the physical nature of the role and societal attitudes towards gender – and women took on risks and responsibilities associated with raising children.

Now, work takes multiple forms for everyone in different places. Increasingly, both partners go out to work. People have transferable skills, side hustles, portfolio careers with squiggly paths and several chapters. We can reinvent, reskill and flex to what's happening around us – our skills and interests, our families, the market, the world.

What we are trying to achieve, the time we have available and the tools we have access to are fundamentally different to what shaped us. Many have said we are now entering the 'human' age of work. The goal is longevity, sustainability, maintaining relevance, making a difference, leaving a legacy for generations to come *and* doing this through feeling part of something, learning and growing, making friends, maintaining health and well-being and experiencing happiness. Elements of this will probably feel familiar. Many people and companies have included these words in their missions and values; they talk about a people-focused culture on their website and employees share a lofty elevator pitch when describing their company. As work has become increasingly knowledge focused, companies have certainly made progress towards this goal. Leaders have recognised the need to focus on people and business and, in many cases, the intent has been good.

However, the road towards this destination is difficult to navigate and full of bumps and obstacles. The bold company statements and words used to describe culture frequently jar in our heads and feel peculiar when we say them out loud. This isn't what we genuinely feel at work. We might have attempted to get here before, but it's a destination few have reached.

To move forwards, we must first understand what is behind our collective state of unhappiness.

## WE'RE LONELY

Interactions were already becoming increasingly sparse before the pandemic, and then Covid made us anxious about meeting people. Whilst most individuals are now re-bounding from this traumatic period, many carry the scars through loss and harrowing experiences. We got used to a more isolated existence and this continues to shape our priorities and behaviour today. Every day, workers weigh up the benefits of going into a shared workspace and seeing real people versus staying home, skipping the commute, connecting virtually with those we need to when we need to and getting stuff (work and life) done. For many, the option to stay at home, save money and time, wins. This comes with a price. It has been well documented that 'having a best friend' at work is a top driver of retention. Friendship is rarely formed through task-based, virtual interactions. It's the shared challenges, laughs, triumphs, and it's not always those we work with directly – people we bump into, or maybe join company training courses or induction pro-grammes with. These are the trusted confidants, the people we can meet for a coffee and vent with, and feel sure that however ridiculous your claims, they will go no further. Friends help guide you, share information and news with you; they can make work feel more than tasks and dead-lines. For many – they are *the* reason to go into a workplace.

Yet a huge number of people today are missing this. Headlines have emphasised the trade we have made – join-ing more virtual meetings over making friends. I recently read an article that said individuals entering the workforce today are Googling more than ever how to make small talk at work. They need to proactively think and prepare to inter-act with other humans, seeking advice on topics to discuss and avoid. This must be a wake-up and smell-the-coffee moment for us all – if we are having to train people on how to talk to other people, something has seriously gone awry. This could serve to broaden the gap between groups with disabilities and minority populations. Reliance on virtual communication can leave more open to interpretation – something those with neurodiverse conditions can find difficult – as body and facial language can be more readily concealed. Perhaps our ability to tune in to others, to sense their feelings and interpret the unsaid will be limited, too, without concerted effort to sharpen this skill.

It's not just connection that is suffering but creativity and problem-solving too. Within sparsely populated work-places, our ability to have chance encounters, overhear conversations, seek guidance and counsel from those we don't purposefully interact with is declining. This affects diversity of thought and innovation, as well as efficiency and speed (with our heads down in our own silos, we make the same mistakes time and again). Across many companies today and despite a plethora of advanced technology at our fingertips (virtual meetings, collaborative tools and platforms), cross-functional working – sharing of ideas and learnings to better our impact on our joint mission – is under threat. Loneliness is also about feeling isolated when hitting obstacles. Tasks and problems can feel insurmountable if we feel alone in our journey to tackle them. How we create the water-cooler chats in a hybrid and virtual world appears to be a question yet to be solved.

## WE'VE LOST SENSE OF HUMANITY

For most knowledge-based roles, work is now synonymous with technology and being online. Logging-in, turning green, being available. Documents are live and shared – individuals can collaborate on the same content from thousands of miles away and across time zones. Our work wardrobes have morphed with our home ones: trainers have been promoted to an everyday item, and if you're like me, there's a whole section of your wardrobe now untouched – waiting for a moment when more corporate dress is required. 'Appearance' is everything. Appearing to be online, doing the infamous mouse waggle to reactivate a hibernating status; dialling into mass broadcasts but using the time to catch up on emails; dressing for Zoom – smart top half, pyjamas or joggers below!

When I first started work, meetings were in person. I spent a lot of time meeting clients at their offices – sharing proposals, delivering development feedback, brainstorming ideas and, at times, delivering difficult messages. How many people have now been fired or made redundant over a virtual call? How many have joined new companies and never actually met anyone in person? How many have never seen and felt the impact of their work on others? That rush of adrenaline when standing up to present to a room full of people isn't the same over a virtual call. Neither is seeing the anger bubble in a client when you must tell them you can no longer meet the timeframes agreed, nor the rush of excitement and feeling of camaraderie when a project team makes a breakthrough. For so many of us now, we simply switch on a computer, tune in to a digital world and then switch it off. I fear we are becoming desensitised – switching off from our own and others' emotions. The road ahead from here could be quite scary: if we are able to disengage our human reactions and emotions to regulate behaviour (of ourselves and others), will there be a limit to what we are prepared to do in a virtual world? Are we heading back towards a world of people as resources, easily replaced should they burn out or become too difficult to manage? Could this propel us somewhere even worse, towards a vision of life without human guardrails? To virtual environments where it is survival of the most callous, where reward waits for those who choose to prioritise themselves, mentally torment, discriminate and destroy those around them to progress their careers and feed their egos. Could a *Squid Game* existence become our reality?

## WE'RE BURNING OUT

With the divide between work and home increasingly blurred, it has become harder to switch off. For many, work is accessible via a laptop, from anywhere, at any time. For those working remotely or in hybrid routines, we have grown accustomed to different or varied work environments. The great advantage of working remotely is flexibility. However, the risk presented through loss of natural 'cues' to trigger a change in activity or end of a working day are often now absent or different. Physically leaving a workplace to go home brings definition. Space between work and life. Now, we are often working at home and living at work. This continues to create challenges around balance, space, burnout and employer expectations (you're online, so you're working). This is reflecting in our well-being. Record numbers of people are experiencing burning out across all demographics, especially those in the early stages of their careers. This could be because many in Gen Z have only experienced working life in and following the pandemic. The connections, friendships, support networks usually developed in person haven't been possible, and this cohort have become very effective at working independently. But this takes its toll.

People in management roles are also experiencing this slightly more than others. The role of a manager has expanded – with constant change, novel scenarios, navigating and brokering new ways of working, the volume of tasks for managers is vast. The content of conversations has become more significant and meaningful, as work and life combine, and work challenges become increasingly hard to unpick from life, e.g. supporting individuals managing the significant rises in cost of living but also needing to encourage people to spend money to come back into offices. Or enabling people with caring responsibilities – an increasing burden on so many as the population ages – to balance work demands. For everyone, things have felt harder, choices more strained, consequences more severe, and this is on top of an inability to separate work from life and growing pressure around job security as organisations rapidly grow and contract, leaving many suddenly without work. Some companies have even glamourised overworking – presenteeism (even if through showing green online) is still a thing. The pressure has become intense and the cracks in us, as humans, are clearly showing.

## WE'RE SEARCHING FOR MEANING (AND STRUGGLING TO FIND IT)

The final aspect contributing to the challenge in finding happiness is our search for meaning. Management consulting firm McKinsey released research a few years ago linking purpose or meaning to the most significant outcome – death. Their research revealed that people who have a strong sense of purpose are five times more likely to report higher levels of well-being. They have a 15 per cent lower risk of dying over the next decade and, at work, are four times more likely to report higher levels of engagement and to help the organisation deliver higher profit margins.

That's huge.

Today, many are struggling to find this. As we began to emerge from the pandemic in 2021, work psychologist Adam Grant described this feeling as 'languishing': 'Languishing is a sense of stagnation and emptiness. It feels as if you're muddling through your days, looking at your life through a foggy windshield.'

Finding individual purpose and meaning can be a game-changer. Yet many people report feeling stuck in jobs and companies where they fail to feel this. Work is simply a list of tasks to tick off. Colleagues and customers are merely faces and voices joining meetings. Decision-making and autonomy are throttled by bureaucratic processes and controls. It can be easy to feel swept up in the quagmire of things to do. We have disconnected tasks and instructions to do following specific rules and processes, without really understanding why. Companies which have experimented with removing controls around expense policies or holiday allowances and replaced these with guidelines such as 'spend in a way that helps the company grow' or 'take the holiday you need to help sustain team performance' have been rewarded with cost savings, retention of talent and increased feelings of engagement. Being trusted to do what's right and understanding how our work contributes to a meaningful mission sets the stage for feelings of accountability and ownership.

A desire for purpose starts at an early age. Many conversations between parents and children revolve around *why* something is important. For most, the moments of motivation come from knowing that there is impact – I painted a picture and now I feel proud sharing my work with my family. I learned times tables and can work out how much pocket money I will have saved in six weeks' time (and plan what I can buy with that!). I trained hard to get better at swimming and now I get to join the group with my friends and take part in the competitions. Tapping into intrinsic motivators will provide more sustainable drivers to guide energy, and whilst the content will differ by individual, a core focus on the impact we make will likely provide a common recipe for success.

Companies committed to purposeful work clearly articulate a galvanising mission bigger than themselves. They successfully ask *why* we exist and what we ultimately need to achieve, beyond financial results. They authentically and constantly link their work to making a difference in the world – to people, communities, the environment. They embed this in everything they do, sharing stories of impact and, importantly, giving individuals space to bring their own flavour and interpretation to this goal. Being part of something, feeling a sense of belonging and community and finding opportunities to learn and grow all feed into this, connected by an overwhelming sense of greater meaning, driving us forwards every day.

The core elements that define us as humans – using our cognitive capabilities to make decisions; solving problems that make a difference to others and the world around us; being immersed in an interesting project where we learn and grow; and meeting our need for interaction and emotional connection with others – have become compromised.

The longest study so far into what makes us happy followed a cohort of people across an eighty-year span. The paper, by Harvard, concluded that there were two key elements that happier people held in common:

1. They prioritised how they wanted to spend their time (in other words, they identified what was most meaningful to them and focused their time on these aspects).
2. They spent time building and maintaining social connections.

If we are to design a new world of work with happiness as our goal, what would we include?

I believe there are three key ingredients we must prioritise to create conditions where we as humans can thrive:

- Autonomy (feeling empowered, trusted and able to make individual choices)

- Meaning (being fuelled by purpose in what we do and experiencing strong social relationships such that we feel a sense of belonging and inclusion)
- Growth (developing, learning and growing through interesting and varied career opportunities)

Could this pave the way to a happier, more fulfilling vision for workplaces in 2038 and beyond?

Here is an alternative vision for my daughter entering the workplace in ten to fifteen years from now. Picture this...

My daughter joined a pan-company early careers programme to design and deliver virtual skill development content. She doesn't work directly for one company, rather a joint venture with investment from four enterprise organisations alongside funding from governments to accelerate national skill development. The programme runs for two years, and she has joined a cohort of twenty-five people across Europe from a variety of backgrounds.

In the hiring process, she completed several psychometric tools to pinpoint motivators, style and understand her current skills. These are used all the time to build individual understanding and maximise learning and growth opportunities. Each person has two mentors, and these can vary based on the individual's needs and objectives as the programme progresses. They have regular conversations evaluating how things are going through the lens of autonomy, meaning and growth and together identify actions and support to ensure these are maintained. Whilst it's clear individuals are responsible for their own career and development, the infrastructure has been designed specifically to enable this.

Everyone works four days a week and success is measured through outcomes, not the hours spent online or being visible. In fact, within the four days, work patterns vary significantly, although there are anchor days in workplace destinations typically one to two days a week. They use this time to collaborate, brainstorm ideas, test concepts with colleagues and gather feedback. This aligned yet personalised approach, with clarity on expectations, widens the gate for people from all walks of life to contribute to the company's mission. This makes for more diverse and inclusive teams, facilitating broader ideas, thoughts and knowledge sharing. My daughter also has regular check-ins, very often in person, with her local mentor, to help solve challenges in the flow of work and seek advice on broader topics and scenarios, spanning work and life.

There is a lot of technology. Countless virtual reality and digital tools, AI-driven chatbots and idea generators. My daughter and her workmates have multiple apps – to gather feedback on themselves, to network with colleagues and work on projects and content. As a team, they are very focused on how they're tracking – both as individuals (well-being, growth and development, and their connection with the project, its direction and purpose) and as a team driving agreed outcomes. I notice they are not afraid to have open and direct conversations; holding one another accountable for the objectives they've set and when navigating challenges. Similarly, they hold a mirror up to each other around work–life balance and the behaviours they demonstrate, asking difficult questions and encouraging reflection. Lessons learned are shared each week – in short burst sessions – and talking about what has been challenging or what hasn't worked well is engrained in the culture. They're focused on bringing a human approach – wanting the best for each other and the whole project team – using a combination of technology, human emotion and judgement to achieve the right blend.

The programme is exceptionally purpose driven. They are focused on reducing the skills gap for every country in which they operate. This has very visible and shared goals and, of course, can be clearly articulated in terms of impact on people, communities and society. They regularly spend time with the people who access and use the content they design, seeing first-hand how they use this, the impact it makes and what else they would like to do with it. At the start of the programme, the group spent two weeks together with a global cohort, immersing in the purpose of the initiative, understanding and adapting to the ways of working and culture and meeting with mentors to support and guide them through this journey (they had a say in whom they wanted to work with too). The core philosophies are very visible: supporting both individuals and the team; getting comfortable with failing and learning from this; providing honest and constructive feedback; and respecting boundaries – the four-day week is upheld and not interrupted – work and life are equally as important.

My daughter is developing fantastic skills, both technical – coding, content development, user interface (UI) design, analytics – and human skills (interacting with diverse stakeholders, working across cultures, presenting and storytelling skills, learning how to cope when things fail or how to manage receiving tough feedback), which she could use in a variety of roles moving forwards. She relishes the focus on understanding her, as an individual, and the commitment to personalising experiences to help keep her learning, growing, feeling included and, ultimately, thriving. At the same time, she enjoys the transparency around accountabilities and objectives. She finds it motivating to have a shared understanding of expectations as well as a clear link with the programme's broader goals. She loves the flexibility, variety *and* camaraderie she gets by spending time with colleagues at similar stages of life, learning and solving things together, as well as the access to diverse, experienced mentors. They work hard, learn and grow, make (and see) an impact, value insights from those around them, enjoy other people's company and place a high value on the time away from work, too.

Both visions for a future of work feel eminently possible and yet each promise quite different experiences and outcomes.

The choices we make will shape the work experiences of

our children and grandchildren. As a parent, an employee, a leader, a work psychologist and a human, I feel we have a duty to learn through our own experiences, to listen to our concerns and anxieties and to prioritise our aspirations for something brighter.

*Make It Human* outlines how we can bring to life a human experience of work.

I believe we all have a role to play. If we step back and allow things simply to evolve, I fear we will slip into an entirely technology-led, always-on, remote, task-focused experience of work within which we, as humans, deteriorate further. Leading isolated, lonely lives where mental health issues are rife, feeling numb to the impact we have, relying on AI to make key decisions and solve problems, we fail to find balance or meaning. This outcome would call into contest every aspect that makes us human.

Now is the moment to create workplaces and cultures where we, as people, can thrive.

I hope you join me in this mission, using the tools, models and insights shared in this book to make it human in your experiences of work and life, every day.

If we don't make it human, who will?

# CHAPTER 2

# WORKPLACE WARFARE

L ift the lid on many well-known companies and you are likely to want to close it quickly.

All sorts of organisations have fallen victim to toxic culture. Experiences of discrimination, abuse, criminal activity, safety breaches, even loss of life if deemed 'systemic' are frequently put down to cultural failings.

Workplaces can be cut-throat, unkind, politically driven, even inhumane environments. Not at all conducive to feelings of safety, support and inclusion, let alone productivity and innovation. A far cry from the conditions we as humans need to thrive. (That's not to say there aren't shining, hopeful examples of organisations where humans are flourishing, which will be explored later.)

First, here are a few stories from companies where workplace warfare has raged. This chapter includes analysis of where these issues might have started – the early signs that cracks were beginning to silently spread – before they caused catastrophic failure. I share these because there are lessons for us all. Culture doesn't just break overnight; it starts with a tiny crack. As you'll see, the well-known, established companies that have been damaged mean that no one is immune. These examples and the culture cracks model (explored in greater depth in the following chapter) can help us to identify how to build and maintain cultures where humans and business can thrive.

## PUTTING THE <u>CULT</u> IN <u>CULT</u>URE

Following the 2008 global financial crisis, people and organisations were searching for the new promise of success. This came in the guise of technology. Apple turned mobiles into smart devices for *everything*. Facebook and Twitter revolutionised social media. App-driven start-ups emerged overnight: Uber turned car owners into an army of taxi drivers; and Deliveroo transformed takeaways into instant meals. Investors went crazy. There was a feeding frenzy, as entrepreneurs and start-ups sought seed funding and the tech industry sky-rocketed (now, in 2024 and beyond, perhaps we're seeing the unravelling of this as several technology companies make mass lay-offs following excessive hiring).

Amidst the foray, a new vision for how we work was being prepared. A utopia of kibbutz-inspired communities, in open-plan, collaborative, tech-enabled, sociable environments for the cool entrepreneurs to mingle, co-create and possibly solve world peace.

But this wasn't just real estate; it was a radical new approach to the very essence of how we work. The 'we' generation, the company's founder and future CEO claimed, didn't discriminate – it saw the best in everyone, as humans. A mission to overhaul the established convention of how and why we work was launched. This was WeWork.

The target market – creatives, independents, entrepreneurs – initially rushed to sign up. The spaces were refreshing, looked edgy and vibrant, and those in the 'in' crowd were leading the way. And it wasn't *just* office space – a technology platform was created to enable people to connect, share and form alliances to do more with their lives. Huge summer camps spanning several days were organised for everyone in the WeWork generation to gather, listen to seminars on their calling and opportunities to make things better. People wore T-shirts emblazoned with slogans such as 'Elevate the world's consciousness' and 'Strive to be better, together'. Groups held hands and closed their eyes to envision a better future.

Looking in, you could easily confuse the company with a cult. Presentations were preacher-like, joint commitments were voiced, stories of how lives had turned around discussed excitedly. The CEO had a Jesus-like status amongst the group. People waited for, and acted on, his every word. He was engaging, inspiring, future focused and enigmatic. They inherently believed he knew the path ahead and would make it, and everyone around him, better and more successful.

The rollercoaster was picking up pace, and more were climbing on board. The 'tech' real estate company was also impressing the investors and valuations were steadily rising. A Japanese investor raised the biggest ever venture capital fund based on the company's projections and put in $4 billion for the CEO to 'go crazy' and take the brand global.

At that stage, the company was valued at $20 billion and the pace of growth was unlike anything ever seen in office space before. WeWork spots would open up with builders and decorators finishing floors as they were unveiled. The brand expanded – the 'we' approach being applied to how we live, how we access education. Even the concept of life itself was up for grabs, and the company eventually reached an epic valuation of $47 billion.

Behind the scenes, all was not as it seemed.

Cracks were beginning to show, and those individuals bowled along by the vision and excitement were beginning to question the reality.

Some employees had been exposed to 'firing lists' circulating the company. Costs were mounting and pressure needed to be relieved. Was this part of the 'we community' mission? Under stress, the CEO's behaviour became unpredictable. It was reported that he would regularly threaten to fire people on impulse, or expose their perceived failings in public settings, undermining trust and fostering fear.

Financially, the numbers just didn't add up. The company invented its own approach to calculating EBITDA (earnings before interest, taxes, depreciation and amortisation) to re-engineer its profits. It was reported that, at one stage, WeWork was burning through $100 million a week.

The CEO and his family were reportedly spending company money on luxurious properties and holidays, flying employees out to meet them in their exotic locations, whilst preaching a modest and community-focused mantra. Profit can be open to opinion, but this was taking it to another level, and it was looking like this tech unicorn was mythical.

Things unravelled quickly when the main investor pulled out. They were unable to deliver on commitments made to their own investors and it quickly became untenable. The company's price fell dramatically from $47 billion to $15 billion.

The bubble had burst. Some rescue attempts via an IPO were proposed but failed to get off the ground. Eventually, the CEO was forced to make the decision to step down and mass lay-offs followed to enable a financially viable business to emerge.

Employees felt angry and deceived. Many had completely bought into the mantra of a 'we generation' and had worked hard to bring this to life. Now it was in tatters.

This story all played out across approximately ten years. From concept, to start-up, to rapid growth, with around 12,500 employees worldwide across 850 WeWork locations, the company had a galvanising mission and people – employees and customers – bought into it. It also had bold growth plans, but initially, people weren't clear what *it* really was. The CEO talked about being a tech company, but it was real estate, right? Yet, its financial projections treated it like tech, and in response, investors did too. It was mysterious, enigmatic, elusive and oh so cool. Celebrities and influencers endorsed it. To be in the 'in' crowd, you needed to be part of the we generation. A lot of this emanated from the CEO. Like the leader of a cult, he was inspiring and believable. What he said made sense. It all looked and felt eminently possible. And yet, behind the glossy exterior, he had created a phenomenal, yet possibly fabricated, narrative of the financial basis of the organisation, was living way beyond his means to finance the 'we' lifestyle and would manipulate and cut down those who dared challenge him. Those around him, colleagues, employees, wanted to believe and therefore saw what they wanted to see. The culture kept the rollercoaster on the tracks, until it veered too far off, and the cracks in double standards and toxic leadership behaviour became too much to overcome. In 2023, WeWork filed for bankruptcy. However, as this book went to print, although looking unlikely to succeed, Adam Neumann had pulled together a bid to try to buy back WeWork. Could the organisation find itself flung back into a similar cycle? Or will the board exercise greater caution, given their previous experience?

## WOLF OF WALL STREET (AND INDUSTRY?)

For many decades, many financial organisations have been portrayed as macho, misogynistic places. *The Wolf of Wall Street*, a film based loosely on the life of Jordan Belfort (a stockbroker ultimately jailed for fraud), is awash with trading floor parties, drinking and drug use, macho 'chest beating' ceremonies, even dwarf throwing. The focus is on the lavish lifestyle of those in investment banking – making millions, taking risks, crossing the line to live life excessively and making a lot of noise about it. Whilst this depiction might be extreme, company collapses and financial crises suggest there is some truth to the cultural experiences and ways of working for some in this sector.

In the 2000s, the culture in multiple banks and financial institutions swirled. Focus shifted towards aggressive selling, risk taking and flexing the rules. Some in key positions saw an opportunity to manipulate the system and achieve phenomenal results. Initially, this seemed to work, and momentum built. Those at the top were said to 'lose sight' of what was happening on the ground – the decisions being made, rules massaged, exaggerated claims made. Risk-takers were being rewarded. Employees who brought in the big deals (millions, if not billions) were rewarded for the results they achieved, no matter how they achieved them. Some employees were likely to have seen the poor behaviour behind the scenes, but few would have felt able or willing to speak up and share their concerns. This was a tight labour market and jobs were at a premium, plus, very often, those at the top were turning 'star' performers into company heroes. Some felt the greed-induced behaviours being witnessed in banks reflected broader societal attitudes towards risk-taking and making money. A banking survey by Deloitte reported: 'There is a societal, cultural problem around acceptance of norms of behaviour around greed and money, which has changed in the last twenty years. The typical person who was a banker has changed in their attitude, values and behaviours.'

Bending the rules appeared to be socially acceptable when the outcomes were deemed worth it – and there was some serious money being made during this period.

That was, until things went too far.

In 2008, a global financial crisis began to unravel. Many will remember scenes playing out on TV of well-known, well-respected financial institutions going under. Whether Lehman Brothers on Wall Street or Northern Rock on the UK high street, the term 'credit crunch' was entering our lexicon, and at pace. Businesses had overstretched, borrowing more than they could afford, and individuals, families, companies and even countries were being swept up in the aftermath.

In subsequent years, there were senior executive casualties. Bob Diamond and Fred Goodwin, ex-CEOs of Barclays and Royal Bank of Scotland (RBS), respectively, became household names, and not for reasons they would have liked. Both were fired, and across multiple banks, a clean-up mission began. Repairs focused on integrity and standards, with organisations resetting their core mission and values to try to instil more ethically grounded behaviour at the foundation. Relationships were tightened with regulators, and new legislation emerged. Codes of conduct, whistle-blowing procedures and compliance training programmes were invested in.

Has it worked? When making money is the main marker of success, a concerted effort to maintain the integrity line will always be needed. As humans, we glorify and seek to emulate those who appear successful, no matter how they get there. Whilst progress seems to have been made, this fascination with exuberant and arrogant characters who appear infallible will always pose a challenge. A recent insight into the culture at Goldman Sachs today would suggest problems still simmer: 'One current junior female employee said that although "on a very theoretical level we are encouraged to speak up ... in practice if you say something controversial it's not well received".'

The bank has recently settled a $215 million lawsuit on the grounds of alleged gender discrimination in terms of pay and promotions. Many women say that whilst bias is no longer explicit, there are hidden cultural norms and expectations that continue to make it far easier for men to achieve success and progress their careers than their female counterparts. Goldman Sachs has made significant progress in improving gender representation, but these barriers still exist, and it would appear to be industry wide as very few CEOs of investment banks are women. According to a *Financial Times* article:

'It's not as though any individual is saying, "Hey, let's keep women back" – that's not how it works,' said Martin Davidson, professor of business administration and global chief diversity officer at the University of Virginia Darden

School of Business. 'It's just in the water ... masculinity is the bread and butter of the investment banking industry.'

In financial organisations around the world, the moral battle of keeping the wolf from the door or letting him in and reaping the (temporary) rewards rages on. Perhaps an injection of femininity is exactly what this industry is crying out for.

## THE THINGS THAT GO ON IN PUBLIC

Governments and public services across the world are also by no means 'safe havens' when it comes to experiences of company culture. Unfortunately, those in the world's highest positions of trust and power can justify flouting the rules and teeter on the edge of ethics; their decisions and actions shaping cultures of bias, discrimination and even illegal activity.

Notably, in 2023, both the US and the UK saw the downfall of former country leaders on very public stages and following similar timelines. When Donald Trump was first elected President, it's probably fair to say there was shock and a sharp intake of breath across many parts of the world. This was reflected in the economy in the levels of uncertainty which spiked following the US election results. A cacophony of events followed: from unexpected changes in his leadership team to the announcement of new legislation restricting travel into the US from Muslim-majority countries. From the infamous wall between Mexico and the USA (and the heart-breaking scenes of separated families) to the building of closer ties with politically questionable allies such as Russia and North Korea. And, of course, we cannot forget Trump's version of the news – which started with wild exaggerations about the number of people attending his inauguration and ended with a ban from Twitter following the storming of the Capitol.

Many of the legislative changes Trump introduced are being re-evaluated and reversed by the Biden administration. The words, actions and relationships Donald Trump used and nurtured in his time as President were frequently called out by others as bizarre and unethical. Yet he survived an initial attempt to impeach him in 2019. Perhaps, had Covid not arrived, he would have survived another term... But Trump's quick dismissal of the impact of coronavirus and then his deranged advice to drink bleach to prevent catching it, arguably, resulted in America suffering one of the largest death tolls in the world and quite possibly delivered the final blow to his loyal supporters. Trump stepped down as President following defeat at the elections in 2021. Now, in 2024, what really happened during his administration is being investigated and Trump has appeared in court on multiple charges.

Playing out in parallel across the Atlantic, there's an eerily similar story.

As Trump became President, the UK woke up to news that Brexit *was* going to happen. The Vote Leave campaign, spearheaded by the then backbench MP Boris Johnson, had become an unexpected reality. It was a vote that literally divided the nation – in a pre-pandemic world, cafes, hairdressers and toddler groups were filled with talk of whether this was a good or bad thing. People were confused; many never really thought it would become a reality. But it had. And with this shift in the UK's political and economic positioning came the re-emergence of Boris Johnson. Known by many for his bumbling approach, clumsy remarks (often from a bygone era), obsession with Winston Churchill and ever-messy mop of blond hair, he became a key player, overnight. But Johnson had to wait a further three years to take the top spot – emerging, again from the back benches, to become Prime Minister in 2019.

Like in the US, many notable moments followed Johnson's appointment. He finely honed his reputation as a lovable rogue – sharing instinctive, poorly worded and ill-considered responses on critical issues but he almost ventured into the status of celebrity – being photographed jogging with his dog, his young fiancée moving into the PM's apartment and gilding the walls with gold (at the taxpayers' expense). Johnson's term was characterised by Covid. His early responses to the virus were, many now say, not enough. He attempted to balance health and economy, delaying national lockdowns until he had no other choice. Perhaps his own spell in hospital following contracting the virus changed his perspective.

Although, as stories now emerge, what went on behind the scenes within 10 Downing Street was often diametrically opposed to that being outwardly preached. A firm ally (at the time), Dominic Cummings, was forced to offer an apology for breaching lockdown laws, and later, 'Partygate' claims dominated the headlines. Whilst millions of Britons were separated from family and friends, missed celebrations and couldn't attend funerals, Johnson was encouraging (or at least allowing) a culture of double standards, hosting gatherings within the confines of government buildings.

Like Trump, Johnson's time at the top also featured various comings and goings from his leadership team. Those in favour quickly fell out of favour. He appeared happy to flout rules and procedures, if it meant bettering his chance of success, and prepared to turn a blind eye to some of the misdemeanours of those he deemed valuable to his leadership (the case of Chris Pincher – whom Johnson appointed into his government despite knowing of past allegations of sexual misconduct). Boris Johnson is no longer Prime Minister and, also like Trump, he now must face the consequences of his decisions in formal parliamentary inquiries.

These individuals were country leaders – voted in to take on, arguably, the two most influential positions in the world – who repeatedly abused the trust placed in them and the power they possessed. Only in years to come will the full extent of the damage be fully understood, as their behaviour undoubtedly influenced and inspired that of those around them. Johnson's Deputy Prime Minister – Dominic Raab – was forced to resign his government role following formal investigation into complaints of bullying. Allowing power, ego and misogynistic behaviours to rule has consequences for integrity, fairness, people's health and, in this case, the longevity of a country.

It isn't just top-flight government where issues simmer. Other public service organisations have experienced a demise of purpose and values, with many saying that they simply lost sight of what's important and where the priorities lie in the services they provide. The Metropolitan Police, in London, has faced multiple claims of cultural failings, including institutional racism (exposed by the failings in the Stephen Lawrence murder investigation), misogynistic attitudes and the normalising of sexual predatory behaviour (as highlighted in the rape and murder of Sarah Everard). Similarly, in the NHS, multiple investigations several years ago revealed that serious cultural failings underpinned the death of 'Baby P', whose neglect was overlooked, on several occasions, by multiple members of his caring team. Moreover, education providers are by no means immune, especially as the pressure of meeting and sustaining external standards grows. In 2023, Ruth Perry, the headteacher of a successful English primary school, committed suicide. The coroner recorded a verdict of 'suicide, contributed to by an Ofsted inspection' and said specifically that the inspection 'lacked fairness, respect and sensitivity'. Perry died before reading a report which downgraded her school from 'outstanding' to 'inadequate' (but it has since been re-graded as 'good'). Many teachers and headteachers feel immense pressure and anxiety relating to

Ofsted inspections. The result often feels personal and carries significant weight, as existing and prospective parents may consider other schooling options on the basis of the report. Ofsted's focus on achieving a single rating on which a whole school is judged brings fear and stress and often relies upon skillsets removed from the core of teaching, in management and administration. Is this a fair, achievable and valid way of evaluating a school's ability to nurture safe learning environments for children?

Sadly, similar examples of cracks in public service organisations can be found around the globe.

## WHY ARE SOME ORGANISATIONS AWASH WITH WORKPLACE WARFARE?

### THE PULL OF PSYCHOPATHIC LEADERS

The values, decisions and actions of those in power, however small, shape those around them. Whether they consciously do it or not, leaders have a responsibility to consider the impact that their own behaviour has on others.

Yet, often, we're drawn to leaders with psychopathic traits, and these, it would seem, are more common than you might think. Research by Professor Simon Croom and colleagues suggests that 12 per cent of corporate leaders are psychopaths, compared with approximately 1 per cent of the total population. This means that psychopathic traits are up to twelve times more likely to be found in those in senior leadership positions. Leadership roles can offer a vehicle for those with psychopathic traits to successfully operate, fulfilling their need for adoration, power and control. And their accompanying skills in charm, manipulation and deception can make this hard to spot: impulsivity can be mistaken for courage and fast decision-making; manipulation perceived as influence and charisma; a grandiose sense of self seen simply as self-confidence; and a lack of remorse, guilt or presence of emotions interpreted as being able to make tough decisions and control their own emotions (the book *Snakes in Suits: When Psychopaths Go to Work* includes great descriptions of this in practice). The behaviours and traits we expect, nurture, hire and promote would certainly seem to be shaping an extreme version of a 'leader' in many organisations. As AI creeps ever deeper into hiring and promotion tools and techniques, this could hold dark consequences for the profile of leaders identified, unless we purposefully interrupt the model and re-programme to identify something new.

In recent years, the 'dark triad' has become increasingly explored in work as well as clinical settings. This offers a view on three 'dark' personality traits:

- Narcissism
- Machiavellianism
- Psychopathy

These traits can exhibit in manipulative, callous, ego-led behaviour from people prepared to do whatever it takes to get what they want. It's very likely that you know, work with or even live with someone with one or more of these traits, and even more likely that they have made it into a position of authority.

The first in the dark triad, narcissism, is characterised by a grandiose sense of self-importance, reduced empathy for others, a need for excessive admiration and the belief that one is unique and deserving of special treatment. Those who have watched the series *Mad Men* will probably recognise this in the lead character Don Draper, an advertising creative who enjoys the limelight, overshadows others with his often surprising and enigmatic approaches to pitches and clearly enjoys the flattery and ego-massaging he receives from clients (especially women) in a 1960s business world. Around him, confusion and chaos reign. Colleagues are unsure what he will do next. Will he turn up to the customer meeting? Is he happy with their work (or indeed them)? Have they said the wrong thing? And in his personal life, his wife and children play second fiddle, seeing him when it works for him and never getting to know the real Don Draper.

Yet, behind the confidence and charm, lies a vulnerable and sensitive core. Most with narcissistic traits are seeking reassurance that they are valued and important. The exterior hides a very delicate ego, pursuing flattery and support to thrive, and those in senior, well-respected roles and professions often display this – their apparent self-belief helps them propel their careers forwards. It is this feature – the grounding of a fragile ego – that makes the narcissist different to a fully fledged psychopath.

The second in the dark triad, Machiavellianism, is typified by being able to detach from any emotion, to frequently, and purposefully, deceive and manipulate others for one's own benefits. Machiavels can be callous in their actions – prepared to trample over others – to achieve their lofty ambitions. This can be observed through actions such as holding back information or deliberately deceiving other people; manipulating scenarios such that others fail or look bad in front of influential people; tricking people into believing it is a good idea to behave in a bold or unexpected way, only to enjoy watching their subsequent demise; and minimising or controlling others' power and influence to benefit their own. The behaviour of those with strong Machiavellian traits can be cold, destructive and cruel. Coercive control and instances of 'gaslighting', if they turn into patterns of behaviour, could suggest someone has a Machiavellian personality.

Machiavellian characters are perfect for leading roles in gripping dramas, and for good reason! Logan Roy – the head of the media family in HBO's *Succession* – is an excellent example. His tussles with his own board, executive team and even family frequently reveal his manipulative, callous and deceptive behaviour. He is prepared to, in a cold and calculated way, plot his own rise at the expense of those around him, even his own flesh and blood. Francis

Urquhart, in both versions of *House of Cards*, depicts the extremes a Prime Minister/President with these traits will contemplate to extend their power (as the series progresses, the trail of deception encompasses secret lives, corruption, illegal activity and tightly executed plots to cover up murders). Those with Machiavellian traits are often very intelligent. The combination of emotional detachment and cognitive capability can result in, for most normal human beings, inconceivable plans and a web of deception very carefully and cleverly managed to avoid exposure. Like narcissism, Machiavellian traits on their own are personality disorders – a presence of traits which can result in patterns of behaviour but can also be professionally counselled and coached, to enable individuals to better manage their impact on others in broader society.

The third area, psychopathy, takes elements of both narcissism and Machiavellianism and adds to the mix the toxic combination of zero empathy, impulsivity, an absence of behavioural control and a lack of conscience or any ability to feel remorse. And this is all often exhibited on top of a grandiose sense of self-worth, great charm and confidence (narcissistic) as well as deception and manipulation skills (Machiavellian).

Psychopathy can turn things very dark, resulting in many infamous criminals being labelled as psychopaths because they feel no remorse for the heinous actions they have taken and devastating impact they have had on others. The belief that no one else matters, that rules are for people of lesser status or capability and being unable to appeal to the raw components of humanity – how you affect others – puts psychopathy in a class of its own.

It has been estimated that approximately 1 per cent of men and 0.3 per cent to 0.7 per cent of women could be classified as psychopaths. Psychopaths exist amongst the normal population and, even more so, in corporate leadership roles, as positions of power are attractive.

These examples are perhaps extremes, but watching for the prevalence of these traits and, importantly, how individuals with them can manage and keep them in check are key responsibilities for those identifying and placing people in senior leadership roles.

Our obsession with confidence, charisma and charm seeps in here, and across society, media reporting, TV programmes, films and books continue to glorify these characters. This shapes our expectations and beliefs around what leadership looks like.

At the heart lies the often-debated question of confidence vs competence.

Psychologist Dr Tomas Chamorro-Premuzic has written extensively on this topic, asking why so many incompetent men become leaders. He explores why there continues to be such an uneven split between men and women in leadership roles and concludes that it is because of our inability to discern between confidence and competence. We commonly misinterpret displays of confidence as a sign of competence – we're taken in by the bravado, flair and promises of better things but fail to check credentials, and so are fooled into believing that men are better leaders than women. Perhaps the statistic that men are more prone to extreme manifestations of personality (e.g. narcissistic, Machiavellian and psychopathic traits) helps explain why more men than women fit the mould of a leader that we have in mind. In fact, research shows, when objectively assessed, that women demonstrate greater leadership potential than men. Our model of what leadership looks like prevents us from seeing what we really need.

Jordan Belfort, the chief executives at Barclays and RBS during the credit crunch, the founder and CEO of WeWork, Donald Trump and Boris Johnson had no shortage of confidence and self-belief. Did anyone look deeply at their level of competence to deliver on the objective requirements of their roles? We often admire and celebrate people who appear to be 'winging it'. Those who put in little effort but appear to shine and be comfortable leading others through the fog, dealing with new scenarios and challenges. They muscle their way through, dismissing naysayers, believing their own rhetoric. Yet, we overlook the quiet, understated competence of others (often, but not exclusively, women) who approach things in a meticulous, structured way, seeking to understand the views of others, to show empathy and build genuine connection, to explore different alternatives and to deliver the best outcome possible for everyone involved. For example, research following the initial waves of Covid suggested, in general, that the way in which female leaders responded led to better outcomes for people in those countries (fewer deaths and better containment of the virus). These leaders, at first glance, would appear to be stronger in competence over confidence (and this is explored in more depth in later chapters).

Who we appoint at the top matters. We are often blindsided by the traits that we have been nurtured to believe equal 'leader'. One of the earliest known leadership theories is Thomas Carlyle's 'great man' theory from 1840. Carlyle suggested that leaders are born with capabilities greater than others, rising to the top in moments of need. Whilst almost two centuries old, the essence rings true in how many people would describe experiences of leadership today: the supreme confidence, verging on arrogance; the superhero able to single-handedly resolve any crisis; the 'been there, done that' delegator whom people are afraid to challenge; the 'man of the people', with 'shared' experiences making them relatable and believable; the gift of the gab, with skilful storytelling, rallying speeches and cries for support; the bullying tactics dressed up as humour or camaraderie; and the ready-to-go explanations, justifications and finger-pointing when things inevitably go wrong.

Particularly in times of threat, history tells us that we are frequently drawn to these leaders.

Companies where these leaders are enabled to prevail will make themselves extinct. The culture they create is one driven by authority, fear, division and conflict.

In our world today, where the only constants are disruption, complexity and ambiguity, the traits we need to nurture for success are the opposite: leading with empathy and humility (and a quest to keep learning and evolving), seeking to create safe, secure and fair workplaces and being guided by a broader purpose (understanding that businesses with longevity require deeper meaning) to build evolving, growing and thriving cultures and businesses.

If you reward, excuse, enable and empower those who display the worst traits in humanity (e.g. greed, selfishness, abuse, discrimination, cruelty), this is the foundation upon which you will build your company and its workforce: an environment where most humans will fail to thrive. In addition, if we allow AI to inform the identification of future leaders based on models of historical data, we will only serve to perpetuate the past. Leadership plays a big role and is omnipresent in experiences of organisational culture. As we explore further in later chapters, this is the moment for us to reimagine the core constructs of good, human leadership to consistently inspire something brighter.

But there are other factors at play, too… And as individuals, we all play a vital role.

# CHAPTER 3

# CULTURE IS CRACKING

*'The standard you walk past is the standard you accept'*

Lieutenant General David Morrison, Australian Army

Whilst confronting issues of derogatory and misogynistic behaviour towards women within the Australian Army in 2013, Lieutenant General David Morrison made this now-famous statement (the incident was later described as the 'Jedi Council scandal'). His message was clear: we all have a role to play in shaping the behaviours we accept and promote within our places of work.

Culture is notoriously difficult to define. Often referred to as simply 'the way things get done around here', it's the character of an organisation – the values, beliefs and, importantly, the visible actions and behaviours that people engage in. But it's also the unsaid and unactioned – the things people hold back on doing, or reframe, for fear of misinterpretation or retribution. Culture is intangible and yet immensely powerful, an invisible force shaping and directing who we are, what we show and how we behave once inside the physical or digital four walls of an institution.

Today, leaders and individuals recognise the importance of a strong and healthy culture. MIT research in 2022 reported that people are 10.4 times more likely to leave an organisation if there is a toxic culture than because of what they're paid. LinkedIn's 2022 Global Talent Trends report also revealed that 40 per cent of candidates consider company culture a top priority when deciding whether to join an organisation.

Toxic cultures have a seriously damaging impact, and the problem is rife. Today, 75 per cent of people report having experienced a toxic culture, and as we've just explored, no company or industry is immune from cultural challenges.

## HOW DO WE KNOW SOMETHING'S WRONG?

Exploring the culture of an organisation is like geology – studying rocks to understand the history of the earth. The layers of minerals and pockets of sediment are built up over years, together creating the environment we experience day to day.

In organisations, cultures evolve constantly and comprise microclimates, subcultures and slices of history – e.g. cultures incorporated through acquisitions and long-serving managers enforcing their own ways of working. It's a living, breathing, ecosystem and this needs very careful monitoring and management to ensure positive experiences and transformation.

Organisational culture doesn't just fail – it starts with a tiny crack.

Through a combination of my own survey-based research, my work as a business psychologist and partnering with hundreds of organisations, I have identified ten culture cracks that I see most frequently occurring. These are the signs that your company culture is under strain. They are the beliefs, actions and behaviours simmering that detract from your goals as an organisation and create feelings of disgruntlement, allow biases and inequity to flourish and prevent individuals and teams from bringing their best. This is the very essence of the phrase 'culture eats strategy for breakfast' – the rituals, nonsensical behaviours, unwritten rules, hidden hierarchies and emotions guiding *how* individuals believe they *need* to work to get on in this place. In many respects, these are the things that make us human: the biases, assumptions and emotions shaping, at times, less positive versions of ourselves and swirling in groups to create social norms and expectations.

Left unchecked, these mount up and can result in catastrophic failure. Whilst leaders set the expectation and are role models for what's acceptable, *everyone* working in an organisation contributes to the culture created and maintained.

To make it human, we need to become more acutely aware of the biases and traps we can fall into as individuals as well as collectively. Like technology and AI, humans also need checks and balances to optimise the impact we have.

You can see the 'ten signs of culture cracks' illustration by using the QR code on page 316.

## TEN SIGNS OF CULTURE CRACKS

### CULTURE CRACK I: WHEN TIME IN MEETINGS EQUALS SUCCESS ('I'M SO BUSY!')

Overhearing casual conversations between employees, or the informal chat before a meeting begins, can provide an illuminating window into employees' perception of what is valued within a company. At so many organisations, there's a focus on measures of 'busyness' – volume of meetings, time spent working, often during late and unsociable hours. Conversation turns to light competition – a fast-paced interaction to determine exactly who is the busiest – and the colleagues return to their to-do lists and back-to-back calls, only coming up for air when essential. Constant and visible activity is almost an addiction.

If you regularly encounter interactions between colleagues like this, with little focus on quality, impact or meaning of the work itself, there could be issues bubbling within your organisation.

In some companies, it might extend to people not taking time away to eat lunch, or even missing lunch entirely, or taking holidays being perceived as a sign of weakness (especially if those at the top never appear to take time out) or maybe even employees working such long hours that sleeping at the office becomes common.

At its worse, this culture can lead to employees burning

out as they feel pressure to work long hours and be *seen* to be contributing. Presenteeism hasn't been eradicated through remote or hybrid work. In some ways, this has made things worse, as being visibly working extends to digital signals around online status, availability for calls and working across time zones. Sadly, many professional and financial services firms have made the headlines for harbouring exhausted, even suicidal, employees. It can spiral to candidates turning down job offers, as the internal culture seeps externally through job sites and networks. It can result in huge inefficiencies, loss of innovation and improvement, as teams feel the route to success is visible time invested rather than outcomes achieved.

This culture crack is silently expanding in many organisations. Microsoft called this the 'productivity paradox' in a study which revealed that whilst 87 per cent of employees felt they were productive working at home, 85 per cent of managers reported that hybrid work had made it more difficult to have confidence that employees were being productive. Trust is of course a critical facet for feelings of security, belonging and empowerment. Our technology-enabled, always-on lifestyles mean there is greater need to monitor and nudge this aspect in the right direction to maintain a healthy approach and balance but equally to avoid a sense of employee surveillance.

Approaches to working hours can vary significantly by country or region. For example, in France, rules for working hours are taken seriously and enforced through regulations.

In many Nordic countries, respect for home life, balance and well-being creates shared expectations for preserving time out of work. Yet, in other places, such as the US, the UK and parts of Asia, social expectations and reward can more often rest on working long hours. These differences in conditions are further explored in later chapters.

## CULTURE CRACK 2: DOUBLE STANDARDS ('THOSE RULES DON'T APPLY TO ME!')

The second culture crack focuses on seemingly small, often unimportant actions that mount up, cause daily irritation and perceptions of elitism. These read like a list of 'pet peeves' – the things that just really get your goat about company life. For example, realising there's another level of catering options reserved for the top executives in the business, frequent abuse of car-parking spaces or electric vehicle charge points at work (it's always the same car parked in the visitor space) or, more topical, leaders setting new expectations around the number of days employees should plan to work in an office and failing to engage in this themselves.

These small actions, particularly from those at senior levels, can evoke anger, create feelings of inequality, feed resentment and ultimately erode trust. At the root of the issue is a perceived double standard. Those setting the standards and writing the rules are simply flouting them rather than acting as role models and following the rules. Partygate in the UK was a clear example of this and the backlash and emotional reactions to it were still felt a long time after the event.

As humans, we want to feel that we're in this together and that we're valued. And whilst a small action, such as picking a more expensive restaurant than the expenses policy stipulates or 'pulling rank' to claim a meeting room which someone else has reserved, might feel minor, these actions add up. This can lead to discontent, a lack of trust in leadership and, if left to simmer, result in significant cultural challenges, including serious toxicity issues as individuals lose sight of where the line needs to be drawn.

## CULTURE CRACK 3: FROZEN CORE – MANAGERS FROZEN BY BUREAUCRACY

A friend recently shared a secret with me. She said:

I'm in a senior leadership role. I have a team of sixty people I need to guide, inspire and deliver critical results through, for the company. My team *think* I have the power and authority to make decisions, to come up with new ideas and change things. But the truth is, I don't. When I started this job, I was really excited. I had the same beliefs as my team – I thought I finally had the opportunity to create something and tangibly improve experiences. But I'm stuck in a daily web of sign-offs, approvals, never-ending email chains, games of hot potato. There's no way I can tell my team that! Then they'd lose all hope too!

The sad thing is that my friend is not alone in this soul-destroying experience of middle management. So many people I speak with share this challenge. Perhaps it's like the widely kept 'truth' around childbirth: no one tells you what really happens until you go through it, then the stories come flooding in!

The tightrope of control and empowerment is hard for organisations to navigate, and a common culture crack extending across the middle of organisations is the 'frozen core'. A group of middle managers immobilised through process and bureaucracy.

So often we tie ourselves in knots through lengthy approval processes. A level of review and sign-off is likely necessary – people miss things – but too much red tape and you risk people feeling devalued. At its worst, this can lead to diffusion of responsibility, boredom, pent-up frustration, reduced engagement and innovation and a culture of blame which can ultimately paralyse your organisation.

The intention is often to empower, but the need to achieve specific outcomes, and fast, pushes us into control mode. In our world today, the pressure caused by uncertainty and disruption creates constant temptation to limit options, to put in place yet more sign-offs or to simply ignore questions and requests until the individual eventually gives up trying!

The risk of a fragmented, disengaged, brain-deactivated group of middle managers far outweighs the risk of enabling them to make well-reasoned, business-aligned decisions themselves. The statistics are everywhere concerning the impact that a skilled and empowered manager has on retention, growth, inclusion and innovation.

## CULTURE CRACK 4: SILENCE
## – CAN BE DEAFENING AND DAMAGING

We've all been there: you're hosting a meeting, reach the 'any questions' moment and – *silence…* Sometimes this is golden, but if it's a regular feature, it could imply broader issues.

As a leader, it is something I have encountered in team discussions before. Early into a journey to build a European professional services team in a technology company, silence occurred frequently, and I felt concerned about the level of connection and psychological safety within the group. Working remotely during the Covid pandemic across different countries and cultures added multiple layers. We hadn't yet reached a level of security to enable individuals to feel confident that this was a safe environment to express views, ask questions or express lack of understanding. So, we focused on ways to build connection and understanding, starting with smaller groups – one-to-one conversation, asking questions to understand people as individuals. Slowly this extended to group conversations, showing the team that this was a safe space to ask questions to learn, grow and challenge, together.

Today, at times, we encounter silence, or the same voices dominate discussion. Sometimes this is fine, but those facilitating will now often pause, check in, invite comment from others or get in touch with people before or after the meeting to ensure that they feel ready, able and comfortable to contribute. Creating psychologically safe environments never ends, and changes will always make it something to proactively manage.

At its worst, silence can result in people not speaking out when they really should. Turning a blind eye to the most awful behaviour because they don't feel supported in calling this out or fear the impact that this could have on them (their future career or own safety, even). In many organisations which have experienced cultural failure, poor behaviours rumble on for months, sometimes years. When people are afraid to challenge, speak their mind or express concern, the accepted standards can slide down a very slippery slope.

Recent high-profile cultural failings in big, successful corporations suggest that years of cover-up and fear have kept cultures of abuse and misogyny well stoked. In 2023, many well-established media organisations exposed that some individuals in positions of power had for years been concealing and overlooking patterns of sexual harassment and abusive behaviour. One incident, or one person, eventually leaking can, in many cases, cause a domino effect. Research over many years has shown that people tend to carefully consider whether to speak up or challenge behaviour that they know is unacceptable. Group dynamics shaping social norms and expectations play a key role. Bystander theory shows that if someone else is present, we are less likely to stop and challenge bad or threatening behaviour if the other person turns a blind eye, and perception of personal risk (what will happen to me and my career if I do speak up?) often serves to keep things hidden.

In September 2023, an incident like this played out live on national TV. Dan Wootton, a presenter on GB News, was interviewing Laurence Fox when Fox went on a derogatory rant, hurling sexist and offensive insults about a female journalist. Wootton appeared unsure what to do, smirking nervously and trying to bring some 'balance' into the views discussed. He failed to directly address or call out the unacceptable behaviour live on TV. Whilst perhaps understandable, given the heat of the moment, the rush of blood and anxiety about how to handle this and the impact it might have, the public, the broadcaster and Wootton himself concluded that he could and should have done better in the scenario.

When someone does pluck up the courage and question poor behaviour, this courage can help others to do the same, as the #MeToo movement demonstrates.

## CULTURE CRACK 5: CULTURE CLOUDS – COMPROMISING ON BEHAVIOUR TO DELIVER BUSINESS OUTCOMES

I once worked with an organisation in the energy sector which had serious concerns about a new member of its leadership team. The individual had all the credentials it was looking for and more: experience in big brand organisations *and* potential to propel the company forwards. But there was a HUGE culture clash and now, six months in, the client wasn't sure if it could turn this around.

The new leader was astute – quick thinking, understood the market and business rapidly – but their style turned people cold. Initially, the pace of enquiry was frantic, no stone left unturned to understand facts and figures. Time was well invested building relationships upwards. Direct reports got used to speedy responses should a request come in from the top and the new leader's reputation be called into question. There were rumbles of discontent; hushed conversations and confused colleagues gathering to dissect requests and understand priorities. The broader team, whilst largely protected by an experienced management team, sensed some tension, and certainly lacked clarity and energy in their mission.

When I explored the behaviour further, a clear picture emerged. Whilst very dedicated to their career, the new leader didn't prioritise people and relationships. These were a means to an end. Team-level communication was limited and financially anchored, which, across a diverse team of roles and professions, failed to inspire and unite. Direct reports encountered command and control situations: tasks were delegated without broader context; underperformance was publicly exposed; and a high-risk, high-performance culture was developing. Other employees were pushed into self-preservation mode – finding ways to keep their heads down to avoid being pressed for more or risk encountering confrontation.

My client was experiencing a 'culture cloud'. Something I've seen on multiple occasions, and I am sure most of you have too, given research estimates that between 50 per cent and 70 per cent of new leaders fail within eighteen months of taking on a new role.

A culture cloud can gather at any level or function in an organisation. Put simply, it is an individual or group who through their behaviour undermine the hard work invested by others into building the desired culture. Often a 'star' performer (see the 'dark triad' explored in Chapter 2) who makes their own rules, and owing to their solid results, the dubious way they've achieved this is overlooked. Unchecked, a culture cloud can lead to excessive turnover – valued employees exiting because they feel unfairly treated, ethically compromised or simply that they cannot shine in the organisation.

My client caught the issue just in time. They were able to use psychometric and 360 tools to provide feedback in a constructive way and have a broader conversation. The individual was also finding the new role challenging but couldn't work out why it felt so different to other companies. Together, they were able to refocus priorities on relationship building, empowering and engaging others to step towards the more positive, trusting and collaborative culture for which the organisation was known.

## CULTURE CRACK 6: PARENT-CHILD – 'WE KNOW WHAT'S BEST FOR YOU'

I experienced this culture crack first-hand when I moved to a new company and stayed less than three months. I joined for the opportunity to build and grow the consulting business and was thrilled to be starting this new chapter. But, three weeks in, I was already starting to question my decision... I told myself it was early days, a very different set-up and I just needed to give it time. Five weeks in and an all-company meeting appeared in diaries. The company was being sold, and to a well-established, global consulting provider. Instantly, I felt betrayed. Overnight, my main driver for joining had turned into a totally different proposition. I had conversations to try to understand more and what this would mean for me. In all honesty, there was one question I wanted answered. Why hadn't they told me? When I asked, the answer given was simply, 'We still thought it would be a good move for you.'

This one line stayed with me, and although I could see opportunities within the broader organisation, fundamentally I felt deceived. My psychological contract had been broken and irreparably so. Why was this so damaging? I think because I experienced the 'parent–child' culture crack. The 'we know what's best for you' tone. Perhaps it could have been a good move for me, but critically, I wanted to be able to make that decision myself.

Slipping into a parent–child relationship at work is

easily done. Often there are good intentions – to protect individuals by holding back difficult messages or worrying information, or to step in and make decisions on someone else's behalf to make things easier. However, over sustained periods, the impact can be damaging to individuals and the organisational culture. People can become overdependent, feel unable to guide their own decisions or actions and resentment at being treated as a child quickly builds. Across the longer term, constant sugarcoating can result in significant gaps in succession planning and leadership pipelines, and if teams fail to see the issues needing to be addressed, it can make change particularly challenging to execute. Ideas, fresh perspectives and people come to a grinding halt. There's only so far wrapping someone in cotton wool will get you.

## CULTURE CRACK 7: HERO COMPLEX – THE CAPED CRUSADERS TAKING CREDIT FOR SAVING THE WORLD!

At the other end of the spectrum, organisations are also prone to over-rely on a small group of people to get things done. The 'company heroes' who are always the first to be consulted or called upon in a crisis. The emergency siren sounds, and a familiar group of caped crusaders gather to take on their next earth-saving mission. Whilst this might deliver quick and efficient results for the company, for those around, watching another rescue by the elite squad can feel totally demoralising. This 'hero complex' culture crack often rewards those who are most visible, outspoken and confident; behaviours which don't *always* equate to competence.

Whether these heroes are capable or not, for those looking on, seeing the same faces selected for critical projects, discussions and opportunities is demotivating. So often people don't put themselves forwards for things if they feel it is a foregone conclusion who will be selected. Worse still, for everyone, is when the caped crusader seriously lacks capability. They rely on others to do the hard work and trample over those around them to take the credit. The business sees a star performer; their colleagues see arrogance, self-promotion and disrespect. Yet by allowing this to play out, the organisation feeds the belief that this is what's valued and these are the behaviours that will drive success.

The hero mindset and jumping from crisis to crisis is also addictive (for those called upon and the broader organisation). This state can ultimately have detrimental effects for those playing this role, creating constant feelings of pressure, resulting in anxiety and burnout. People leaders also frequently fall into this trap. Team members regularly share challenges and setbacks, seeking support and advice on how best to move forwards. From personal experience, I know how tempting it can be to jump in to help save a deal, rescue a client relationship or ensure the delivery of a project – often this is the fastest and easiest way to resolution (you've likely dealt with this countless times before). Fixing the issue will help in the short term (and provide a nice hit of dopamine for the leader), but won't help in the longer term, because it masks underlying issues. The greatest value a people leader can add is to establish safe environments for teams to practise and access constructive feedback, equipping them to tackle varied and unpredictable scenarios themselves.

## CULTURE CRACK 8: HISTORY LESSONS
## – 'IT'S JUST HOW THINGS ARE DONE AROUND HERE'

Picture this: a new employee joins a company full of ideas and optimism for the path ahead. Several weeks in, having been met with 'we tried that before and it didn't work here' from multiple places, they retreat and begin reconsidering whether this was the right move after all. An organisation shaped by legacy and with a clear identity can be powerful when this opens doors and fuels progress. But if it hampers and holds things back, blocking learning and enabling the same mistakes to be made time and again, it could be a sign of a simmering issue.

People often fall into the trap of narrowing influences. Building what they know, surrounding themselves with people who see the world the same way they do.

In good times, this strategy might work. Things 'feel good' and excitement and belief build momentum. The group and the whole company seem unstoppable.

What the group fail to see is the obstacle lying just around the corner – be it tougher trading conditions, a new competitor, advances in technology changing the way business gets done or employees seeing and accessing better deals elsewhere. Without perspectives – different eyes, ears and thought processes – to see what might lie ahead, or how things could be interpreted differently, this could become a lethal fracture in the organisation.

In 1971, psychologist Irving Janis wrote about the phenomenon of groupthink. Janis described this as situations when individuals refrain from expressing doubts or disagreeing with the consensus. In the interest of making a decision that furthers their group cause, members may also ignore ethical or moral consequences. Essentially, a closed, homogenous group can fail to see the oversights of a proposal, and collectively press on with making a poor decision. The famous examples shared by Janis are military incidents – the Bay of Pigs (a mission in 1961 involving the CIA training Cuban exiles to return to Cuba to overthrow the Castro regime. Despite the many expert advisors consulted, who later reported having held reservations about the plan, no one spoke up, thinking everyone else believed it was a great idea, or perhaps not daring to share a dissenting view. The mission was a disaster, ending in defeat to Castro's troops within just a few days) and the bombing of Pearl Harbor (the Japanese attack on the US naval base in Hawaii in 1941, resulting in thousands of US casualties, might have been intercepted had intelligence of a potential offensive been taken seriously. Instead, the group talked themselves out of this possibility, convincing each other they had far superior capabilities to defend any attack should it occur).

Given our human tendencies to flock to those like us and to support the consensus, it is easy to see how these conditions can be created.

Today, groupthink occurs in governments, industries, and businesses around the world.

Swissair – a company previously known as the 'flying bank' because of its legendary financial stability – went bankrupt in 2001. Many studies have explored the downfall of such a solid organisation and a theme is consistent throughout: the board of directors got to a position of collective superiority, feeling that they couldn't be thwarted and believing that every decision would be a success. The executives felt that they were so effective as a group, they further streamlined the board, removing those with industry expertise and potential to bring opposing views. This was the action that came back to bite.

How can leaders and organisations protect against groupthink? Jeff Bezos introduced an empty chair during internal meetings to physically force people to consider the current needs of 'the most important person in the room' – the customer. He also encouraged future-focused thinking, famously sharing this statement: 'Avoid copying the past when creating the future.'

Creating a conscious stream of outside-in thinking can help keep this in check. The recent recovery of the UK bookstore Waterstones is a good example of this. Historically, physical booksellers have turned a profit by focusing on deals with publishers. Agreeing volume in return for prime product placement. James Daunt, CEO at Waterstones, instead concentrated on pushing responsibility down to the bookstores themselves: empowering teams to choose what gets placed at the front of the store, to share their own reviews and recommendations on best books; judging that they were best placed to know what their local customers wanted. Where other booksellers failed, Daunt and team are succeeding. He went on to buy Barnes & Noble, a similar chain of bookstores seriously underperforming in America, and a comparable, customer-needs-focused approach appears to be paying off.

Daring to see things differently, to challenge convention and *start with why* the customer comes into a bookshop helped Daunt to achieve what many likely saw as an impossible task in the face of rising online channels. And I bet he drew upon the thoughts, ideas and challenges from a diverse team to help confirm his plan.

## CULTURE CRACK 9: CORPORATE CLONES – NEPOTISM FILLS CRITICAL ROLES

The phrase 'you're going to love her!' might feel familiar to many employees, when their leader announces the arrival of an ex-colleague into their firm. This might be the hire of the century, but have they bypassed the standard objective hiring processes because they're a 'known entity'? Or is this a leader bringing their past with them to build what they once knew, rather than what's needed? If people feel that new hires have come in via the backdoor, or customers and shareholders start to comment on the lack of representation in meetings and events, perhaps there is a latent issue to address. (This approach can also make things challenging for the new joiner, who likely lacks a thorough understanding of the situation they are walking into and can find the relationships they attempt to build impaired by their relationship with the person who ushered them in.)

As we get older, the number of people we interact with steadily declines. Throughout our working lives, this hovers just over twenty people each day: family members, brief conversations during commutes and on the school run, chats at coffee shops, interactions with colleagues and calls with customers. Our perceptions are constantly shaped and reshaped; hypotheses formed and reworked. At retirement, the average number of interactions more than halves to around ten each day. We have a smaller circle of thoughts, opinions and information shared, and this is often shared in a more homogenous group – partners (children have likely flown the nest), neighbours, the lady delivering the milk, friends in a local walking club. Without a diverse group to interact with at work, we're naturally drawn to those most like us – people at similar ages, stages, living in the same neighbourhood, with shared upbringings and interests.

Without a concerted effort, the forces shaping what we think and feel narrows. It can be easy to live life with perceptions and opinions firmly set in stone – everyone else around seeming to completely and utterly agree with how you see things!

Despite the ample opportunities for diverse and frequent interactions in organisations, very often this isn't what plays out. Even with chances to broaden our views, we can fall into the habit of returning to strong ties – the people we trust and know well and from whom we can easily elicit support. This is true particularly in moments of stress or strain. It is possible, too, that remote workforces, despite improving global connection, could exacerbate this problem further and our tendency to flock together with like-minded people could serve to create silos and functionally or regionally separated groups. Workforces could find themselves stuck in loops, failing to share learnings across teams, repeating the same mistakes and feeding a culture of isolation and failure.

That's why it's so important to tackle the 'corporate clones' tendency we all have. Pick up the phone to an old friend and encourage them to apply for a new role in your organisation – certainly. But make sure they're objectively assessed and compared with other applicants, from other disciplines and walks of life, to ensure that the optimal decision (for them and you) is made – regardless of your own network.

## CULTURE CRACK 10: PROFIT OVER PURPOSE – 'COMPANY SUCCESS MEANS NOTHING TO ME'

How do you measure success and communicate progress within your organisation? If it's mainly financial performance, you risk demotivating and alienating employees. Executives and shareholders find financial growth metrics very motivating, since, personally, they are likely to directly benefit from these results. However, for most, this doesn't hold the same reward. Much has been said about the need for galvanising missions and purpose statements. It can mean different things to different people but must align and propel action in a meaningful and sustainable way.

Today, work is more complex and tasks often digitised. Jobs, functions and companies evolve constantly to remain competitive. Industries and professions remain varied, but most now incorporate an element of knowledge work – people are paid to make decisions, manage emotions, collaborate, interpret information and motivate teams.

These same advances have enabled humans to live longer. Planning and financing a 100-year life is now a likely reality and opportunity for many.

Our objectives have shifted. From outputs, production rates, a job for life (until physically I can't do the tasks any more) and retiring on a final salary pension (knowing about twenty years should cover it) to being valued for cognitive and emotional skills and the ability to keep reinventing and reskilling to meet demand.

As individuals and families, we need to finance longer lives, work for longer (possibly across multiple careers, perhaps working independently) and, essentially, maintain our health and well-being. Having an impact, doing something meaningful and leaving a legacy have become increasingly important, too – and people are willing to leave well-paid jobs if the culture grates or the work itself lacks purpose.

Despite being a long time coming, this is a shift that many companies continue to find challenging. A business needs to produce *things* at pace, often at scale, and in a profitable way. The principles of scientific management resonate – make it quicker, cheaper and get it in the hands of customers ahead of the competition. Make money, make some people rich and stay viable.

In our complex, constantly changing world, this simply isn't enough. In fact, a sole focus on profits can really grate. The gap becomes a chasm between the haves and have-nots, regardless of the skills in demand and the effort invested. Individuals will speak with their feet if financial gain is *the* main marker of success.

Successful individuals and businesses today play the long game. As inspirational business speaker Simon Sinek depicts, this is the infinite game. They value the journey – the experiences they enable, the human assets they nurture and the careers they shape – as much as the destination: company longevity and meaningful impact.

The goal is the same – for an individual and a business – to cultivate sustainability through engaging experiences, meaningful work, learning new skills and prolonging our value. Profit and purpose do not need to be either/or.

Are there culture cracks simmering in your team or organisation? Complete a less than five-minute diagnostic and receive personalised insight to help you target action to strengthen your culture. Access the diagnostic using the QR code shared on page 316.

## WORKPLACE WARFARE – REVISITED: WHERE DID THESE CULTURES START TO FAIL?

### PUTTING THE CULT IN CULTURE

Although hard to see for those immersed in the WeWork culture at the time, looking back, there were likely signs of fatal culture cracks in the foundations of this organisation:

- There was complete reliance on one leader to inform strategy, make decisions and report success. Was the organisation suffering from a 'hero complex'?
- There was clear evidence of 'double standards' – the CEO certainly seemed to regularly say one thing and personally do something else. Integrity, trust and transparency appeared rocky from the start.
- There were suggestions that some workers did ask questions and felt uncertain about the strategy and claims made. But did they feel able to voice this? Were there clear channels for employees to flag concerns and share alternative perspectives? It's possible WeWork was also suffering from 'silence'...

### WOLF OF WALL STREET (AND INDUSTRY?)

Although hard to see for those immersed in the culture of many financial organisations during the 2000s, looking back, there were signs that fatal cracks were silently simmering:

- There was a tendency to hire in 'old pals', creating 'corporate clones'. Bypassing recruitment processes and building teams with very similar profiles can contribute to building tight-knit, closed groups, 'cut from the same cloth'.
- Accounts during this period also suggest toxic behaviour was overlooked and even rewarded from certain individuals bringing in the money. These are the 'culture clouds' that can form and set the tone for acceptable behaviour.
- Were whistle-blowers encouraged and listened to? Given that for many organisations the issues appeared to start at the top, it is very likely there were cover-ups and people lacked feelings of psychological safety to express how they felt and what they saw. 'Silence' also seems very likely to have contributed to these cultural failings.

---

### THE THINGS THAT GO ON IN PUBLIC

It is not just the organisations and public bodies mentioned in the previous chapter that are suffering from culture cracks. Indeed, there are common threads emerging throughout society which indicate that certain human tendencies and behaviours are increasing and negatively affecting those working in or interacting with these services:

- Accounts of organisational culture across these institutions suggests evidence of 'parent–child' relationships. The withholding of information and sugar-coating of messages by some people in positions of power likely create dependency and resentment, blinkering the masses from activities going on inside
- A tendency to revert to what's happened in the past also suggests 'history lessons' could have contributed to more inward-focused organisations, preoccupied with process and form-filling and overlooking the broader impact they were making
- There are definitely signs of 'double standards' throughout most of these organisations, and in particular, at the very top in key leadership positions (e.g. public leaders prepared to flout the rules they set and, in doing so, breach trust with their teams and the general public)
- There appear to be obvious challenges with 'silence' – employees lack confidence and trust that they can and should speak up when they see something wrong (perhaps there's even confusion about what constitutes 'wrong')
- And, in the tragic case of headteacher Ruth Perry, the distilling of a school's performance into a single rating created extreme levels of stress, perhaps because of its fixation with achieving metrics that are often removed from the daily focus and real value of the school (it's not quite 'profit over purpose' but a similar concept)

---

## COMPANY CULTURES ARE CRACKING

Having identified ten culture cracks often experienced across organisations, I developed a survey to help identify where issues might be simmering and enable targeted action before serious failures occur.

In total, 305 people completed the survey, across multiple countries, job roles and organisations. This enabled exploration of the trends in experiences of culture, providing an understanding of the extent to which company culture is cracking. (You can complete this for yourself by accessing the QR code shared on page 316.)

Here's what I found:

## EXPERIENCES OF CULTURE CRACKS ARE PREVALENT

Overall, 88 per cent of people were experiencing at least one crack in their organisational cultures, and 82 per cent reported two or more. Organisational culture *is* cracking.

## MOST COMPANIES FACE 'HISTORY LESSONS', CREATE 'HERO COMPLEXES' AND SUFFER IN 'SILENCE'

The culture cracks most often reported were 'history lessons' (67 per cent), 'hero complex' (60 per cent), 'silence' (57 per cent) and 'frozen core' (55 per cent). Typical challenges included a lack of openness to new ideas, being stuck in the past and feeling threatened by the outside. This is likely to seriously hold individuals and organisations back from embracing transformation and anticipating change.

Companies also appeared to form an unhealthy reliance on a small group of caped crusaders to 'save' the day – a reliable team of 'stars' who swoop in to solve issues and deliver great results when the pressure is on. This tendency is often accompanied by bouncing from crisis to crisis. This state is not sustainable, and dependency on the same 'heroes' to come to the rescue can cause resentment, block learning and succession and stifle progress. This is likely contributing to a steady stream of undiscovered talent quietly flowing out of the organisation.

Being stuck in the past and struggling to truly understand the whole workforce's potential and capability would seem to be a common state for many.

## WOMEN REPORT MORE CULTURE CRACKS THAN MEN

Notably, the data revealed a slight difference in the average number of culture cracks reported by women and men. Women were higher at 4.3 per person, versus men at 4.1 per person. In addition, the specific culture cracks rated top differed by gender. Women were most likely to experience 'hero complex' and men 'silence'. This is an intriguing difference – are women seeing more men play the role of the 'hero'? Other research suggests that this might be the case, and that those playing heroic roles feed on confidence over competence. Men are more likely than women to put themselves forwards for new roles and opportunities, even when they lack direct experience. Men apply for roles when they meet just 60 per cent of the criteria; women only apply when they meet 100 per cent.

This appears more significant when considering the recent finding that women are 41 per cent more likely than men to experience toxic cultures. Based on an analysis of more than 3 million US Glassdoor reviews, an MIT Sloan report found that women spoke more negatively than men about most elements of culture, including the work–life balance and collaboration. The largest gap between the genders, by far, was for toxic culture, which the report described as a workplace culture that is disrespectful, non-inclusive, unethical, cut-throat or abusive.

The need to identify when and where toxicity could begin is critical, and even more so in the quest to nurture diverse and equitable organisations.

On the flipside, men encountering silence when attempting to engage with people and spark debate might suggest that there is a skills gap to be addressed. It has often been purported that women demonstrate greater natural people skills than men – empathy, emotional intelligence and reading social cues. Professor Richard Boyatzis and psychologist Daniel Goleman found that women are twice as likely to demonstrate social awareness and 45 per cent more likely to show empathy. As we continue to engage with people across hybrid settings, it is quite possible that investment in social skill development is desperately needed for many, particularly as limited dialogue is symptomatic of a lack of psychological safety (without which it is exceptionally difficult to build a healthy organisational culture). Could this intervention help change behaviour and gendered experiences of culture? And could a reframe on what constitutes good leadership enable those with stronger people skills to nurture fairer, kinder and more inclusive environments for growth? This is something explored in more detail later.

## THE US FACES 'HISTORY LESSONS' WHILST THE UK AND IRELAND NURTURE A 'HERO COMPLEX'

From my study, the only regions with large enough data sets to explore differences were the US and the UK and Ireland (UK&I). In the US, 'history lessons' came top and in the UK&I, 'hero complex' was number one. Do American-based teams have bigger challenges around moving forwards, bringing the outside in and driving continuous transformation? And in the UK&I, is there more credit-grabbing behaviour going unchallenged? Are leaders more inclined to rely on the same people they regard as stars to solve tricky problems and, in doing so, more likely to crush the engagement, commitment and development of others?

## COMMON NEGATIVE EXPERIENCES WHICH DAMAGE OUR CULTURES

Digging a little deeper, the following are the most commonly reported daily experiences, which combine to define – and often damage – the cultures we create:

1. Leaders rely on the same 'star' performers to drive solutions (74 per cent reported this)
2. Employees often evaluate proposals based on what has happened in the past (72 per cent reported this)
3. Business success is primarily measured and shared through financial metrics (63 per cent reported this)
4. Managers are often caught in a web of approvals to drive any action (61 per cent reported this)
5. Individuals are concerned about the reactions of others if they share genuine feedback (59 per cent reported this)
6. It is common to encounter silence in meetings when inviting questions (59 per cent reported this)

At the root of these experiences lies the core elements of what makes us human: a need to feel valued and belong, to feel supported and secure and to be able to make our own decisions so that we can learn and grow. For organisations, this boils down to creating environments where individuals and teams experience trust and empowerment, feel able to express thoughts and ideas, see their contributions and achievements recognised and rewarded and access honest and constructive feedback to progress their careers.

## ORGANISATIONS ARE AWASH WITH WEIRD AND, AT TIMES, NASTY, INHUMANE BEHAVIOUR

In groups, we can lose sense of our own identities and behave in ways we wouldn't normally, having a detrimental impact on those around us. Often, our actions – failing to speak out or challenge, going along with the crowd, not pausing to ask why or invite views from others – collectively create the grounds for toxic cultures to breed. These very human tendencies, ironically, hold us back from building environments where humans can flourish. This can pave the way for the extreme examples explored in Chapter 2, across well-known corporations and public service institutions.

As individuals, we have a choice to make. Our actions and decisions, however small they may feel, make a difference.

How can we do better? And what do we, as humans, need to flourish?

# CHAPTER 4

# HAPPY HUMANS (PART 1)

Ironically, it is our human tendencies that often threaten the foundations that we need to have in place to nurture the best in humans. The culture cracks prevalent in so many organisations are a result of humans struggling to navigate the complex web of thoughts, feelings, pressures, drivers and instincts swimming through our heads, often leading us to choose the most damaging path.

To understand how we can do better, let's first consider what contributes to happy experiences.

Looking back, the moments in my life when I have felt most fulfilled contained several key ingredients.

I share these to bring personal meaning but do so with great awareness that they are set in a position of privilege. Sadly, for many people, their starting point is very different. I am fortunate to live in a part of society where safety and security are rarely flung into consciousness because it is largely assumed. I haven't experienced war, had to flee my home or country; I have had stable relationships and very few brushes with tragedy and grief. These experiences and moments can shape a different perspective: one where purpose is painfully focused on survival rather than fulfilment.

However, I hope that these personal reflections bring connection and meaning to many.

The first, the build-up to getting married – knowing someone wanted to share their life with me created a huge sense of belonging and security. Like most, I had wondered whether this moment would ever come. I knew I desperately wanted to find a partner for the journey ahead, and I had hoped this would mark the beginning of a much-sought-after next chapter. It was exciting and daunting in almost equal measures, yet it was a time when I found that everything else bounced off me. Challenges felt achievable, decisions easier to make. I even found I *could* eat healthily and regularly go to the gym. There was an aligned future path, I was fuelled by purpose and had a strong foundation to provide support and guidance for the journey ahead.

The second standout moment was being pregnant with my daughter. This was a period marked by contentment and a clear mission. The path to pregnancy hadn't been straightforward, and once through the early stages and into the safer zone – a visible bump, regular midwife appointments to reassure everything was OK – I felt clear on my aim. To grow this baby in a safe, nurturing and warm environment, and prepare for the next phase of parenthood soon to hit us both head-on. Things I might usually worry about felt irrelevant. I was calmer, more self-assured and clearer in my thinking. This reflected in my approach at work and improved my ability to evaluate scenarios and guide actions. I distinctly recall being on the way to the hospital to have the baby and receiving a call from my boss to confirm I had been successful in my application to take on a promotion. It was a role I would start once I returned following maternity leave (an opportunity I am still grateful to have received, despite being about to embark on a significant period out of work). The path ahead seemed to be falling into place.

These life moments share similarities. They were key transitions – creating a commitment to my husband and beginning our lives together, preparing to welcome our daughter into the world and taking on new responsibilities as parents. I felt safe and secure. I had the foundations and right conditions to thrive. I experienced clarity in my role and responsibilities, shared values and perspectives and could work through new expectations and realities. I had a strong sense of belonging. I could be myself, share my thoughts and ideas, even make mistakes and feel supported. And, with these building blocks in place, I experienced the liberating feeling of trust and purpose. I felt empowered to make choices – for myself and on behalf of others – because we shared an aligned view on what was important. Overwhelmingly, I felt propelled by purpose – as a wife and then as a parent. This created opportunities for growth. I relished the moments I learned something new, developed a skill, navigated a different challenge – and in both phases, there were many!

These elements are just the same when considering what humans need to thrive at work.

## FIVE ELEMENTS FOR HAPPY, HEALTHY, HUMAN WORKPLACES

I have captured this in a model, to help us all embark on building workplaces where people can thrive. There are five elements, each requiring focus and monitoring to protect from culture cracks and to optimise impact.

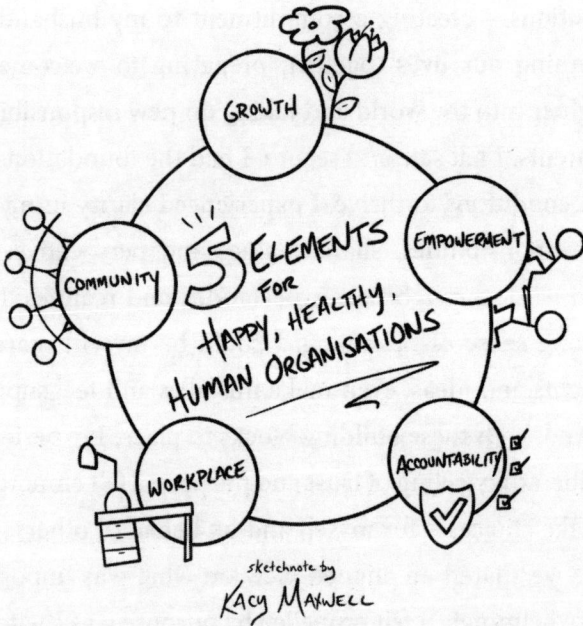

sketchnote by
KACY MAXWELL

This chapter focuses on the first two elements – creating the conditions for people to thrive and ensuring clarity on how people can contribute to an organisation's success.

Two key questions can help assess an organisation's ability to do this:

1. Do people and teams have what they need to thrive?
2. Is there shared understanding of what 'good' looks like?

Just as national cultures can define values, beliefs, rituals, traditions and holidays, they also play a key role at work. A quick look at countries leading the way on work–life balance and satisfaction reveals a pattern. Many Nordic countries – including Denmark, Sweden and Norway – are consistently ranked within the top ten, whereas countries frequently struggling to make the mid-way point include Japan, the USA and the UK.

Perhaps it is no surprise that there is a word in Danish specifically meaning 'happiness at work' (*arbejdsglæde*) and in Japanese for 'death from overwork' (*karoshi*).

Cultural traditions often stem from practices which enable balance, rest, sharing, learning and celebrating. They have been designed to provide opportunity to pause and reflect, give thanks, celebrate and enable people to have time off with others. The structure of the year, the placing of public holidays, even the phases of the moon and circadian rhythms help us to sustain ourselves with periods for rest, social connection and growth – as if by design. So, why as communities (organisations, teams, countries, families) do we so often overlay norms, expectations and reward systems undermining these principles?

Whilst many workplaces might start with a similar structure and logic, in practice, the foundations can be rocked as boundaries become frayed and goodwill tested.

Work can feel like a leash. Digitised ways of working offer tangible benefits by enabling connection and co-creation across time zones, but this also creates risk of 'always-on' cultures, especially as our notions of home and work intertwine. In France, a 'right to disconnect' law was introduced to restrict out-of-hours contact and requests. Specific 'rules' might not work for all (flexibility around time can be a great enabler), but the unwritten norms and cues need to be carefully managed to ensure that people don't feel 'leashed' by non-stop work.

We are inclined to follow others, even when they do questionable things. Early psychological experiments in the 1960s, such as Stanley Milgram's obedience studies, demonstrated our willingness to follow the orders of those seemingly in authority and inflict pain on others. Albert Bandura's experiments showed that children are more likely to engage in aggressive behaviour if they see others doing this. These core elements – role-modelling the behaviour of others and obeying authority – are still observed in social groups, workplaces included.

We rely on cognitive shortcuts to speed up the processing of information. This makes us innately biased. Naturally, we seek to sort information and people into groups. Confirmation bias (seeking evidence to support an already-held belief) and optimism bias (overstating the likelihood of success) are reasonably well known, and proximity and presenteeism are becoming more prevalent as divides simmer between those in and out of an office environment.

Finally, a key feature clouding our work experiences today is that models and norms for how we work have been designed for a bygone era. A time when jobs, responsibilities and structures remained consistent across the year, and rhythms were set according to an annual cycle. Goals and targets were agreed and cascaded at the start of each year. Tasks and duties were clearly outlined in job descriptions. Those at the top could access information and build knowledge ahead of those in the layers below. Criteria for promotions were outlined and opportunities to progress were shared in a programmatic way, alongside annual development programmes to improve managing and leading capabilities. This was a time when things were more certain and predictable. Now, everything moves and evolves. Roles and tasks shift, individuals have access to live information and organisations are flat – people and knowledge can be accessed at all levels and career development facilitated in multiple ways.

It's clear that the conditions we create play a key role in shaping our ways of working. Our experiences *could* be different, if we shape something better by starting with what we need to survive and thrive (as Abraham Maslow's hierarchy of needs depicts) as human beings.

## ELEMENT I: WORKPLACE – CREATING THE CONDITIONS FOR PEOPLE TO THRIVE

Hopefully this goes without saying (although isn't always the case), but ensuring that people have the foundations in place to work in safe, secure work environments is a prerequisite. This includes providing the right equipment, space, lighting and warmth to enable people to perform their role. With this in place, how do we build stronger foundations?

### SPACE FOR FLEXIBILITY

Appreciating different preferences and enabling choice is critical. This is where the underpinnings of trust are set. We need to recognise that employment plays a key part in people's lives for so long and that we all need to make it work for the duration. Today, so much debate centres on controlling when, where and how often people attend in-person workplaces. What's more important is creating an environment that people *want* to come in for – and this is so much more than pizza and ping-pong. Knowing that others will be there is a driver; there's nothing worse than walking into an empty office. We need dedicated time to collaborate, share ideas and be creative and to not spend all our time joining virtual meetings, headsets on, hidden in meeting rooms. Time to interact with and hear from senior leaders is another strong driver, but not just the lip-service townhalls or staged interactive Q&A sessions. Genuine two-way interactions – where individuals can engage, ask questions, share feedback and make suggestions – take time and practice to achieve. We also want time to build social connections – make friends, share funny moments, learn through overhearing others and be able to access guidance and support in the moment. Guidelines to provide choice, not rules to drive uniformity, will bring out the best in all. Work without social connection, belonging and meaning is just a list of tasks, and something we are unlikely to approach in an engaged and productive way.

## DEFINE RITUALS AND TRADITIONS

This is something that so many great communities have front and centre. Take any religion and you'll see that they have a calendar of important and shared events that bring the group together, as well as rites of passage – often linked to age or to symbolise commitment, including ceremonies to welcome people into a faith, partnership commitments and end-of-life rituals. Each religious community brings their own flavour, but at the core is creating a sense of belonging and meaning within the group. For many, this community, whether religious or not (e.g. sports clubs, hobbies, social groups etc.) offers social connection – sought-after regular interaction, something to look forward to and build identity. Many companies have taken to sending out a package of swag – hoodies, pens, water bottles, laptop cases – emblazoned with company colours and logos to welcome new starters. Personalisation – with the new recruit's name

– is proven to instantly boost feelings of engagement and belonging, which last for several months to come. Feeling part of something is so important, and powerful, to us as humans.

In our disrupted and ambiguous world, moments really matter. Taking time to develop and maintain how your company marks key moments for employees can make a massive difference. What happens when a new employee joins? How do we share this with others? What about milestones for years' service? How do we celebrate this? What happens when someone leaves – do they simply disappear, never mentioned again, those who work closely with them only finding out via an out-of-office email reply? These moments matter, for the individual themselves but also for those around them. Consistency, fairness and a human approach are all key – this is what people remember and form judgements on. Considering how you communicate and encourage others to adopt these rituals is important, too. Getting the right mix of group identity and autonomy to make it your own is delicate – e.g. a manager might choose to celebrate birthdays or work anniversaries in a certain way within their own team, using the budget allocated but bringing their own style. Carefully treading the line between being part of a community and not part of a cult, as WeWork discovered, is key to a healthy, sustainable culture.

Check out the accompanying visual for the 'messy middle' via the QR code shared on page 316 for ideas on creating your own moments that matter.

## INTEGRITY AND FAIRNESS

This is fundamental to have at a business's core. As humans we are biased. Yet we expect to be treated fairly and this starts from a very young age – who gets what and when is intensely scrutinised. This expectation remains with us and is felt at all decision points in organisations: who gets hired, who doesn't, who advances, who gets left behind, who gets fired and who remains. We need to create and maintain fair and objective processes to build meritocratic and inclusive slices of society. Considering reward and promotion mechanisms is key. Which behaviours do you really value and want to reward? And what happens if someone achieves a desired outcome but gets there in an undesirable way? Sales performance can often cause organisations a headache if the individual hits targets, bringing in money to the business, but does so in an aggressive or ethically questionable way. By paying them a bonus, the behaviour is being rewarded; the individual receives the message 'keep doing what you're doing!' Those around them might choose to disengage or move on as this doesn't appear to be a place where they can be successful. Unchallenged, tensions fester and cause divides, feeding toxic cultures.

Defining *how* results should be achieved is fundamental in building a fair, integrity-led culture. Training and guidance must be repeatedly provided for those in decision-making roles doing the hiring, promoting and moving people on. A strong culture can be enhanced through a well-informed hire or promotion, recognising objectively the potential for growth. On the flip side, a poor hire or ill-informed promotion decision can undo years of hard work in an instance. Having clear, transparent approaches to objectively assessing people is key, as is ensuring that these processes are upheld by all. Frameworks of skills, behaviour and potential can enable shared understanding of what 'good' looks like (and what it doesn't). Committing to involving people from outside immediate teams in panels to inform critical people decisions can help broaden perspective, and including objective measures of future potential can also help combat biases when it comes to evaluating capability. People processes must be reviewed and improved regularly – as humans we find shortcuts, and tools and techniques continually advance, so there is always room to refresh and improve.

## OUTSIDE-IN MINDSET

Fostering curiosity at the base of an organisation can provide a pillar of strength. Communities are, by nature, about the group within, but the stronger ones encourage interest and learning from those outside, too. The group's identity can feature curiosity as a strength. Many successful organisations have had this at its core. Crossrail, one of the greatest engineering achievements of our age, connected the east and west across London via the Elizabeth Line and involved 75,000 people working over twenty-two years. Mark Wild, who was CEO, has reflected on the need to shift from a conventional mindset of individual parts working in collaboration to every leader and team owning the whole system and genuinely standing in the shoes of others. This project involved multiple companies, partnerships and alliances, to achieve delivery of a brand-new railway. Wild notes: 'A key lesson for me is spotting the difference between collaboration and everyone seeing the whole and truly acting in its service.'

As organisations become larger, span time zones and national cultures, demonstrating genuine commitment to understanding and appreciating diversity can be a differentiator. This can involve building cross-cultural understanding – sharing and acknowledging different traditions, holidays, festivals etc. Making a concerted effort to build diverse and inclusive teams, through hiring, development opportunities, promotion and reward. By establishing partnerships with other companies and institutions, such as schools, colleges, business schools, charities, local community groups and maybe even competitors. Acknowledging that the organisation exists as part of a broader ecosystem can bring great advantages – sharing of talent, knowledge exchanges and creating meaning and purpose for employees through community projects. Organisations must recognise that learning and growing through connection with others is a core element for enabling people to thrive at work.

## CUSTODIANS OF CULTURE
Your leaders must embody your culture. Countless cultural failures stem from leaders being unable to walk the talk.

Yes, they've joined sessions to agree to the organisation's vision, mission and values, but has anyone asked if they are personally prepared to commit to displaying these behaviours, day in, day out? This is possibly *the* most important element because everyone is watching and waiting for their move... Positive examples of 'walking the talk' include actions such as providing open access to diaries, so people really can access a leader's time, and regularly spending time on the front line, whether with customers (Uber's CEO regularly moonlights as a driver), patients in healthcare providers, diners in restaurants, guests in hospitality or with employees. TV programmes like *Undercover Boss* and *The Hotel Inspector* show the power of insights gained through regularly pausing and seeking to understand what it's really like to work within an organisation.

On the flip side, a leader's actions can become a boulder in the stream if they don't align with cultural aspirations. If a leader works long hours, leaves late, sends emails at the weekend, that's the expectation set of others (remember the images of employees sleeping at Twitter offices in early 2023?). If a leader disregards processes for hiring and promoting and ushers in their pal from a previous company, fairness and integrity are flung out the window. If a leader regularly shouts, argues and dismisses others' ideas, the organisation's commitment to two-way, open and honest communication is shot to bits (as is any feedback, progress and innovation). I have often seen leaders loudly proclaim that 'their door is always open', but this is a long way from the reality of a hidden calendar, time fiercely guarded by an assistant and abrupt statements in meetings shooting down others' suggestions.

Leaders must be able to commit to role-modelling inclusive, sustainable and human work behaviours. This has to feature in regular meetings – discussing examples of living the organisation's values and sharing incidents of navigating tensions (e.g. profit vs purpose, being agile yet decisive, inclusive and meritocratic). Leaders, like everyone else, don't have all the answers and experiences to draw upon to sustain and evolve a human culture, so sharing their experiences and learning from each other (including leaders in other businesses) needs to be a constant feature.

A leader who stands out in this regard is genuinely focused on the longer-term success of the organisation. Regardless of the ownership structure or the opportunities to make a quick buck, leaders must buy into, and invest in, the long-term durability of the organisation, recognising that nurturing a workplace where people thrive is paramount. This driver will likely reflect in actions such as: routinely spending time getting to know and understand people across the organisation; proactively seeking and listening to feedback; demonstrating empathy; transparently sharing the path and challenges ahead; being prepared to share when they get things wrong; valuing difference and learning from others; and engaging in activities to build social connections and have fun!

They are *accountable* for the conditions they create.

| ELEMENT I: WORKPLACE<br>– CREATING THE CONDITIONS FOR PEOPLE TO THRIVE<br>A key question to understand the strength of workplace conditions:<br>*Do people and teams have what they need to thrive?* | |
|---|---|
| START HERE... | KEEP FOCUSED ON... |
| **Prerequisite: ensure people have the right tools and a safe space to do their job** | |
| • Create a workplace people *want* to come into – for social connection, meaning, and belonging<br>• Provide guidance (not rules) on where and when people work, but leave space for personalisation<br>• Define your community's rituals and traditions to build moments that matter<br>• Embed integrity and fairness at the core of everything – hiring, developing, progressing and leaving<br>• Nurture an outside-in mindset through valuing curiosity<br>• Ensure your leaders can be custodians and role models of your culture | • Time spent in shared workspaces and how they're used – nudge people toward social connection and collaboration<br>• Gathering feedback – what's working, what isn't? How do people interpret the guidelines? How can they be refined?<br>• Reviewing the strength of community – explore engagement and exit data for signs on what's working and what could be improved<br>• Ensuring fairness and integrity is felt in all processes and decisions. Each year, there will *always* be opportunity to make this better<br>• Building two-way dialogue between leaders and teams |

## ELEMENT 2: ACCOUNTABILITY – SHARED EXPECTATIONS AND CLARITY ON HOW TO CONTRIBUTE

The second essential element in human organisations is a shared understanding of expectations and how to contribute.

Despite managing change every day (within us and around us), we organise our lives around agreements, understanding and commitments. Some are formally contracted, most are not, and yet they guide our expectations and influence our feelings. Jobs are just the same: interviews culminating in the agreement of contractual terms – location, working hours, salary, benefits, company policies, bonus schemes etc.

When taking on a new job, we are also, psychologically, signing up to a much longer, *unwritten*, list of expectations. Like booking a holiday: the hotel website, package and deal are closely reviewed, but it's the Tripadvisor reviews and conversations with friends who have stayed before which muster images of once-in-a-lifetime experiences, incredible food, world-class service and the promise of a truly relaxing break. *That's* what we expect when we get there. Like Tripadvisor, Glassdoor and other similar websites offer potential employees a look at what life is *really* like inside companies.

One of the challenges with how we design and set up organisations – roles, responsibilities, structures – is that nothing stays still in today's world. The days of clearly defined job descriptions are disappearing; once written, out of date. The pace of transformation and disruption is immense, and constellations continually shift. We have all learned that we don't want to be working for the Blockbusters of today, looking at a sorry collection of videos collecting dust.

How can we enable people to consistently and positively contribute?

Crucially, most people *want* to do this. Feeling part of something and being able to use our capabilities to propel an organisation forwards provide meaning and connection. We are much more likely to be productive if we feel engaged and happy about the work we do. There are things leaders and organisations can do to help people feel this…

## FIND YOUR NORTH STAR

Following the pandemic, research has shown that our motivators and priorities have been reordered. Having had the foundations of our lives rocked – health, friendship, security – many are now searching for a new North Star. McKinsey's great attrition report revealed that people are leaving jobs in search of caring leaders and supportive teams, achievable goals, growth opportunities, meaningful and purposeful work, balance and well-being. Purpose plays a key role and when captured well creates the red thread running throughout an organisation, pulling people together, aligning actions and creating meaningful work. Successful individuals and businesses today are focused on enabling long-term impact for people and environments outside of themselves. Critically, however, they also balance this with an appreciation for the journey itself – the experiences they enable, human capabilities they nurture, careers they shape – as much as the end result (if this is, indeed, ever reached). Patagonia's CEO, Yvon Chouinard, in 2022 announced that he and his family would transfer all profits to a not-for-profit trust to fight climate change, bringing together very explicitly the mission of the company and its purpose through financial means. Unilever's twenty-eight 'sustainable living' brands (i.e. brands focused on reducing Unilever's environmental footprint and increasing social impact), such as Dove, Vaseline and Lipton, delivered 75 per cent of the company's growth and grew 69 per cent faster on average than the rest of its businesses in 2018.

Through promoting the products in a purpose-aligned way, they changed the growth and mix of the company.

Adidas has been making strides to become a sustainable company, something the fashion industry has notoriously struggled with. From 2024, only recycled plastic will be used, and by 2050 all production will be climate neutral. One of the ways Adidas is making sustainability part of its culture is its new employee training called 'How to Think and Act Sustainably', where it offers employees the opportunity to contribute towards a more sustainable world through their day-to-day actions. This four-week training combines self-study and conversations with colleagues from across the globe to make employees aware of how they practise sustainability through a different lens, with a different starting point and with diverse possibilities to make a change.

Linking organisational strategy and priorities firmly to a broader purpose works because it unites people together through a shared cause. Individuals, managers and leaders must work hard to continuously review and reset goals throughout the year, as context changes but keep these true to the reason why the company exists. Purpose can cut through rank and hierarchy; it doesn't divide based on financial means but pulls people from all walks of life together, behind a meaningful cause. Compellingly, research shows that people who feel purpose driven are healthier, happier and more likely to live for longer. It is well worth the investment in finding and defining your own North Star.

## FOCUS ON OUTCOMES AND SKILLS

Jobs for life now rarely exist. Careers are not singular tracks. Jobs can't be captured in a single description of tasks and responsibilities. A focus on outcomes and skills can help because it enables clear linking of contributions to a broader mission and purpose (creating alignment amongst disparate functions and meaningful work for individuals), as well as agility (a tight definition of a job role can make it hard for organisations to flex to the context and for individuals to break out of the box they have been placed in). Used well, this can provide a recipe for longevity for both individuals and organisations. Outcomes can be reset on a regular basis – e.g. a healthcare company sets the following outcome goal for a continuous improvement specialist: this quarter, the key outcome to achieve is an improved response time to customer calls, which will directly contribute to our organisational mission of providing rapid healthcare and support to patients in our community. The following quarter, as call response time improves, the outcome is reset to another priority area, still clearly linked to the organisation's mission. The employee understands the skills likely to drive success in their role – a mix of technical and people-based skills. For both the individual and the organisation, there are huge gains to be made through understanding capability and potential to demonstrate these skills. It enables targeted improvement (e.g. access to coaches, mentors with matching skills to share or digital learning) and mobility within the organisation as other priorities and opportunities emerge.

## DISCUSS THE UNSAID

We all make assumptions about what has been agreed and what hasn't. Yet, our expectations on what will happen and when, what we will get and by when, are frequently only recorded in our own heads. It's true – to assume, can make an ass out of 'u' and me. The psychological contract we establish can be wide ranging. From flexibility and autonomy (ultimately driven by trust), timeframes for progression and how interesting or challenging the work will be, to whom I work for and with. It is incredibly powerful, and if compromised, is hard to regain. I have seen many people struggle and have felt this tension myself, ultimately resulting in a decision to leave the role after a short period of time. Breaks in the psychological contract often happen following change – e.g. a different manager steps in, a new function is established or an individual returns to work following a period of extended leave (as our lives change, priorities and commitments also shift).

Having open, ongoing dialogue about this is essential. A colleague has helped me to try to embrace a more northern European approach to giving feedback and sharing feelings of misalignment as soon as they occur. It's wise because, unchecked, the small things mount up; and eventually the straw will land and break the camel's back. My colleague would always phone me immediately after a shared important interaction – a client meeting, team workshop or interaction with a senior stakeholder – and very directly ask for feedback and share suggestions with me. At first, I found it a bit unnerving; I needed some time to prepare and order my thoughts! But quickly I came round to the benefits. The feelings we experience in the moment are often what stays with us – and being able to pinpoint what action, phrase or question led to this is immensely powerful. Otherwise, we do the same thing again, and again. My comfort increased so much that I found myself doing the same with others, and soon a culture of sharing feedback, embracing suggestions and understanding that there is always room to improve and grow began to take root. Having regular conversations about our expectations – perhaps on a quarterly or even monthly basis – can be advantageous for all. It can create a channel to reveal the misalignments, confront tensions, broach honest 'I can't see that happening' type conversations which otherwise fester, growing arms and legs. In a constantly changing and ambiguous world, it is a no-brainer in enabling transparency, trust and autonomy.

### INSTALL A RIPCORD (AND ENSURE PEOPLE FEEL ABLE TO USE IT)

We also need to establish clear expectations on *how* work gets done to ensure that this is ethical and sustainable. As well as providing a compass, we must make sure people feel they can pull the ripcord if needed. This includes articulating what 'good' doesn't look like and being prepared to act when people engage in counterproductive behaviours. Huel captured this simply in the slogan 'Don't Be a Dick'. Over-simple, perhaps, but it gets the message across memorably! As humans, we follow others. Philip Zimbardo's prisoner experiment (everyday members of the public seamlessly adopting the roles of prisoner and guard) demonstrated deindividuation, a state when you become so immersed in the norms of the group that you lose your sense of identity and personal responsibility. This experiment might feel dated, but there are many similar modern-day instances: the storming of the Capitol in the US in 2021; the London riots in 2011; and the cultures of abuse that simmer in organisations every day where people are paid bonuses for results they have achieved in unethical ways – with many watching on, knowing what's happening but feeling too scared or alone to do anything about it.

The social taboo of speaking out and raising concerns often stops people from acting. There's the fear of retribution (what will they do to me?), of facing aggressive behaviour and of the impact it could have on their future career prospects. Recent examples include McDonald's and the Confederation of British Industry (CBI), which were both alleged to be harbouring cultures of sexual misconduct, abuse and toxicity. The insights published reveal a hidden abusive culture spanning years, and undoubtedly affecting thousands of people, directly and indirectly. Establishing psychological safety is essential to building a culture where people feel confident in identifying what poor behaviour constitutes and empowered to pull the ripcord, shining a spotlight on what's going on.

In all organisations, examples of poor behaviour will be encountered. A strong supportive culture will ensure people feel able to flag what they see and have faith that those in leadership will do something about it. Showing teams what is acceptable and what isn't is a daily task for managers and leaders, and it is critical they are aligned on what falls where. A culture with strong foundations in two-way communication will very often help steer behaviour and attitude in the right direction before any significant breach occurs and more official channels need to be used. But these must still be there and accessible. Raising the alarm to abusive, coercive, bullying, unethical or irresponsible behaviour takes courage (the individual likely feels torn about whether they should flag concern and fear an impact on their own career and reputation in the business), and how an organisation responds will shape the behaviour of others. If the whistle-blower is ignored or punished, this tells the whole workforce that the behaviour they experienced is endorsed here. If they are listened to, the situation investigated and actions implemented to ensure alignment with the culture moving forwards, this also sends a strong message – that the company has clear expectations for behaviour and is committed to maintaining a safe and inclusive environment for all. The #MeToo movement demonstrated the power of one voice and how this can build momentum and shift willingness of individuals and leaders to stamp out unacceptable behaviour through building a culture where it is known and understood that such behaviour will not be tolerated.

## DON'T PULL THE RIPCORD! THE TRAGIC UNRAVELLING OF A SAFETY CULTURE AT BOEING

For years, Boeing had the reputation for safety and quality in the aviation industry. Airlines depended on Boeing's proven designs and meticulous production, and it dominated the market. Boeing employees worked there for years; they felt a strong alignment with the organisation's core values of safety, quality and working together. They didn't give a moment's thought in pulling the ripcord, and delaying a launch, or questioning the detail of a design or scrupulousness of a quality check if they felt there was a safety risk. Boeing's purpose was clear, its culture aligned and its unrelenting focus on passenger safety at all costs created an unyielding feeling of psychological safety for all employees. Their shared responsibility was to ensure that the highest-quality aircraft carried passengers in the utmost safety to their destination.

Then, something changed. A merger was announced – Boeing joined forces with manufacturer McDonnell Douglas in 1997. Very quickly, the culture changed. The new organisation had different priorities – the goal was to manufacture more planes, more efficiently, to maximise profit and performance on Wall Street. Ex-Boeing employees sensed the shift. Previously well-established processes were overhauled, reinvented to streamline and improve efficiencies. Quality checks were removed. Production rates picked up, but so too did the volume of errors. The leadership team seemingly didn't mind – they were cranking the handle and financial performance was rocketing. The new regime sensed some 'slowing down' and cynical questioning from the old guard – mainly those in technical roles with expert understanding of aircraft design and the aviation industry. Management made the decision to move the headquarters from Seattle to Chicago – many believed to enable greater free rein in decision-making, as the technical engineers were seen to hamper decisions which would fuel financial growth. However, commercial growth was faltering. Airbus was making up ground, and fast.

During this period, employees also noticed a distinct change in attitudes to whistle-blowing. Previously, Boeing, driven by safety and quality, reportedly had a strong culture of support for people who spoke up and shared concerns. Now, they were being shut up or removed. People raising problems were attacked – the messenger was shot down. This was a culture of placating and hiding – don't bring problems, bring solutions or simply bury your head in the sand. The ripcord, previously always visible and frequently pulled, was now hidden in a restricted area, with a 'do not touch' sign clearly emblazoned above it.

In response to Airbus's advances, Boeing rapidly developed the 737 Max. Based on the Boeing 737, a model introduced over forty years ago at the time, the planes were designed with modern, energy-efficient engines and could carry more passengers. The beauty of it, though, in Boeing's eyes, was that the use of an existing model meant that the design could be positioned as a derivative – not a brand-new model – speeding up production and, importantly, flight approval from the Federal Aviation Administration. Boeing sold around 5,000 737 Max aircrafts to airlines all around the world and quickly reclaimed the top spot from Airbus.

The 737 Max might sound familiar, and unfortunately not for any good reason. In 2018 and 2019 (just five months apart), two Boeing 737 Max aircrafts crashed, killing all crew and passengers on board.

In total, 346 people died.

For the first time in history, airlines across the world made the decision to ground an aircraft model.

Subsequent inquiries revealed the extent to which the safety culture at Boeing had been lost and years of silencing of those who dared to question internal processes and decisions. Although a derivative of the previous 737, the Max did have a new design feature – the Manoeuvring Characteristics Augmentation System (MCAS). The energy-efficient engines were heavier and needed to be positioned higher on the aircraft than previous models and this (in layman's terms) created a risk of weight imbalance, causing the plane's nose to push upwards. MCAS was a system automatically deployed to help counteract this and enable the pilot to keep the plane on course.

No one outside Boeing had heard of MCAS. No pilot had

been trained in how to manage the system. Information eventually retrieved by investigators who trawled through thousands of documents evidenced that Boeing had deliberately kept any reference to the MCAS system within the organisation. The production rate and sales trajectory couldn't be interrupted by delays to approvals or time for pilots' simulator training. Concealed documentation also later revealed that multiple concerns had been expressed by technical staff about the functioning and use of MCAS, and internal testing had demonstrated that pilots only had ten seconds to respond and rectify any malfunction with the MCAS system. They recommended training for all pilots before flying the 737 Max.

The two pilots killed in the fatal crashes had ten seconds to try to respond to a system failure they didn't even know existed and certainly had never been trained to manage.

The families of those killed attended the inquiries, holding up photos of their lost loved ones. They ensured that the Senate and Boeing executives had to face the human consequences of a corporation's actions and relentlessly sought explanation for their irreplicable loss. The families say Boeing never apologised nor admitted accountability to them directly. The Boeing CEO during this period was forced by the board to resign several months later. He did have to face the families of those lost during the final inquest, but he also walked away with $62 million in pensions, stocks and shares.

Today, in early 2024, Boeing is still struggling to get its reinvention right. The company has made headlines again as whistle-blowers testify to US Congress about the continued safety issues going apparently unaddressed within the organisation. Tragically, another whistle-blower, who had flagged safety concerns and was waiting to testify, was found dead, appearing to have taken his own life. Amongst all of this, another change in leadership is in motion, as the current CEO has shared plans to step down at the end of 2024. This will be Boeing's second CEO since 2019.

As a new leader takes the helm, hopes rest on them being able to finally put right the overarching mission and priorities of this leading aircraft manufacturer. Will restoring the foundations of its culture – a purpose to ensure the safety of passengers across the world through combining technical excellence with commitment to quality shared in clear processes and ways of working across teams and functions – be the primary objective? Hopefully ensuring a visible, readily accessible ripcord, which, if pulled, is met with support from those in senior positions to help resolve any concerns, is high on the list, too.

This example shows the extreme impact an organisation's culture can have on life-and-death outcomes. It highlights the crucialness of clarity in understanding the North Star – the company's reason for existence and impact on the world – ensuring that the skills and expertise driving success are valued and listened to, and that people feel supported and able to freely express concerns to help the collective team deliver on its mission. There is so much for us all to learn from through this case.

| ELEMENT 2: ACCOUNTABILITY – SHARED EXPECTATIONS AND CLARITY ON HOW TO CONTRIBUTE | |
|---|---|
| A key question to understand the strength of accountability: *Is there shared understanding of what good looks like?* | |
| START HERE... | KEEP FOCUSED ON... |
| • Find your North Star (as an individual and as a company) – use this to create a compass for contribution<br>• Focus on outcomes and skills to provide a meaningful and agile framework for work and careers<br>• Openly and regularly discuss the unsaid with your manager and those you manage – psychological contracts (the often-unsaid assumptions and expectations we make in our heads about what will happen and when), if not aired and reviewed, can break us all<br>• Define, and commit to enforcing, expectations on *how* work gets done – outlining what good does and, critically, *doesn't* look like<br>• Install a ripcord to enable people to flag risks and concerns – and ensure people feel psychologically safe to use it | • Sharing examples of work, across the functions, teams and countries contributing to your North Star<br>• Enabling mobility within your organisation – through projects, teams and experiences<br>• Bringing managers together to share how they have regular honest conversations with individuals to align understanding and expectations – this is a skill in itself and requires honing<br>• Discussing the behaviours rewarded and promoted, and those not. Constant calibration will be required to ensure alignment and reinforce culture<br>• Exploring how frequently risks and concerns are raised – are there teams where this never happens? In every culture, this will happen, and absence could indicate support is required to build psychological safety |

# CHAPTER 5

# HAPPY HUMANS (PART 2)

Continuing our exploration of the foundational elements of happy, healthy and human workplaces, up next is how we create and maintain balanced and positive communities. Places where people feel empowered and able to grow.

Three key questions can help assess an organisation's ability to do this:

- Do people ask for help?
- Can people say what they *really* think?
- Are people able to grow?

## ELEMENT 3: COMMUNITY – WE'RE IN THIS TOGETHER AND EQUALLY VALUED

The first question is fundamental to community belonging. The second and third questions build on the first and relate to nurturing empowered teams and facilitating continuous growth – both of which we will explore later.

You are likely part of many communities: neighbourhoods

(perhaps you're the one who organises the street parties, or maybe you hide inside, pretending not to be in!), sports clubs (increasingly these are virtual, like the digital community Peloton has created of people working out remotely), religions, parent, child and school groups, perhaps book clubs, societies or classes where you learn new skills (again, many are now virtual and spanning geographies) and social media sites (Instagram, Facebook, LinkedIn etc.). The good ones make us feel great. It's a place where we belong. We're part of something. We feel valued, respected and that we're doing something worthwhile.

## WHY ARE COMMUNITIES IMPORTANT TO US AS HUMANS?

To answer this, let's explore how it can feel being 'rejected' from a community. I have seen many people experience redundancy. I have even made business decisions to initiate change and as a result put roles and people at risk. The experience exposes the jagged edge of an organisation: a sudden change in tone, hushed conversations or consultation periods, ultimately resulting in colleagues quickly and often quietly exiting. A company needs to evolve to maintain relevance and growth – but the business rationale doesn't make this any less challenging to deal with.

It hurts because it threatens our core human drivers. Firstly, we read redundancy as 'I'm no longer valued' – my skills, experiences and loyalty are not an asset to this business any more. Secondly, the ability to make a choice has been taken away. 'Your role is at risk' instantly removes the power we take for granted to decide when it's time to move on. And thirdly, the very acute realisation that you might not work here any more – the daily rituals, purpose, identity and friends all linked to a job and workplace are in jeopardy. The feeling of rejection is intense and the risk of not belonging again feels very real.

Experiencing belonging feels good and there's scientific reason for that. Social connection triggers our brains to release oxytocin, a hormone producing a happy feeling. Whilst often associated with bonding between parents and children, it is activated by social bonds at any stage in life. It's also addictive – the more we feel, the more we want – and, conversely, scientists say it can also elicit feelings of jealousy and suspicion if there is threat to the dynamics of the group. Historically, social belonging has resulted in survival; those threatening the tribe being left for dead, literally. Throughout childhood and in education, belonging is both actively sought (e.g. in attachment with children) and used to manage poor behaviour through exclusion. Feeling and creating belonging is a highly sought-after prize and in many ways a life's work.

It's no surprise that even the word redundancy can stimulate our fight-or-flight response system. Our brain moves to high alert. The amygdala releases cortisol (a stress hormone) which moves throughout the body spreading the message of danger – pupils dilate, heart rate increases, breathing gets faster, adrenaline is released – our bodies get ready for the next move: to stay and fight or flee to safety.

We feel much better – mentally and physically – when we are part of something, have purpose, feel appreciated and know that someone has our back. The Hawthorne studies in the 1920s and '30s unintentionally illustrated this. Starting as a productivity experiment, the research intriguingly discovered that people worked harder whatever change (positive or negative) was made. In essence, the researchers had stumbled upon the power of belonging – being observed, feeling valued and part of something drove people to deliver more.

Being observed will only have an impact for so long. Friendship, however, has the power to influence and shape behaviour across the longer term. If you're lucky enough to have friends at work, you will be familiar with the great benefit this can bring. Personally, I know the huge value that going for a walk or having a coffee with a friend can bring. Accessing warm, supportive advice, having a laugh or simply venting in a safe place can change a gloomy perspective and inform more balanced decisions. Unfortunately, recent research has shown that 22 per cent of people don't have a friend at work and that those with low social connection experience higher levels of anxiety, burnout and stress. An engagement survey by Gallup includes the statement 'I have a best friend at work' and it is this that is most predictive of turnover; if you have a close friend at work, you are much more likely to stay. Work communities, crucially, are not families. We don't fire or rate the performance of our partners, children, siblings or parents.

Companies and people can confuse a strong community with being part of a family. The distinction is important – although there are things that both families (nurturing long-term relationships, open communication, honesty, respect) and workplaces (offering care, forgiveness, kindness, support) can learn from each other – and founder-run or family-owned businesses typically evolve to appreciate and value the differences.

Post-Covid, the debate about work rumbles on. Companies are confused about how to manage the return to offices, carefully treading the line between autonomy, flexibility and creating physical presence and collaboration. Many are now stipulating rules and expectations for when people are in offices. Where this will land it's not yet clear, and economic uncertainty is pushing many companies back towards command-and-control models – something many leaders in their fifties and sixties have experienced themselves and revert to in times of pressure. Central to the debate appears to be 'what *is* work?' If I achieve the list of tasks I need to each day, is the rest of that time mine? Or do I *need* to join cross-functional working groups, attend knowledge-sharing sessions, mentor others or read up on the latest company successes? The question is now how much of our work should we devote to contributing to a community as well as delivering results. We know that quality, innovation, productivity and engagement can all increase when a diverse team works effectively together, but how can we create effective communities at work?

## CREATING STRONG COMMUNITIES IN OUR WORKPLACES
### In this together

Establishing psychological safety has become a marker for success across many teams. Professor Amy Edmondson has led the way in defining and advocating for this as a key foundation for high-performing and healthy teams: psychological safety is 'a belief that one will not be punished or humiliated for speaking up with ideas, questions, concerns, or mistakes, and that the team is safe for interpersonal risk-taking'.

A psychologically safe group isn't about comfort. Rather, it is about getting comfortable dealing with discomfort. Creating an environment where people can share what they really think – whether that's supporting or challenging an idea. Where people can ask any question and not feel stupid for doing so. And where learning is seen as success – sharing what went well and what didn't (and not brushing this under the carpet) is an attribute of a psychologically safe team, too.

At university, I failed my statistics module. The course took place in a computer lab (a distant era before smart technology!). We learned statistical techniques through applied case studies using software and textbooks. The room was dark (so dark I can't recall the lecturer's face), the only light coming from the rows of computer screens. Computers were enormous machines in those days, so students sat miles apart. If you missed a step in the process, you were gone. It was very hard to recover and catch up because the computer programs were complicated and didn't exactly match what was outlined in the textbook. I had no idea, really, what was going on or what I was doing. I rarely reached the outcome the lecturer shared. People didn't ask questions or seek help. Just put your head down and try to keep up seemed to be the mantra. Despite this being the same group of students I shared many other classes with, there was no psychological safety in the room and, ultimately, this resulted in many people having to resit their statistics exam (second time round, I sought help from someone outside the university, asked the stupid questions and began to get my head round what this actually was all about, and managed a pass).

Psychological safety can vary between settings, leaders and topics. It must be continuously worked on to establish, maintain and evolve.

### Success = social connection and making an impact

We spend so much of our lives at work, the measure of success cannot simply be business outcomes: how much money we made, how long it took us, the size of the company, how well-known the brand is. When people leave organisations, it's unusual for someone to just talk about these achievements. Most reflect on the relationships and friendships they've built, the skills they've learned, the team they've felt part of and the impact they have had on those around them.

Yet, it is still reasonably uncommon for companies to

really talk about the importance of these elements in their success. Certainly, there will be a nod to being people focused, having an impact on the community, but is this really embraced from the outset? And when compromises need to be made, does the company's impact on the community and its people get prioritised over financial results?

When leaders talk about wanting to get teams back into the office, are they doing this because they really value the collaboration this could bring? Or is it to reassure shareholders that they have got a motivated and visible workforce, putting in as many hours as possible to deliver growth?

In other communities, social connection and impact come top of the list. I recently attended a ceremony for appointing the new head at my daughter's school. It is a faith school, so there was a religious tone, but the sense of community and the role of the new head within this was paramount. A room full of pupils, teachers, parents, church leaders and school governors all gathering to contribute to this special moment. The new head explicitly commits to their responsibilities across all these groups – creating a safe learning environment for all pupils, taking on a key role within the broader community and church, leading a supportive and growth-focused workplace for all staff and running a financially effective business. The calling out of responsibilities across all stakeholder groups made this feel tangible and meaningful for everyone. There was a genuine sense that the new head understood their responsibilities and that everyone in the room was aligned in supporting his success. In organisations, new leaders are often announced with a cursory email, if at all. Perhaps there is a place for a more significant acknowledgement of the breadth of responsibilities of leadership, to ensure shared understanding and commitment to this path? Creating long-term value for all stakeholder groups will ultimately serve to drive business outcomes, in any case.

## Empathy is the enabler

Favourite lessons at school were so often shaped by a teacher who cared. Someone who checked in, asked if you were OK if you looked down, who personalised feedback to help you achieve more (because they believed in you). This is a feature in many great teams. The youth squad that Sir Alex Ferguson built at Manchester United in the 1990s turned around a 26-year wait for the Premier League title in 1993. In his time at the club, he led the team to win thirty-eight trophies. There are many accounts of how Sir Alex and his team achieved such success. One key aspect that players talk about is the sense of belonging he created. Many great players – David Beckham, Paul Scholes, Ryan Giggs, Gary Neville – joined the club as teenagers. They spent long stretches of time away from their families, yet they joined another one. Sir Alex was a father figure – encouraging and coaching and, equally, setting high expectations, embedding discipline and commitment. He understood each player, what motivated them, their aspirations and anxieties. For the players, being at Manchester United wasn't just about playing top-flight football – it was being part of a club.

Gregg Popovich was head coach of the San Antonio Spurs basketball team, ranked as the third greatest basketball coach in history by the NBA for his 170 play-off wins. Many described him as a grandfather-type figure and, fittingly, his nickname was 'Pop'. Grumpy at times and, like Sir Alex, focused on discipline, he cared. He showed genuine interest and empathy for each of his players. People describe how at social events, he would work his way round the whole room, engaged in conversation with every individual. He remembered details – family set-ups, interests, ambitions – and he made each person feel important and part of the group.

As he said:

Yes, we're disciplined with what we do. But that's not enough. Relationships with people are what it's all about. You have to make players realize you care about them. And they have to care about each other and be interested in each other. Then they start to feel a responsibility toward each other. Then they want to do that for each other.

To create feelings of belonging, small actions and attention to detail go a long way.

### Be curious, not judgemental

This next feature involves another sports coach, this time the fictitious Ted Lasso. In the Apple TV series, there's a wonderful scene when Ted highlights the power of curiosity over judgement. Ted finds himself in a high-stakes darts game in the local pub with Rupert, the co-owner of Richmond FC (the team Ted has been appointed coach, by Rupert's ex-wife, Rebecca). At stake – Rupert being evicted from the owner's box, whilst Rebecca is still in charge. Ted starts by giving the impression he is clueless when it comes to darts, before 'remembering' he is left-handed and nailing every throw. As he secures the victory, he shares a childhood story of always being underestimated by other kids at school and a quote, from Walt Whitman, 'Be curious, not judgemental.' He says, 'If you were curious, you would have asked if I have played a lot of darts. And I would have said, "Yes, sir, every Sunday afternoon with my father at a sports bar from age ten until I was sixteen, when he passed away."'

A community needs to be a place where everyone is accepted and can be themselves. There might be common threads – we are all talented footballers, we all attend the same church, we are all interested in photography – but an appreciation for the value that difference brings is also key.

This is easier said than done. Our brains classify moments when different views are expressed as a threat. Our fight-or-flight response system activates, and we seek to close conversations, get out of situations and save ourselves (sometimes even in scenarios when we feel embarrassed or threatened simply because we don't know the answer).

Blood rushes to our heads, our hearts pump harder and louder, our palms feel sweaty. It's not just life-or-death scenarios, any of these everyday situations could trigger this physical reaction:

- Someone challenges the proposal you have worked weeks to prepare
- You encounter uncomfortable silence or intense conflict in meetings
- You don't know the answer to a question
- You need to ask someone for help
- You receive difficult, perhaps unfair, feedback on your style and impact
- You work with someone who sees things differently to you

An unavoidable side effect of belonging to some extent is that others are excluded. This starts early on in socialisation, as children develop friendships and begin to measure enjoyment through being part of something bigger than themselves. It extends to habits, use of language and in-jokes – defining the character and norms of the group. Parents experience this as their children get older – being cast aside often quite dramatically into their out-group! Whilst this is an inevitable part of growing up and identity, in other scenarios, being on the fringe can be exceptionally tough and unfortunately for many is a common experience. Social identity theory suggests that the groups we belong to give us a sense of pride and increased self-esteem. It says we go on to develop prejudiced views through dividing the world into 'us' and 'them' by exaggerating the similarities

of the in-group and differences of the out-group. To understand and appreciate difference, sometimes we must work
against our human instincts.

| ELEMENT 3: COMMUNITY<br>- WE'RE IN THIS TOGETHER AND EQUALLY VALUED<br>A key question to understand the strength of community belonging is:<br>*Do people ask for help?* | |
| --- | --- |
| START HERE... | KEEP FOCUSED ON... |
| • Establish psychological safety and a feeling that 'we're in this together' – safe environments where people can ask questions and share learnings through failure<br>• Ensure people know collaboration and social connection are important and valuable parts of work (as well as tasks and outcomes)<br>• Identify people who lead with empathy. Place them in crucial roles to create a foundation of genuine concern and care<br>• Nurture curiosity, not judgement. Make asking questions and seeking to understand difference the norm<br>• Build visions and stories to demonstrate the value of the whole. Deliberately and repeatedly show how everyone contributes to the journey and success of the community | • Developing key habits to strengthen psychological safety – retrospectives to share successes and failures and fuel learning; regular meetings where leaders simply ask questions and listen<br>• Showcasing and rewarding examples of communities working well and having impact. Talk about *how* results were achieved, not just what<br>• Embedding empathy as a core skill into talent processes – hiring, developing and promoting. Measuring 'caring' in surveys, e.g. 'My leader cares about me', and targeting development<br>• Establishing strong diversity, equity and inclusion communities across the organisation, enabling awareness, understanding and belonging for all<br>• Encouraging employees to recognise and reward people who have contributed to their success (e.g. within recognition programmes) |

## ELEMENT 4: EMPOWERMENT
## - PEOPLE ARE TRUSTED TO DO THE RIGHT THING

The feeling of being empowered to tackle something difficult, gaining new knowledge and coming up with a solution
that makes a visible difference is wonderful. Time literally
flies, you feel immersed in the challenge, exhilarated by
the rush of making progress and sharing updates with key
stakeholders. Psychologists call this being in 'flow', and key

to this is achieving the right balance between challenge and skill – not too challenging so we feel overly anxious and not too easy so we get bored.

Creating opportunities to experience flow isn't always easy for employers, and navigating the spectrum of control and empowerment can feel like a tightrope. It is tempting to default to directive approaches to leadership, particularly when times are tough, because organisations are led by humans, too (well, currently!). The game of hot potato – passing decisions around, deferring action, quashing ideas… Spending our days in a quagmire of meetings and endless email chains. Ugh.

Psychologically, having a lack of autonomy to steer our own actions and decisions can be catastrophic. Having autonomy scientifically makes us feel good and is proven to improve well-being and satisfaction at work. Without it, we can burn out, spiral into learned helplessness and engage in destructive behaviours.

Empowering others isn't always our default. Habits, anxieties and egos creep round the edges, telling us to do things ourselves or take the 'simpler' route. Sometimes an urge to protect others from the prickly stuff can mean that we wrap them in cotton wool, inadvertently blocking their understanding and growth. Or, as a leader or manager, we believe that this means we should take charge all the time, know all the answers and dominate conversations. Adopting the role of master and commander can get in the way of motivating and enabling. Then there's the familiar temptation to just do something yourself. It will be so much easier, quicker, if I do this task. Yet the investment in time upfront can quickly pay off; providing time for you on tasks where you can experience flow.

Tobi Lütke, CEO of Shopify, embedded the concept of a 'trust battery' within his organisation. He describes it in this way: 'It's charged at 50 per cent when people are first hired. And then every time you work with someone at the company, the trust battery between the two of you is either charged or discharged, based on things like whether you deliver on what you promise.'

I love the visual image this creates and believe in many ways that empowerment is what makes trust feel real and tangible. The trust battery charging up might look like people being empowered to take on vital projects; individuals asking for help and receiving support; colleagues sharing their work and ideas across the business; and leaders openly sharing challenges, inviting ideas on how they could be solved. At the other end, behaviours such as micro-managing, lying, gaslighting, blaming others and credit-grabbing will drain the battery and leave people feeling dejected, isolated and burned-out.

Empowerment can be the secret sauce within an organisation's culture, but it's an exacting recipe. Too much and people feel lost and isolated; too little and they switch off. Feeling trusted and empowered, valued and invested in, gives people fuel – you can almost see the lightbulb go on and burn bright, enticing others to follow.

## HOW CAN WE BUILD TRUSTED AND EMPOWERED TEAMS?

### Communicate an inspiring vision <u>and</u> report progress

A compelling and inspiring mission with meaningful impact that everyone can relate to is a must. But this can't be unveiled and forgotten. Or only remembered and celebrated when big milestones are achieved. To align and empower people around a shared vision, it must feel in reach, something each person can contribute to. Importantly, people must feel that progress is being made. Sir Dave Brailsford led the British cycling team from 2002, in the build-up to the Beijing Olympics in 2008. British cyclists previously had very limited success – only a scattering of medals at Olympic events. Brailsford's squad won seven out of ten gold medals available in track cycling, and they matched the achievement at the London Olympics four years later. Famously, Brailsford adopted a marginal gains approach to cycling. He believed that if the team made 1 per cent improvements across the board to small things (such as bike aerodynamics, nutrition, the pillows they slept on, even hand-washing techniques to minimise sickness), they would achieve a significant increase in performance. And they did.

As he said:

When we first started out, the top of the Olympic podium seemed like a very long way away. Aiming for gold was too daunting. As an MBA, I had become fascinated with kaizen and other process-improvement techniques. It struck me that we should think small, not big, and adopt a philosophy of continuous improvement through the aggregation of marginal gains. Forget about perfection; focus on progression and compound the improvements.

## Learn to let go

Some slack in the reins is necessary for new directions and growth. Letting people in, to find their own way and make their own mistakes is all part of the story. This is something that founders can really struggle with – it's their idea, their baby, after all! Yet often the idea, the entrepreneurial mind and approach that got the business started need some new strands and perspectives to enable scale. This is where being clear from the outset that growth is about people as well as financial milestones can help. But it's not about delegating and disappearing. Facilitating connections, sharing thoughts and guiding can provide ideas with air and nutrients to breathe and grow into something better and stronger.

Leaders play a key role in this, and showing their own vulnerabilities can help create a psychologically safe environment. For example, showing interest in someone else's views or knowledge, admitting their own mistakes, initiating rituals around learning through failure, listening more than speaking and appearing at ease with not knowing everything can help build the foundations. These actions can pave the way to let others in.

## Trust people with the truth

An empowered team needs to understand the reality of

the business. Letting people in can help charge feelings of trust. This needs to be balanced with responsibilities for confidentiality and sensitive information, but often what we communicate is shaped by what makes us feel better more than what the audience needs to hear. Being transparent about the key elements (cost constraints, what the future path holds, how this will change experiences) says you see them as adults, part of this journey, with choices to make. For example, in one global manufacturing company I worked with, a leader openly shared with their team a requirement to save costs. Rather than launching into a redundancy process, they invited suggestions from the team on how this could be achieved. The team came up with a proposal to each reduce their working hours, equating to the savings made, enabling everyone to keep their jobs. In general, people will respect and respond positively to this approach; treat people as adults and you will get the same approach back. This can help embed a culture of accountability. Being trusted with the truth means that you're in this together. The conversation shifts to 'how can we use our skills to move forwards', and everyone has a role to play. In addition, ensuring efforts and successes are accurately attributed communicates a meritocracy, not a hierarchy, and encourages accountability, not blame.

### Welcome failure as part of the journey

Embracing failure as opportunity to learn helps create the conditions for people to stretch and try new things. If failure is rare, hidden or punished, people will naturally look for places to hide, wait for instruction or work to strict rules. Making failure an expectation and part of the journey can help people feel confident to voice opinions, share ideas and develop new skills. It's no good just saying this: people need to see it in action to believe it. Regular sharing of lessons learned and equipping individuals with skills and tools to talk about these instances in a constructive and helpful way will help build resilience and openness. In the early 2000s, Netflix overhauled its approach to talent management. At the centre was a commitment to candid feedback. Understanding that in most groups, honest feedback is rarely given, Netflix created a model – the 4As – to assist employees in providing regular and constructive feedback.

The 4As are:

- Aim to assist – give feedback with positive intent, not to get something off your chest
- Actionable – make sure what you share enables the individual to do something differently
- Appreciate – when receiving feedback, show appreciation, acknowledging it is being shared with good intent
- Accept or discard – appreciate that the decision to act (or not) on the feedback shared is entirely with the individual receiving it

Getting the right blend of trust, support and guidance to nurture empowered teams takes focused thought and coordinated effort, but it can prove a transformative asset within a happy, healthy organisational culture.

| ELEMENT 4: EMPOWERMENT<br>– PEOPLE ARE TRUSTED TO DO THE RIGHT THING<br>A key question to understand the strength of empowerment is:<br>*Can people say what they think?* | |
|---|---|
| START HERE... | KEEP FOCUSED ON... |
| • Picture trust as a battery within your organisation. What actions can you take to energise your teams through feelings of trust?<br>• Communicate an inspiring vision and share progress made. Break down big goals into small, achievable steps that everyone can contribute to<br>• Learn to let go, and let others in. Long-term sustainable growth is about finding multiple routes to delivering value<br>• Trust people with the truth. Being transparent with constraints or opportunities can tell others that you're in this together<br>• Welcome failure as part of the journey. Embracing failure as an opportunity to learn can encourage people to share and contribute more openly | • Indicators that trust is an issue, e.g. people choosing not to apply discretionary effort; repetitive failures; high attrition<br>• Coaching and supporting individuals and teams to identify the best actions to make progress towards bigger goals<br>• Single points of failures. Individuals who are overloaded and overwhelmed. Help them to let others in<br>• Stress-testing communications – is what you're saying benefitting you or the audience? Often, we hold back from sharing the truth because it can feel hard to deliver<br>• Equipping individuals and managers to embrace a true feedback culture with tools and skills to have confronting yet constructive conversations |

## ELEMENT 5: GROWTH – PEOPLE FEEL SUPPORTED AND INSPIRED TO DEVELOP AND GROW

Building a community and nurturing empowered teams of people who feel trusted to do the right thing can create the foundations for growth.

The final question is: Are people able to grow?

To bring this part to life, I share a story from my own leadership experience and highlight the elements I believe helped build an environment where people could grow.

It starts amidst Covid – a time when everything felt

strange and uncertain. But companies couldn't simply stop their transformation and growth plans. Business needed to continue, and in September 2020, we embarked on a significant piece of change. To bring together locally managed professional services teams into one aligned European function.

This was a multifaceted group across six regions, covering more than ten languages, and a mix of consulting, sales and project management roles. There was also a lot of heritage – many had been in the company for more than ten years (several twenty years plus!) and had strong regional identities. This change was critical to company strategy – enabling growth through scaling solutions, enhancing client experiences and delivering in a consistent and efficient way. It simply landed at a time of great uncertainty and change.

Despite this, within two years, we achieved revenue growth, improved margins and enhanced client experiences; but more than that, we created a community where people felt a sense of belonging, were trusted and empowered to do the right thing and supported to develop and grow. Here are the key components that helped:

DESIGN FOR HUMAN GROWTH (AND KEEP IT FRONT AND CENTRE)
We started with this as a key goal. Business outcomes were there too, but at the foundation was building a culture where our people could grow. If we could get this part right, I felt confident that the results would come. In the first few months, I invested a lot of time in meeting, understanding

and connecting with the team. Who were they? What was important to them? What were they worried about? Of course, there were differences. Some anxious about job security; others fearing loss of regional identity and local connections. But there was excitement too. What could this new chapter bring? And, unanimously, what could it mean for me? I focused on this in more detail – asking questions about what a positive experience would look and feel like. Here, commonalities emerged – a place where I can learn and grow, where I am treated fairly, where there is team spirit and I can be myself and use my skills and expertise to contribute to our success. This was a diverse and disparate team spread across Europe – professionals with specialist qualifications and skills, interacting with clients, delivering high-value work. Having a strong manager who really cared, and had the time to care, would be vital to success. So, too, was continuous improvement – making things easier, sharing knowledge and generating new ideas. This was a group of people who wouldn't be satisfied sitting still – they wanted to move forwards and have impact.

I designed a new structure to enable just that. A pan-European management team including dedicated team managers and senior individuals with specialist responsibilities. This enabled managers primarily to manage. Managers interacted with team members regularly to really get to know and understand them and their needs. They provided support – when facing challenges in client delivery; how to navigate internal processes; and to discuss their career aspirations and development opportunities. Alongside, specialists drove improvement and managed service lines. They worked collaboratively across the teams, identifying pain points, risks and opportunities to make things easier and partnered with colleagues across the organisation to enable transformation.

In companies around the world, temptation is there to ask managers to manage *and* be responsible for client portfolios, take sales targets and deliver client work. Star-performing individual contributors are asked to keep doing what they're doing *and* just manage a few people. The truth is that management is totally different to being a strong individual contributor. Achieving through others takes specific motivation, and facilitating growth in others demands distinct skills for success.

The division of focus and responsibilities worked exceptionally well (it also provided different options for career progression – managing people and applying expertise at a more strategic level). Crucially, it created a sense of ownership – empowering managers and their teams to take accountability and deliver on their own commitments. As the CEO of Shopify described, the trust battery was beginning to charge. As we explore later, managers *can* bring work to life, but only if they're not overloaded, overworked and lacking in energy to make the magic happen. Designing teams and structures to optimise this dynamic can be the game changer.

The most successful and durable business plans start

with unwavering commitment to fuelling and enabling human growth.

## NURTURE GENUINELY <u>KIND</u> ENVIRONMENTS

This was a group for whom achievement, progression, learning and fairness were non-negotiables. Creating a culture where these elements were characterised was key. However, this didn't mean an environment where everyone always got what they wanted; understanding how they can contribute, get recognised and develop their careers was essential. This meant designing a 'kind' learning environment, as psychologist Robin Hogarth defined. Not to be confused simply with kindness (although a feature), this involves transparency around expectations and routes for progression. In kind learning environments, feedback is abundant and accurate – e.g. when learning to ride a bike, we wobble and learn to rebalance, go too fast and feel out of control so we slow down. Or, when playing chess or tennis, we understand the rules, the conditions and get instant feedback based on the move or shot we played. Conversely, in wicked environments, feedback is incomplete, delayed or unreliable. We feel blind – venturing into the unknown without any sign that we're moving in the right direction.

As a management team, we worked on producing clear guidelines for roles and expectations. Fewer job descriptions (these can become out of date very quickly), more guiding principles for ways of working. We spent time co-creating promotion criteria and how we would measure readiness for a move. This empowered individuals and their managers to discuss career aspirations and identify opportunities to gain the skills and experiences required to progress. We incorporated more flex to timing – rather than building up a waiting list for one period in the year (and creating risk of attrition through perceived lack of pace in career growth), we moved to a 'when we're ready' approach, meaning that individuals could complete a readiness assessment and the business need could be reviewed at multiple points in the year. From the outset, we spent time discussing high-stakes moments for this group, such as promotions, new opportunities and pay reviews, recognising that these would need to be managed carefully, in a structured and transparent way to ensure fairness and rigour. Whilst we didn't always get these things totally right, our intent was clear and appreciated by the team. (See the accompanying visual on the 'messy middle' and creating moments that matter via the QR code shared on page 316.)

At a management offsite in Italy, we explored the memorable moments we had experienced as individuals and tried to identify the core ingredients to charge trust batteries. There were standout instances when people had felt trusted and empowered by the business – e.g. being offered new opportunities just before heading off on maternity leave – and moments of achievement and pride, such as seeing their work and impact appreciated by others at conferences, through recognition or promotion. There was also a big cluster linked to working and learning as a team on exciting and stretching projects – high-profile clients, new challenges, in interesting international locations. We made a commitment to architect these opportunities for everyone within the team in a fair and proactive manner. We knew that these moments would fuel growth and engagement and this became a key feature in the culture we created.

## GROWTH HABITS

As American psychologist Carol Dweck highlights, people with growth mindsets believe that success is determined by effort and that their own traits and skills are only the starting point: 'I haven't learned how to do that, yet.' In the 1990s, many automobile organisations adopted this approach. They put in place learning hubs, enabling anyone to access development of interest to them, regardless of their role. They were ahead of the curve in realising that creating opportunities for growth would nurture engaged and motivated teams. Building a space where people felt supported and able to adopt a growth mindset was something we wanted to incubate. However, when you hire and develop people with a drive for high achievement, it can be difficult to also encourage the open sharing of development needs and challenging experiences. It is still a work in progress, and as team dynamics naturally evolve against an ever-changing business context, this will continue to be something to work on. There were, however, some activities we introduced across the team that really helped. The managers each ran weekly 'stand-up' meetings.

A fast-paced start of the week, teams shared what was on their agendas, asked where support might be needed and identified opportunities to improve across the whole company – e.g. sharing challenges and learnings (and very often the specialists took these things back to work on team-wide solutions). This was a safe space to talk practically about what needed to be done, and how.

Being a European team, we naturally incorporated a combination of cultural tendencies and perspectives. In Belgium, the Netherlands and Germany, in particular, there was greater comfort in giving and receiving feedback. This was a habit we captured and developed across the European team, encouraging short, focused feedback conversations immediately after key interactions (so things didn't fester or turn into a big deal – it was genuinely about helping each other to grow). We introduced the practice of 'dry runs', scheduling time with a small group to act as an audience for high-stakes interactions, to enable preparation and feedback. Initially, many were reluctant. We persevered, and the impact on confidence and delivery was significant – enough for word to get out amongst the team that this was a safe space and worth the time investment.

Injecting moments of light-heartedness was important, too. Feeling able to share a laugh with colleagues is a good sign of a strong and balanced culture, and whilst it certainly takes time to get there, we had many laughs. Two moments stand out. The first was early into our journey as a European team. We couldn't meet in person owing to

Covid restrictions but wanted to bring social connection and sharing of cultures into our time together. The management team organised a virtual bar crawl. Small groups created their own 'bars' – with themes, dress codes, a menu of drinks and songs available on the jukebox. Some even created mingling activities to help the conversation flow. Our screens were awash with '80s gear, Finnish, German and Dutch drink choices and a whole plethora of music options. It was silly but talked about for many months to come. The second moment was Christmas during Covid, again seeking an opportunity to lighten the mood and share in some festive celebrations. I rewrote the words to 'Twelve Days of Christmas' and merrily handed out song sheets ahead of our final team get-together. Turns out, this particular Christmas carol is not as widely known as I thought, and varying broadband speeds made for more of a medley rendition than an in-synch choir! It was slightly awkward but in a festive, fun and bonding way.

These were all actions eminently in our control – they depended upon people and time. Prioritising them made a big difference to the work we delivered but more importantly, to the relationships we nurtured across the group. Trust and respect flowed – we were able to show how we could support each other to achieve more – and at the heart of this was kindness. Not simply telling people what they want to hear, or what's easiest to share, but being honest about their capabilities, impact or the likelihood of making promotion or receiving a pay rise in the next six months. Equipping ourselves and the teams with the skills and a safe environment to make this a habit was a critical pillar for human growth in the company.

## VALUE AND REWARD LONG-TERM PERFORMANCE

The emphasis was always on the long term: building a function and team that would make things more fulfilling and have a lasting impact. However, along the way, it was tempting to put in place quick wins to enable focus on short-term results, such as an additional incentive or initiative to drive the activity required at that moment – e.g. completion of customer surveys, faster deployment of transactional services or 'tick box' items to demonstrate progress. We did this a couple of times, but it generally distracted and confused. I learned it was much better to try to get the set-up of the year – the mission, cadence for communication (the big plays) and incentives – as right as possible from the start. We kicked off each year keeping these goals simple. Picking a theme (creating connection was one, great explorers another) and three to four things, as a team, we wanted to achieve. Importantly, these were also things clearly contributing to the broader organisational strategy. We were all swimming in the same direction. These tactics helped align, connect and provide meaning and a framework to demonstrate our impact – within the team and for our executives – throughout the whole year. Like marginal gains and the

British cycling team, this created momentum – breathing life into everything we did, and providing markers that we *were* making progress.

In addition to team and company growth, we spent time showcasing stories of personal growth. Illustrating how team members were progressing against their own ambitions. Sharing and celebrating milestones – delivering a new solution, improving skills, helping a client, achieving promotion or tenure anniversaries. Finding regular ways to recognise, reward and illustrate personal growth can become an energising feature of a high-performing, healthy, inclusive culture. Identifying the smaller moments, changes and examples that demonstrate progress must be a core feature, since the 'end' never comes (every stage, quarter, year or role, we start again). It provides lasting reason to stay involved and connected with the team.

### NURTURE POTENTIAL

The final feature that helped us to create a growth culture was a commitment to objectively understand what people wanted to, and could, do in the future. An eye to what's next is always helpful. As humans, we want to know and understand what could be round the corner. Falling into the trap of making assumptions about what people can do or want to do based on what they have done in the past is common but can be fatal: people are misunderstood, opportunities overlooked and exits sped up. Embedding these tools and habits can ensure regular discussion and alignment of opportunity and potential between individual and organ-isational needs.

We used measures of personality and motivation when hiring and on-boarding new starters. This is enlightening for building, understanding and exploring future oppor-tunities as capabilities and potential develop. This insight, alongside performance metrics, engagement data and one-to-one conversations to explore priorities (e.g. how life stages and needs are affecting their requirement for work right now) and aspirations (what individuals want to devel-op and how they would like their career to progress) pro-vided a treasure trove of insight to fuel alignment as context evolves. Managers within the team met individuals regular-ly, updating views and understanding, as people changed and grew. This helped identify risks – e.g. potential flight risks and to put in place personalised actions, or individu-als ready for more, including stretch assignments, different roles or promotion. It fed a detailed review of our readiness to adapt and evolve, stress-testing different scenarios – e.g. a surge in demand, a drop in demand, acceleration of new solutions requiring different skills etc. We explored engage-ment survey data in depth, identifying changes over time, exploring trends (and the potential drivers behind this) to identify macro actions that we could take forwards to keep nurturing a culture where people felt able to grow.

We were acutely aware of the molten nature of the land-scape, for individuals, the team and the business. Much like a garden, growth is always precariously balanced and demands constant attention, tailored support and coordinated effort to bloom.

---

**ELEMENT 5: GROWTH**
**– PEOPLE FEEL SUPPORTED AND INSPIRED TO DEVELOP AND GROW**
A key question to understand the strength of growth in a culture:
*Are people able to grow?*

| START HERE... | KEEP FOCUSED ON... |
|---|---|
| • Design for human growth. Create time and space for managers to manage<br>• Nurture kind learning environments. Identify significant moments and stages and purposefully shape these for growth<br>• Embed growth habits. Dedicate time and structure to actions that support ongoing learning (e.g. project reviews, preparation support and rhythms for feedback)<br>• At the start of each year, capture how your team needs to contribute to the company's success in a mission theme. Pull out three to four goals you all commit to driving and measuring | • Ensuring managers are allowed to manage. That they're not overwhelmed and have the tools and skills to nurture positive relationships with their teams<br>• Keep an eye on fairness and inclusion – this is likely to be something you need to regularly nudge to improve<br>• Power-up capabilities via tools and training (e.g. giving and receiving feedback) and showcase how learning and development have led to success<br>• Constantly review and discuss progress one to one and as a team and regularly share and celebrate examples of personal growth<br>• Regularly review macro-level insights to spot trends, identify risks and opportunities and inform purposeful people planning |

---

This is where the five elements in the make it human model come together to ensure that individuals feel able to ask questions, empowered and supported to try something different (even with the risk of failure) and able to grow. In these environments, people can step into the learning zone – where new ideas are formed, improvements are realised and people experience understanding – and find unique ways to create value, for themselves and the collective.

# PART 2

# HOW TO MAKE
# IT HUMAN

## CHAPTER 6

# BODY: FOUNDATIONS FOR GROWTH

So far, we have examined the current state of human experiences within companies today and revealed a messy picture. However, by understanding where we're going wrong, how our human attributes can hinder progress and focusing on the five elements which can ensure more human workplaces, we find hope and opportunity – if we act on it.

In the second half of this book, we shift to exploring the things we can do to make happier, healthier, more human workplaces a reality, learning from the people and organisations already carving out new possibilities and imagining what else might be possible in our lifetimes and beyond.

To build a human workplace, we need to consider the organisation as a human being – positioned, fuelled and strengthened to bring out the best in people. In many ways, this is something we have been doing for years – describing and assessing the character of an organisation, its values and attributes, and the mood of a team. The collection of people working for a company is, after all, what makes the culture something living and breathing. The human traits we assign are how we describe companies to others – e.g. 'it's a friendly, supportive and conscientious place to work' or 'this company is tired and cut-throat'. Humanising companies brings both the challenge of fear, stubbornness and selfishness as well as the promise of hope, dedication and capacity to change.

Yet, within organisations, particularly when under pressure, we can bury the human features deep down. We move to talk about people as resources and overheads, to review outputs such as sales performance, profit margins and utilisation rates in isolation from the people driving them. This dehumanises our perception to enable seemingly more objective decisions – where cost efficiencies can be achieved, or productivity pushed harder. At times this can be helpful. However, the optimal approach to such scenarios is undoubtedly a blend. From personal experience, I know that a view on outputs can tell only one half of the story. The value an employee brings is rarely captured simply through quantitative data. I was asked to manage a cost-out exercise in a business and approached the task in an 'objective', business outputs-led way. This revealed an answer, suggesting who could be let go, and an interview focused on the future role requirements appeared to validate this. We made the decision to explore an exit for this individual. However, several conversations later, I was left wondering whether this was the best outcome. Colleagues who worked closely with them revealed that they contributed a huge amount to the business in other, less measurable ways. Their absence had a detrimental impact on the day-to-day running of the office, to interactions with clients, to morale and to engagement across the team. The lesson is that measuring outputs only reveals one side of the coin; the inputs could be more valuable than you realise.

To appreciate the value of the whole, I believe we need to consider three aspects to nurture human workplaces: body, mind, and heart and soul.

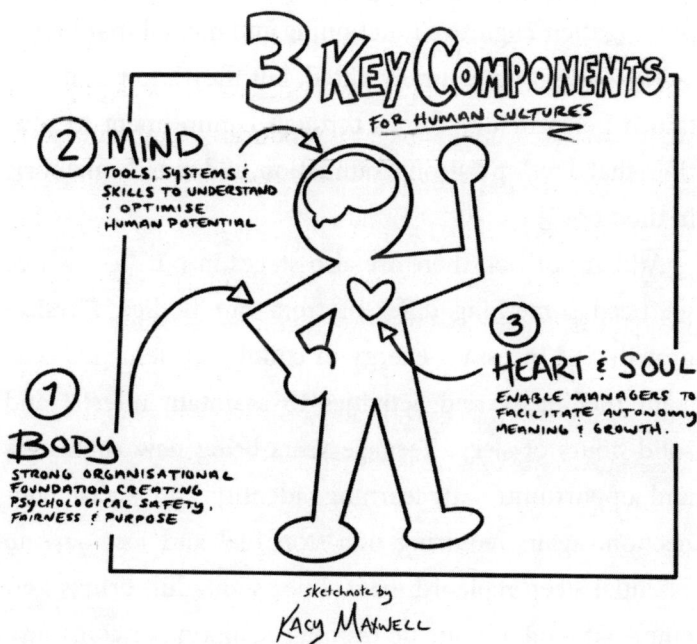

## 3 KEY COMPONENTS
### FOR HUMAN CULTURES

(2) MIND
TOOLS, SYSTEMS &
SKILLS TO UNDERSTAND
& OPTIMISE
HUMAN POTENTIAL

(1) BODY
STRONG ORGANISATIONAL
FOUNDATION CREATING
PSYCHOLOGICAL SAFETY,
FAIRNESS & PURPOSE

(3) HEART & SOUL
ENABLE MANAGERS TO
FACILITATE AUTONOMY
MEANING & GROWTH.

sketchnote by
KACY MAXWELL

Athletes spend a considerable amount of time building and nurturing the body they need to sustain results. Cyclists and runners carefully strengthen muscles, follow warmth and ice routines and meticulously eat dull, yet nutritious diets, whilst weightlifters look for ways to gain weight and manufacture muscle, eating several small, protein-based meals throughout the day. Formula One racing drivers need to focus intensely on strengthening their necks, to enable them to deal with the extreme pressure their bodies face driving at excessive speeds. Some athletes choose to train at high altitude where oxygen is less dense, to help stimulate improvements to oxygen delivery and lung capacity. All will also focus on getting enough sleep and on constantly improving their cognitive functioning and mental well-being.

They might be naturally gifted, but they know that sustained performance comes through commitment to routines that develop a strong foundation, and muscle memory, in their bodies.

Athletes or not, there are also stages in our lives where we need something different from our bodies. Physical growth and incessant energy in childhood demands constant fuelling, varied activities to maintain interest and solid hours of sleep. Teenage years bring new challenges and opportunities in learning, identity and social connection, again requiring non-stop fuel and lost days to essential sleep replenishment. Life as an adult brings new emphasis – often more on training, sculpting or constraining intakes to try to ward off the inevitable middle-age spread. Other periods might require nurturing a body to grow and feed babies and, as parents or carers, adjusting to lack of sleep and putting others' demands before ourselves. Many change eating and sleeping habits to ensure their bodies can provide what's needed throughout this period. Later in life, focus again shifts to ourselves – sustaining and maintaining health perhaps through vitamins and exercise routines to strengthen muscles we didn't realise existed, let alone needed strengthening!

Yet, in organisations, we rarely purposefully consider the 'body' we need to strengthen, fuel and replenish to optimise the results we seek.

## WE BECOME WHAT WE MEASURE

We have certainly come a long way from the harsh, impersonal work environments of the past. There's no doubt that companies have modernised approaches, realising they need to nurture conditions for people as well as results to thrive. Measures of engagement (and whole teams managing these processes) have become key features, employee experience is discussed and invested in and holistic benefit programmes are developed to support the whole person at work. We have stepped onto a path to something better, and yet there is still work to do. Adoption and results are mixed. The sea of data we have access to and our human instincts can detract from the broader ambition we are developing.

How often do businesses focus solely on financial performance to measure success? Organisational updates and company-wide communications are fixated almost exclusively on the growth of the company – sales, revenue, growth rates, margin, profitability. It's a very common scenario. Yet take a look at the feedback on sites such as Glassdoor, and you will need to search hard to find reference to financial success as a key reason for joining (or staying in) a company.

There's a major disconnect between what companies track and proclaim as 'success' and what people value (and is proven to deliver long-term success). Financial performance in isolation simply isn't enough to build a durable business – hundreds of studies attest to the importance of broader factors – yet few companies visibly prioritise these metrics. Financial metrics are important, but they're only one part of the equation. The challenges encountered when focus shifts almost exclusively to these measures are multifaceted and not always immediately attributable to this element of design.

Firstly, it can divide. Business growth by numbers only *really* motivates those whom it directly benefits. What does 10 per cent growth mean for 90 per cent of an organisation? These metrics might provide interest and some aligned motivation in the short term, or for a subset with aspirations to lead businesses or specialisms in finance, but across the long term, they can create divisions. These numbers mean very little to me (as an employee) but a lot to you (as a leader with a stake in the business's financial success) – is this company just about making a small group wealthier?

Secondly, it can split audiences. Talking numbers can turn many people off. Looking at charts, graphs or projections can feel complicated and confusing. Numbers aren't what most people remember or feel energised by. It's the stories, emotions, challenges overcome and breakthrough ideas that really bring work to life and make it meaningful. Bringing investor-style calls into everyday communications can create a detached and alienated workforce – unsure about how their work contributes to the organisation's performance or what they need to do next.

Thirdly, it's exhausting. A tireless focus on financial performance naturally creates a year with many ups and downs. The quarter starts well, then tails off. The next quarter *must* be huge! In sales teams, the ups and downs and the 'you're only as good as your last quarter' feeling is common, yet sales teams expect this. Many thrive on the risk and reward environment, the relentless chase, the intense highs and gut-wrenching lows. However, for a whole company, this can deplete energy and resources. Multiple 'finish lines' makes efforts feel futile, work meaningless and never-ending. The motivational rollercoaster can feel draining and debilitating.

If athletes, artists, singers and parents tracked outputs only, they would likely stand still. They'd lack motivation to keep going, feel exhausted, like every day is a failure. 'I haven't made the qualifying time for the championships.' 'My baby will only sleep for two hours a night.' 'My debut song only got 200 downloads.' 'What's the point in continuing with this?' Learned helplessness can replace feelings of energy, motivation and progression. How we measure and perceive success is so important. It's what shapes attitudes, behaviour and beliefs. If we feel we're not making progress, success isn't meaningful or it saps our energy; the body, or foundation, we are nurturing is unable to thrive.

In today's people-centric world, there's a need for a more holistic model to guide a company's success and enable inspiring and motivating communications. This could even help organisations to pinpoint what drives and multiplies results and identify the levers to pull in changing scenarios.

## WHAT REALLY MATTERS?

Behind every result, output, metric or outcome are people. People have choices – where to invest time, how to behave, the amount of effort to put in. What we measure, how we report progress and share updates must reflect this, to motivate, align and inspire discretionary effort, hard work, loyalty, commitment and belief.

Glassdoor published the top companies to work for in 2024 in the UK, based on employee reviews. The top ten include companies such as Bain & Company, Mastercard and Boston Consulting Group, as well as smaller organisations, such as Housing 21, Equal Experts and NetCompany. The employee reviews cite experiences such as: 'People-centric. Cares about individuals, developing them and giving them what they need through the highs and lows of life' (about Bain & Company), 'Good benefits. Lovely people. Huge organisation but you don't feel like a number' (Mastercard) and 'Exciting projects and career opportunities, inclusive and supportive culture. Flexible, family-friendly work-patterns' (NetCompany).

The metrics that matter to employees are clear – a collaborative, inclusive culture; flexibility and balance; interesting and meaningful work; opportunities to progress and grow.

How many organisations proactively and objectively track these elements? Some report on engagement surveys, but there is always opportunity to massage the data, to select what is reported (and what isn't). Many organisations talk about these components, but dig beneath the surface and are these really measured, reported and targeted? Some genuinely do, but this is often the exception, not the norm.

In their quest for finding workplaces offering these experiences, employees often display a better instinct for what truly matters in sustainable organisations and businesses. Research has found positive relationships between purpose and company earnings; employees today demand more than pay and benefits (and they can access this in a much broader array of companies); nurturing diverse and inclusive organisations increases company profits; and people who don't find opportunities to learn and grow their careers will leave the company.

So, it's time for something new.

## NEW WORLD OF WORK, NEW MEASURES OF SUCCESS

I believe we need a new holistic model (see the 'new measures of success' model via the QR code shared on page 316) to target, measure and share what success looks like, across workplaces today. This enables us to capture both outputs (what) and key inputs (how), in a model with humans at the front and centre of the equation, because we inevitably become what we measure. Organisations will adopt their own versions and flavours, but ensuring balance across all these elements is critical to enabling healthy, inspiring and sustainable growth cultures.

## EMPLOYEE VITALITY

This must be first. Are people healthy? Is this a culture focused on long hours, presenteeism or input over outcome? Are people burning out? Or does the company treat people like adults – trusting them to work in a flexible, balanced way? In the 1990s, many companies introduced benefit programmes offering gym memberships. Employers recognised the need to maintain healthy employees, but the conditions created within the workplace prevented these from having a broad impact. How connected do people feel at work? Gallup's engagement survey item 'I have a best friend at work' is one of the best predictors of retention. When we feel part of something and that we belong, we feel happy and therefore more likely to work harder and stay at a company.

## CULTURE HEALTH

Culture is often described simply as 'how things are done around here' and yet a positive or negative experience can have a far-reaching impact. Having some regular tracking of culture is so important, to examine elements such as diversity (how representative the workforce is and how this changes over time) and who gets promoted and who doesn't, as well as the extent to which collaboration, learning and growth happens across the organisation as a whole (or only in pockets) and taking a measure of psychological safety – do employees feel they can say what they really think and not get shot down for it? Techniques such as organisational network analysis (ONA) and natural language processing (NLP) offer advanced ways to gather insights on company culture, through providing information on how, when and where networks are established across organisations as well as the words and phrases being used. With thought and proactive data collation, objective, data-led views on culture experience can be gathered and monitored to inform action.

## PURPOSE AND IMPACT

Meaningful and impactful work is increasingly prioritised as a top driver (amongst knowledge workers) and is often why people explore side projects or take time out to pursue new adventures. McKinsey research has even found links between purpose and life expectancy. As an employer, building and maintaining a galvanising purpose is critical as it can help drive and align workforces. Tracking the strength and position of this, therefore, feels like a no-brainer. Many companies provide employees with time for charity work or organise company-wide initiatives to give back to communities. Our next step is to ensure this is woven into the day-to-day experiences of work. Mastercard, for example, includes a 'decency quotient' when identifying new employees. Bringing in people who are talented, can get on with others and do the right thing is fundamental to the company's success.

## COMPANY PERFORMANCE, TODAY

Understanding the performance of the company today is vital. This might include metrics such as financial growth (sales, revenue) as well as profitability (margins, EBITDA etc.) but should also reference things such as productivity (are we working smarter, not harder?) and the longevity of the business (do we have a model that will last? E.g. are new customers signing up, buying more? How quickly do innovations arrive and how successful are they?). Of course, this section is intricately related to, and driven by, those previously outlined. Many organisations are getting good at including 'lead' measures to business growth. Technology companies track and beta test incubated innovations; enterprise companies examine their customer buying behaviour, modelling journeys and nudging customers between offerings with personalised marketing; and sales pipeline information has grown significantly – many companies have developed their own data models to test and build confidence in strategies. Data is abundant, but choosing carefully what is useful and informative is key to avoid drowning in it.

## TRANSFORMATIONAL POTENTIAL, TOMORROW

A final component, often overlooked, is the potential of the organisation and its people to evolve and remain relevant in the world, tomorrow. This is where aspects like constant learning in the flow of work (e.g. mastering skills, adopting new tools, accessing courses, completing badges etc.) and the ability to deliver change (whether programmatic or through reconfiguring organisational designs and enabling internal talent mobility) can be key indicators of future durability. In addition, objectively measuring potential within the workforce – e.g. for leadership and to develop new and emerging skills (technical and human) to deliver future needs – provides valuable insight, too. Macro views on objective assessment (psychometrics, skills assessments etc.) can provide a means for organisations to quantify the latent potential and transformational capability they have within their workforce, focusing efforts on improving this to sustain company growth.

## START SMALL AND BUILD

It's certainly not easy to measure and track *all* these elements but start small and build from there. Look at the data sources you have available today e.g. engagement surveys – can the questions themselves be used to provide insight into different components? HR systems such as applicant tracking, psychometric tools and assessments, learning and development platforms, skills portals and talent marketplaces could also provide great data sources. Customer feedback, buying behaviour analytics and sales metrics can provide great intelligence, especially when combined with other sources. Activity streams such as Microsoft Viva (tracking collaboration, time spent working etc.) and even ONA tools showing how information flows around the organisation could offer some fascinating insights.

Make it manageable, practical and insightful and quickly extend your view beyond financial metrics. Reporting on these will help people understand the company better (and vice versa); it will help attract even more talented people (from a diverse range of backgrounds); and it can help identify the action required to drive continuous improvement and future agility. Financial metrics provide a snapshot of an organisation's position today. You need to understand and tell the broader story about the journey, how this can be sustained and what's needed to build readiness for tomorrow.

Carefully considering what to include and report on is critical. We can access data on anything. The trap many companies are falling into today is analysis paralysis. Disappearing into data holes, stifling action and decision, because there's always something else to explore or an alternative projection that can be pulled together. The key is to consider the problems you wish to solve and keep this clearly linked to purpose. Once you share data, people expect follow-up and ongoing reporting. Suddenly teams grow arms and legs; there are more people reporting and analysing than creating! Of course, AI brings methods to scale, but it still requires human oversight. What is measured is a commitment you need to get right from the outset.

When this is designed and managed well, insight across each of these elements is gold dust, equipping leaders with the means to build agile and dynamic organisations. To understand which levers to pull and when, to achieve specific outputs in certain scenarios, the balance between controlling and enabling is fundamental. So often metrics tell a leader only one half of the story, failing to provide insight on how to change the outcome. That's why leaders revert to command and control when things get tough; they can't sit back, they know the results aren't where they need to be, but they lack the data to understand what's needed to change this. Their seizing of the reins, slowing down of autonomy and empowerment, ironically, does more damage than good. Results might increase in the short term, but undoubtedly a decline will follow, as those with ideas, suggestions and insights exit or stay silent. A lack of information flow – reality checks, stemming of innovation, honest feedback – has seriously damaged multiple businesses (e.g. Blockbuster, BlackBerry, Kodak) and will continue to do so, unless we break the knee-jerk control reaction on which we rely.

## FOUNDATIONS FOR HUMAN GROWTH

Carefully considering and establishing holistic measures of success is a key ingredient, but these must be grounded in an understanding of an organisation's foundations for growth. This is the first step in enabling a climate for human growth. The second two steps (fuelling the organisational mind and empowering managers to create the beating heart) are discussed in the following chapters.

Strong organisational foundations shape the body within which heart and mind can be connected and activated, enabling humans to experience belonging, meaning, growth and happiness at work. It is about capturing the essence of the company.

Being able to answer the following questions provides a great starting point:

1. Why do we exist? What's our purpose and mission?
2. Who are we? How do we ensure we work with trust, integrity and fairness?
3. How do we work? How do we build environments where all people and ideas belong?

All companies are people companies. Therefore, all companies need to create and nurture foundations where humans can grow if their business is going to stand the test of time.

There are some doing this exceptionally well because they are crystal clear in their answers to the above questions. People and organisations will undoubtedly change and evolve (if they are to survive), but the durable ones do this around a clear and solid core.

The B-Corp certification takes a holistic look at a company's entire environmental and social impact. Certified

B-Corporations are leaders in the global movement for an inclusive, equitable and regenerative economy. This is quite a shift in focus and recognition, and is encouraging employers, large and small, to consider their broader purpose and role within society. B-Corps are legally required to consider the impact of their decisions on their workers, customers, suppliers, community and on the environment. This involves not only having a social conscience as an organisation but putting in place objectives and work to reduce inequality and poverty, contributing to a healthier environment and treating their workers well. They also commit to using their profits and growth for the greater good.

To become B-Corp certified, organisations complete a rigorous assessment across multiple aspects of their organisation: governance, workers, community, environment and customers. An overall score is achieved and if successful, they can publicise their certification and score, seeking to improve on their rating each year. Companies can also be discredited if they fail reaccreditation or breach the standards set.

A new era in 'doing good business' is fast emerging, and it's in high demand.

This provides a great way to identify the companies leading the way in running more holistic businesses. Here are a few B-Corp accredited (at time of writing) companies and the aspects I feel make them likely contenders for strong human workplaces.

## ABEL & COLE

Abel & Cole, a UK-based food delivery service, is clearly purpose driven, as its website states: 'Since 1988, we've believed that food has the power to help change the world. We're on a mission to make shopping sustainably simple, putting people and our planet first every step of the way.'

Abel & Cole sources and delivers fresh organic food and groceries from sustainable producers. This means supporting independent growers, cutting carbon emissions, reducing unnecessary packaging and using sustainable materials to build a greener future for all.

As a customer for several years, I have seen this in action multiple times. All packaging is recycled (box, string, ice packs), produce is seasonal and from local suppliers and, more recently, the company has branched out to provide plastic wrap recycling collections, as well as reusable milk bottles. I once enquired about changing the delivery slot we had, because we started to include refrigerated items and would prefer an earlier time to guarantee getting them in the fridge before everyone leaves for the day. However, the very friendly response I received explained the driver's routes were carefully planned to minimise carbon emissions and the packaging provided would keep the produce chilled for a whole day, so it wouldn't be possible to move the delivery time. Fair enough, I thought! A refreshingly purpose-aligned and transparent response.

I also admire Abel & Cole's focus on people. Food boxes arrive with information about the suppliers, their stories and sustainable production approaches. They share insights on how they're growing and evolving as a business and what they've learned along the way. I enjoyed updates about recyclable packaging solutions for milk (really!), honestly outlining that they'd had several failed attempts but kept trying and eventually got there. It sounds like a work environment where psychological safety, support to experiment when there's opportunity to make progress, fairness and respect are prominent features.

This feels like a company where its purpose permeates everything, and as a customer, you feel part of the greater good.

## PATAGONIA

Other B-Corp organisations leading the way include Patagonia, another strong, purpose-led organisation: 'Patagonia is in business to save our home planet.' It has partnerships across communities and grassroots organisations and has established Patagonia Action Works with this objective at the heart. This is mirrored in the culture and ways of working for employees. There is a focus on creating flexible, supportive communities where like-minded people can use their skills for a distinct cause. In 2022, the CEO announced all of the company's profits would be put towards tackling climate change and protecting undeveloped land.

## DANONE

Danone (across multiple sites) aims to create a food ecosystem that works in harmony with people, the environment and the communities in which it operates. To create a positive impact on both people's health and the planet, Danone's mission is to engage consumers in healthy eating habits through education and specific nutritional commitments. There is a focus on early ages to ensure future healthier lives, with change and school programmes. In addition, Danone integrates the importance of reducing its impact on the environment with projects through the company's value chain, which is striving to use 100 per cent renewable electricity and have zero waste in factories by 2030.

## NESPRESSO

Nespresso is the pioneer of high-quality portioned coffee. The company works with more than 120,000 farmers in fifteen countries through its AAA sustainable quality programme to embed sustainability practices on farms and the surrounding landscapes. Launched in 2003 in collaboration with the NGO Rainforest Alliance, the programme helps to enhance the yield and quality of harvests, ensuring a sustainable supply of high-quality coffee and improving livelihoods of farmers and their communities.

## FATFACE

FatFace is a British, family, lifestyle clothing brand that is made for life. With a unique heritage, FatFace creates product ranges for the whole family to live life in. FatFace products are designed with purpose and built to last. This is a brand with sustainability at its core with a clear strategy based around three key pillars – product, planet and community. FatFace appears devoted to style and sustainability, in equal measures.

## TONY'S CHOCOLONELY

Finally, an early adopter of B-Corp is Tony's Chocolonely. An Amsterdam-based chocolatier with a simple yet ambitious mission: 'Alone we'll make slave-free chocolate, together we'll make all chocolate 100 per cent slave free.' The founders had noticed a big problem – a handful of chocolate giants profited from keeping the price of cocoa as low as possible, resulting in farmers being forced to live in poverty, illegal child labour and modern-day slavery. They set up Tony's Chocolonely to do things differently, and slave free. But, like many of these organisations, this isn't just a business; it's a movement, with a mission beyond the reach of its own people. They educate and act as a role model of how chocolate can be produced sustainably and slave free, and foster relationships with local farmers, NGOs and other providers to champion dialogue around slave-free chocolate production. They certainly appear crazy about chocolate, and serious about people.

Permeating these distinctive companies is a crystal-clear sense of why they exist. Their purpose has become their North Star for empowering and guiding individual actions and decisions, even in how multiple people describe the company for which they work. They take running a strong, ethical, good business seriously. This is present in all aspects – how employees experience work; how suppliers and distributors are managed; and how customers interact with the company.

They bring clear understanding of how and why they add value to their customers and stakeholders and build their company around this core mission. The talents, skills and behaviours most highly valued are those that deliver on this, and in many cases, this is the unique combination and learning interfaces they create. When these elements purposefully collide, the ideas and magic flow. For example, creative designers, content writers and technology teams who are equally valued and co-creating in successful advertising agencies. Or the technical engineers, project managers and commercial teams who each contribute, have a voice and career development options, in successful engineering businesses. They are acutely aware of the importance each of these teams bring, but they also understand that their success depends upon the whole organisation. These groups might deliver the exacting recipe or enable a leap forwards in invention, but they need those around them to deliver and sustain success. It is always clear that everyone has a part to play.

Crucially, these companies recognise that their commitment to a greater cause will mean that some decide to leave and go elsewhere, or that some distributors or suppliers are not the right partners. This creates a strong identity: this is how we work; these are the principles we hold close; this is what we expect and reward. Yet, around the core mission, they embrace individuality within the foundations – create space for new and different ideas by making people feel connection, meaning, belonging and psychological safety. Purpose led doesn't mean cookie-cutter uniformity. They recognise that their future depends on human growth, and that whilst their core purpose might remain constant, the streams they operate within, the context, their work and products will all need to evolve and grow, to survive and thrive.

In 2022, BrewDog, a UK-based beer brewer, lost its B-Corp accreditation. A documentary exposed a 'culture of fear' and the company found out the hard way that failing to sustain the high standards required to attain the B-Corp accreditation would seriously come back to bite it, damaging both employer and consumer brands.

Being purpose driven can go hand in hand with financial success, as a tale of two retail pharmacy chains in the US shows. CVS has a clear purpose: 'Help people on their path to better health.' In line with this, in 2014, it made the bold decision to eliminate tobacco from its stores at a cost of $2 billion in revenue. It hurt their shareholders, with stock declining, and over the following months, the sales of cigarettes tumbled. But, across the longer term, through increasing sales of nicotine patches and staying true to its core mission, its stock price doubled over eighteen months. This is in contrast with Rite Aid, which has a similar purpose to 'offer everyday products and services that help our valued customers lead healthier, happier lives'. It chose to continue selling tobacco products, directly conflicting with its foundations for growth. Due to large debts and lawsuits filed during the ongoing opioid crisis, Rite Aid filed for bankruptcy in 2023. Drug stores are having to undergo considerable transformation in the US to survive, so a commitment to a meaningful mission will enable agility and durability.

Just like the human body, resilient and agile organisations must keep strengthening their foundations. They should stay true to their core drivers for existence, their identity and nurture strong psychological safety to enable individuals to use their talents to propel the collective forwards.

## THREE ACTIVITIES TO ESTABLISH AND STRENGTHEN FOUNDATIONS FOR HUMAN GROWTH WITHIN YOUR TEAMS AND ORGANISATIONS

### ACTIVITY I

| REVIEW YOUR ORGANISATIONAL FOUNDATIONS |
|---|
| In small groups, discuss the three elements of organisational foundations and what you see in your team and/or company:<br><br>• Why do we exist? (What is our mission and purpose? What impact do we have on others and the environment?)<br>• Who are we? (How prevalent are attributes such as integrity and fairness in our identity?)<br>• How do we work? (Do we create psychologically safe environments to enable new ideas and suggestions to propel us forwards?) |
| Evaluate the strength of your organisational foundations:<br><br>• Give a score from 1–10 for each of the categories and total these up as a group<br>• Discuss and capture the things you are doing well and want to strengthen<br>• Discuss and capture the things you would like to improve<br>• Are there other teams within the business or companies outside that you see doing this really well? What can you learn and apply? |
| Agree what you will do to act on this as a group, and identify someone else in your company to share these findings and suggestions with to continue the momentum |

# ACTIVITY 2

## ACTIVATE AND ALIGN PURPOSE

Business author Daniel Pink has a short but incredibly impactful exercise that groups can complete to evaluate the strength and alignment of an organisation's purpose. He gives everyone an index card and asks them to write a single sentence to answer the question 'what is the purpose of this organisation?' You might also decide to explore individual purpose and how this relates to the overall organisational purpose (as everyone's unique, these two purposes don't have to and are unlikely to be completely aligned, but having threads of commonality will help galvanise energy and momentum). Here's a version of this exercise you can tailor to meet your needs:

- Write your own personal purpose statement. E.g. 'I exist to...', 'My mission in life is to...' or 'I feel most energised when I am...'
- Think about the things you're passionate about, what makes you get up in the morning and where your talents lie
- Provide examples of company mission statements or purpose drivers from well-known leaders and celebrities, to help get thoughts flowing
- If the group wants to, you could ask them to share their purpose statements with each other (in pairs might feel more manageable)
- Ask the group to write down scenarios, periods in their lives or types of work they've engaged in where they have felt strong alignment with their purpose
- Reflect on how this made them feel (they're likely to say things such as energised, driven, positive, clear thoughts, most impactful work etc.)
- Explore areas of conflict/compromise – noting down skills and approaches that are likely to help minimise any negative feelings
- You might choose to close this activity out at this point and ask the group to identify one or two ways in which they will take accountability for increasing the amount of time they spend doing work they feel aligns with their purpose. Or... If you're feeling brave and the moment is right, you could seek to explore how individual purpose interacts with company purpose:
  o Where is there consistency?
  o Where is there potential rub?
  o What steps can you take, individually, to strengthen the moments of alignment between your purpose and the company's?
  o (Beware – this topic could cause some individuals to reflect that there is too much of a gulf between their individual drivers and the company's mission. But most will likely identify some commonality and, importantly, work out what they can do to amplify these moments further.)

There are many great materials on the topic of purpose to add to your understanding and conversations. Here are a few suggestions:

- Find your calling with the napkin test, a less than one-minute self-reflection exercise to help understand your purpose. This was developed by executive life coach Richard Leider (and shared by Daniel Pink on *The Pinkcast*). It involves answering the following statement with these prompts to calculate the equation G (Gifts) + P (Passion) + V (Values) = C (Calling). *I gain a sense of purpose at work when I use:*
  o My Gifts...
  o To serve my Passion...
  o In a culture that Values...
  o What gets me up in the morning... (my Calling)
- Explore how KPMG convinced its employees they could change the world with a campaign focused on articulating how the accounting firm's work was linked to a broader purpose. The team produced an advert illustrating how KPMG employees had shaped history e.g. how employees managed the Lend-Lease programme to help defeat Nazi Germany; resolved conflicting financial claims to lay the groundwork for the release of the US hostages in Iran in 1981; and certified the election of Nelson Mandela in South Africa in 1994. Crucially, KPMG took a co-create approach, asking everyone from interns to the board to share their own stories about how their work is making a difference. This was used to create powerful stories sharing how their work shaped people and society. The purpose-driven approach enabled KPMG to improve engagement scores and rise seventeen places in the Fortune 100 Best Companies to Work for list. (There's a great *Harvard Business Review* paper on this called 'How an Accounting Firm Convinced Its Employees They Could Change the World'.)
- The quest for purpose-led work grows: read McKinsey's research highlighting the huge impact purpose has on our health, longevity, happiness and willingness to stay or leave companies and Simon Sinek's *Start with Why* and *The Infinite Game* for purpose-related personal inspiration

## ACTIVITY 3

### MEASURE WHAT YOU WANT TO BECOME

As a group or individually, review the metrics your team and/or company regularly measure and what this means you will likely become (and not):

- Looking at the new world of work model (see the accompanying visual 'new measures of success' via the QR code shared on page 316), note down the metrics you regularly track and report on today.
- Where is there good coverage? Where are there gaps?

Fast forward to two years from now. Looking at the metrics you are tracking, paint a picture of what your likely performance could look like. Through focusing on these areas, what have you likely improved? Which words would you use to characterise the organisation? Is this the organisation/team you want to become?

- Reflect on your organisational foundations. Does this feel aligned? Looking at the areas where there is less or no coverage, what does this mean that the company is lacking? Is it important, or not?
- Discuss and identify how you can refine what you measure, to enable better alignment with what you would like to become:
  o What data or insights could you gather to improve the current metrics you report on?
  o Identify two to three new success measures you would like to move towards measuring in the future, to enable better alignment between your organisational foundations and the company you would like to become
  o Testing these out across a few months can help you to see whether it is possible to measure the metric, and if it has the meaning and relevance you require to embed in the longer-term picture of your organisation

*These exercises can be completed by anyone, in any role, level or function within the organisation. They can be used as part of strategic planning exercises, or simply to build awareness and improve collaboration within teams. It is recommended that they are repeated regularly, as people and organisations never stand still.*

# CHAPTER 7

# MIND: FUEL THE ORGANISATION

When I ventured into the working world twenty years ago, things operated in a structured and cyclical way. In the early days, I had a good understanding of what I needed to do to progress my career. I could scan upwards and steadily climb the ladder ahead of me. Looking back now, I can see that this perspective evolved quickly, as digital ways of working emerged, information became more freely available and career paths got blurry.

The macro landscape has been evolving, too, with significant changes to demographics and technological capabilities. In many parts of the world, birth rates are declining and people are living longer. Multichaptered careers are fast becoming a necessity to sustain healthy, meaningful lives, and for employers, engaging and developing workforces with four generations working together, often at different career stages, is an everyday reality.

The world has felt exceptionally strange and unpredictable in recent years. Many are now saying we're entering a new phase of 'normality', a BANI (brittle, anxious, non-linear and incomprehensible) era. This landscape is characterised by the interconnections we feel as globally linked and digital societies. Ripples are felt across the world in job markets, talent pools (e.g. declining birth rates, political changes such as Brexit, motivational shifts which make service workers a scarcity), supply chains (e.g. climate change, freak-flooding or excessive heat turns avocados into the most-valuable item in the supermarket – because how can we possibly survive without it?), cost of living, essential services (e.g. strikes continue to be a key feature in developed economies), communities and families. And we are glued to our phones, scouring social media and news stories to ensure we feel one step ahead and avoid FOMO (fear of missing out).

Technology continues to reshape how, where and who we work with. Accessing shared documents, interacting virtually across time zones and cultures and collating data on everything is our everyday norm. The advance of artificial intelligence (AI), virtual reality (VR) and machine learning continues at pace, and speculation on the impact on jobs has moved towards the new skills required to augment these advances, from robots simply replacing humans. Finding the optimal blend between automated technology and human emotion and interpretation to enhance productivity is our next challenge.

In this context, the moments that matter are often buried

in the day-to-day experiences that organisational life throws us. The clock starts ticking the second an employee joins a company. LinkedIn research revealed that an employee is 12 per cent more likely to stay at an organisation if they move internally within their first year, and 19 per cent more likely to stay if they move internally within two years. How we move, explore and grow within a business is possibly more important now than how we get in, because people have greater choice of where they work, when, who they work for and for how long. Life and career stages play a role, yet more frequently it's the navigation between an organisation's objectives and an individual's priorities that gel or create tension.

Across multiple sectors, a talent crisis looms. As technology, context and organisational needs constantly shift, there simply are not enough skilled people for jobs. Employers are having to become more creative in acquiring talent and designing new and improved approaches to nurturing effective teams, very often for tasks and roles they haven't yet imagined.

Within organisations, the traditional game of snakes and ladders has made way for a giant game of Tetris. (See the 'messy middle' model by using the QR code provided on page 316.)

Today, organisations are live ecosystems with new roles, new teams and functions constantly emerging. Employers must find ways to align their people with the opportunities (skills, projects, roles, teams) to deliver value and maintain relevance in a market where industries converge (e.g. fintech and edtech). A new taxonomy is emerging – skills and projects over roles and qualifications – enabling agile evolution and exploration of different and diverse talent pools (within and outside organisations).

In this dynamic ecosystem, the challenges for people and businesses are:

1. To constantly transform
2. To find moments of alignment to fuel growth
3. To build environments where humans can flourish

To succeed as humans, we need to reinvent the processes, tools and insights we use within workplaces to understand and align people with business needs.

I see six main shifts we need to make:

## 1. FROM STATIC JOB ROLES AND CAREER PATHS TO SKILLS AND MARKETPLACES

Breaking down jobs into skills and experiences so we can put them back together in the optimal way to deliver critical outcomes in ever-changing contexts is a critical step. The World Economic Forum suggests that a skills shortage crisis is only a few years away – having frameworks and technology enabling anticipation, identification and matching of individuals to key tasks, projects and teams will prove essential.

## 2. FROM TOP TALENT TO EVERYONE HAS POTENTIAL

Switch your focus from top talent only, to everyone who has potential. Businesses that stay ahead in the game of remaining relevant will have their finger on the pulse of objectively understanding who has got potential to take on something different. Who could learn a new skill? Who could deliver a business transformation project? Who will thrive in an environment of uncertainty? Very often, the next right answer lies in front of you – you just haven't seen the potential, yet.

## 3. FROM SUPERVISORY MANAGEMENT TO HUMAN MANAGERS

The old model of managers as supervisors and providers of tasks and deadlines is no longer fit for purpose. Good management is shifting to empowering, coaching, personalising (in terms of jobs, interactions, experiences) and empathetically supporting a whole person, with life outside of work. Understanding and nurturing a team, across countries, cultures and in hybrid settings is often undervalued and yet can make or break a business.

## 4. FROM CULTURE 'JUST HAPPENS' TO MANAGING CULTURE AS AN ASSET

Employees are now more likely to judge a workplace on its culture than the salary they are paid. Culture creates happiness and loyalty through experiences, forging friendships and enabling feelings of inclusion and belonging, and if set up and managed as an asset, it can fuel productivity, innovation and growth. Employees expect organisations to be purpose led and this creates the foundation for psychologically safe, constructive and fair environments in which to work and thrive.

## 5. FROM RULES TO EMPOWERING PRINCIPLES

Employees want and can access flexible approaches to work. Embrace hybrid working; it is here to stay and could become a catalyst for sustaining longer, multichaptered working lives. Understanding people as individuals, personalising experiences, connecting stages in the employee journey (e.g. hiring to on-boarding) and providing access and time to learn in the flow of work will provide quick returns in a motivated, agile and skilled workforce. Are you empowering your teams to own their careers?

## 6. FROM REPORTING THE PAST TO FUTURE-GAZING WITH TALENT INTELLIGENCE

Finally, a race begins to design talent systems enabling organisational agility through harnessing the collective power of human potential. Capturing objective people insight on skills, motivation and potential, as well as data such as engagement, performance and customer impact, will enable organisations to confidently connect the dots and curate seamless employee experiences as well as mobilise growth-focused teams.

## INTERRUPTING HUMAN HUNCHES

At the core of the human organisation (with strong foundations in place as explored in the previous chapter) is a culture enabled by tools, systems and skills to drive good people decisions and nurture collaboration and learning. This is step two in creating a climate for human growth.

This is about interrupting our cognitive shortcuts and human hunches with objective data and insight, in the right place at the right time, to fuel predictive and fair people decisions. This ecosystem must be skilfully designed to ensure tools and processes are not too complex or overbearing, that insights are easily and instantly available and that the people accessing them have the right training and skill to use them in the optimal way.

Left to our own devices, chaos can ensue. We make decisions based on opinions, what we've seen before or what feels most comfortable (they remind me of me!). We misinterpret pace for progress and impact. We get lost in the tasks and forget the impact we each have on the ecosystem and culture we create. This is where many of the cracks in cultures begin. At the core, we need to equip organisations to make fair and objective people decisions.

Research shows that we repeatedly underestimate the potential of women and overestimate that of men (despite women, objectively, showing greater natural leadership potential). People who are promoted are actually more likely to leave than those not, in the following six months (due to politics, bureaucracy or opinion getting in the way of recognising and rewarding top talent which means the promotion comes too late or feels uninspiring). In 2023, a team of psychologists and I examined the personality and motivational profiles of thousands of people managers. Surprisingly, we discovered that the typical profile of a 'people manager' across organisations and countries looks much more like an individual contributor than a manager. It would seem we're confused about what management looks like and often promote the star, ironically often resulting in losing our top performer – because they really don't want to manage – *and* disengaging an entire team. We frequently overlook talent within our own teams and organisations, instead going external to fill critical roles (despite ample capability and motivation lying within).

As humans, we need prompts and insight to remind us, at times, to be better humans. This is exactly what a strong human-centric organisation purposefully designs and maintains. Our organisational mind needs to be equipped and ready to nudge and guide us on the best path forwards.

## REWIRING THE ORGANISATIONAL MIND
### OBJECTIVELY UNDERSTAND PEOPLE AND POTENTIAL

Historically, talent has been explored in silos – e.g. by function or layer – and many talent initiatives and programmes have focused on 'top talent' only: individuals selected into elite talent pools to be nurtured for senior positions when key players exit the business. Today, 'critical roles' are broader and dispersed. Skills (using emerging technologies, AI, data, as well as human skills – storytelling, leading with empathy, creative thinking) and moments in time (we need to capitalise on an opportunity now to scale our operations; who can lead on a new business acquisition; designing a new product to beat a competitor to release) require a wider and more detailed view on entire workforces to inform great people decisions. Mobility isn't just upwards; it could be sideways, diagonal, even a step down to reskill. Matching individual motivation and preference, as well as capability and potential, with organisational need is key to delivering long-term value.

Many companies are moving towards free-flowing, employee-driven approaches to talent management, through marketplaces where individuals are empowered to develop their own careers and learn new skills. This is creating a self-directing marketplace where people trade skills and experiences and move to take on new roles, projects, secondments, mentorships etc. A fundamental shift here, too, is that managers are no longer the gatekeepers for employee development. This has been changing for several years, as learning and development content became digitally accessible, enabling individuals to plot their own routes for growth. Managers are rewarded not for hoarding their talent but for nurturing and mobilising individuals, enabling them to find opportunities to flourish within the broader organisation.

Many companies have started to adopt more inclusive, broader approaches to developing their people. Standard

Chartered Bank (SCB) has embarked on this journey to 'democratise development' by putting access to learning, projects and people into the hands of their employees. It saw this as a great mechanism for further building on its commitment to diversity and inclusion, by removing hurdles ahead of development opportunities and enabling access and support for all. SCB identified a technology-fuelled talent marketplace solution to bring this to life and has seen significant improvements in productivity, feelings of inclusion and access to career development across the organisation.

Objective assessment tools can be used to collect insights to optimise and accelerate experiences and outcomes for individuals and businesses. But how many organisations *truly* understand their people? In many companies, it feels as though we are just scratching the surface. Impressions are constantly built and shared, and doors opened or closed because of these. However, an objective understanding of an individual at a holistic level can create new views and opportunities for all involved.

I have long been a fan of this simple model to build a comprehensive understanding of people:

- Results (the experiences, achievements and qualifications that the individual brings with them from their past)
- Behaviour (how they achieve these results – the capabilities, skills, style and ways of working, relied upon day to day)

- Potential (what they could achieve in the future, if supported and developed in a positive way – their motivations, personality preferences and cognitive reasoning
  abilities)

Frequently, we make people decisions with one, maybe two,
pieces of this jigsaw puzzle, and most fail to incorporate a
view of future potential into this equation. This is a huge
mistake and leads us to the wrong, 'right' answer all the
time.

Chosen well and used in the optimal way (by people who
have had training in how psychometrics work), objective
assessments bring incredible insight. Quick confession – I
have worked in the talent assessment industry for many
years. I've seen the good, the bad and the ugly! Used well,
objective assessments say to employees that this leader or
company cares; they want to understand more about me,
when I'm at my best and how I can grow and thrive. I have
helped many people use this insight to start a journey of
revelation and self-discovery – to explore hidden ave-
nues, flex new muscles, appreciate difference and improve
relationships.

For employers, it brings the science, objectivity and predictive power we yearn for when making people decisions.
Well-designed, appropriately selected and implemented assessment tools can significantly improve the prediction of
job performance. In 2021, Professor Paul Sackett and other
psychology researchers released a revised meta-analysis

of work assessments, providing insight on the predictive validity of a wide variety of tools. Structured interviews can achieve predictive validities of *c.* 0.42 (that's broadly in line with the relationship between height and weight). Work sample tests (for example, case studies, presentation exercises, tasks mimicking the job) can deliver validities of *c.* 0.3 (better than the relationship between sleeping pills and reducing insomnia), ability tests land at a similar level of prediction, and aspects of personality, such as conscientiousness, produce validities of *c.* 0.2 (higher than the relationship between pain killers and pain reduction). Better still, when used in combination in efficient and effective ways, the predictive power increases further. (Although simply piling up assessments for the sake of it won't lead to better outcomes. They must be carefully reviewed and selected based on the requirements of the job, to ensure robust and fair approaches, and incorporated within processes that deliver positive participant experiences.)

Personality in adults remains reasonably stable. Our preferences for ways of working might change slightly, particularly following key life events or traumas, but in general, how we feel energised, approach problems, cope under pressure and the way we build relationships remain broadly consistent. Yet, through building self-awareness and targeting development to further strengthen the things we naturally feel good at doing, and developing skills in others, we learn and grow. Add in a view on motivation – what makes you get out of bed? What does success look like? – as well as assessments of skills and abilities and you begin to develop a more sophisticated understanding of any individual. From there, you can discover how to maximise potential and exponentially increase opportunities for impact, happiness and fulfilment. It helps us move from making assumptions to asking questions and exploring possibilities. (The whole field of assessment and personality in particular is very widely researched and written about – *Personality: A User's Guide* by Nikita Mikhailov and Georgi Yankov offers a great overview, if you want to find out more.)

Who we are can be distinctive, but who we can be is defining. At the core is the belief that as humans, we can harness our potential and grow.

## UNTAPPED UNDERSTANDING
Many organisations use objective assessments as part of hiring processes, to help attract and select the best-fit applicants for a role. The structured and clear insights can help tackle the biases we rely upon, forcing us to breakdown assumptions, challenge grand statements and open our eyes and ears to possibilities. Some companies then use the insight collated to inform on-boarding – providing feedback using personality and motivational insights, or to share strengths and development areas observed during the assessment process to help set new employees up for success.

Very few organisations use these powerful insights for

anything further. Despite experiencing a revelatory process and feeling better equipped to make a good people decision, most of us quickly drop the wisdom gained in favour of our human hunches when the next opportunity to shape a good experience appears. This is a massive missed opportunity, especially in the dynamic landscape we operate in today. The insight captured during hiring processes can be gold dust – helping identify themes in the profiles of teams, motivational drivers, capabilities and development gaps – and can be used to embed more impactful ways of working, inform development programmes and even identify individuals for future roles and opportunities within the company at later dates. Connect the technologically driven concept of a talent marketplace with the powerful objective insight through assessments, and there could be something game-changing for people and businesses to come. An organisation which commits to truly understanding its people through well-selected, integrated and maintained technology platforms enabling connection, understanding and the democratisation of opportunities (e.g. projects, mentorships, roles, learning), combined with well-embedded and optimised use of objective assessment tools, across employee experiences and stages, can fuel a people-focused, inclusive, agile and growth-oriented culture.

## EVERYONE LEARNS

In a fast-paced, complex and ambiguous world, learning is fundamental. But putting ourselves in positions to learn and sharing with others that we want to and need to learn (because we don't know everything) can make us feel vulnerable. After-all, for centuries, leading others (tribes, families, communities, teams, businesses) has been associated with being authorita-tive, clear and certain, having all knowledge and understand-ing (or, at least appearing to) even in the face of adversity.

We, as humans, need support to help us untangle the models and innate drives we have instilled through evolu-tion to embrace learning as a lifelong habit.

The steps above are connected to this – understanding and appreciating that we are all different, offering varying strengths and possessing the ability to learn to develop and grow. In addition to this, layering in tools, practices, skills and, importantly, continually role-modelling at leadership levels can embed and reinforce the principle that everyone learns across the organisation.

A snapshot of an organisation with learning running through it like a stick of rock features feedback conversa-tions, every day. Leaders talk about their own mistakes and learnings, encourage others to share new ways of working, discuss interesting insights and explore what this could mean for their work. Tools are instantaneously integrated into the flow of work (e.g. generative AI) to provide feed-back on communication style and impact, including relay-ing use of words and the percentage of time spent talking vs listening. On-demand learning content is genuinely used (not just because it's compulsory or helps with pro-motion, but because it works and provides visible value).

Individuals offer to share their skills and new knowledge with colleagues. Groups are comfortable talking about failures and don't fear what this could mean for them. Rather, they embrace the opportunity to learn and improve.

Amy Edmondson, professor of leadership at Harvard Business School, describes this process as 'intelligent failures' in her book *Right Kind of Wrong*.

We associate failure with losing. It's difficult to naturally feel any pride when talking about a failure, and most of us will seek to brush it under the carpet or quickly change the narrative. And yet, the most successful in society fail frequently. From award-winning scientists to elite athletes, novelists and engineers. Guaranteed, they all have experiences of failure in common.

Edmondson says such successful people understand, as a baseline, that not all failures are created equal. They work hard to avoid the unintelligent failures – the slip-ups through poor preparation, lack of understanding or making the same mistake again. Instead, they embrace intelligent failures with these four qualities:

1. They take place in new territory
2. They are in pursuit of a goal
3. They are driven by a hypothesis
4. They are as small as possible

Examples of failure pioneers whom Edmondson describes include celebrated American entrepreneur Sara Blakely, founder of the apparel company Spanx, who famously endured countless setbacks on her path to becoming in 2012 the youngest ever billion-dollar entrepreneur. Edmondson also discusses Madame Clicquot, born as Barbe-Nicole Ponsardin in France in 1777, who was sadly and suddenly widowed at the age of twenty-seven. Instead of giving up on the tiny struggling business she had recently started with her husband, she persisted through staggering business and technical failures for years, ultimately building Veuve Clicquot, one of the most successful and enduring companies in the wine industry.

Intelligent failures move us into uncharted territory, new explorations and possibilities previously untested. And, crucially, each experiment enables learning to progress in this mission.

Fortunately, it wasn't simply luck that drove the team at Pfizer to develop a vaccine for Covid-19 in record time. Intelligent failures made many years prior to the pandemic (as well as foresight, preparation and establishing a strong learning culture enabling high-potential employees to interact regularly with senior scientists) enabled them to achieve this remarkable feat.

A series of small thoughtful experiments, driven through curiosity and propelled through applied learnings, are essential to making sense of and success in our world.

## FACILITATE DISCOVERY

Novartis, a global pharmaceutical organisation, has been

completely overhauling its approaches to talent for several years, and with fabulous effect. The company is frequently featured in 'best places to work' lists and accredited with awards for progressive changes (including diversity and inclusion accomplishments and HR awards). As such, it is worth taking the time to explore what's behind its success. A constant feature is letting go. Novartis realised it needed to step away from controlling and managing and towards facilitating, empowering and enabling. This runs through the key principles it has adopted, such as focusing on the entire workforce with regard to talent management, the belief that everyone has potential (and can grow) at the heart, putting individuals (not managers) in the driver's seat on their careers and approaching talent as a shared resource.

These principles, supported by well-selected frameworks, partners and technology, fundamentally transformed Novartis's approach to nurturing people. At the fulcrum is the belief that growing people will grow the business. One way it brings this to life is through deconstructing work into projects and gigs and moving from jobs to skills. This creates an open and fluid way of communicating business priorities and enabling individuals to use their skills to optimise impact, whilst expanding their networks and their capabilities. This came with risk – how would people move to the next project? Would all business priorities be delivered on (or just the most exciting looking ones)? And how would it ensure consistent and fair adoption? (And not simply those who shout loudest getting the biggest bite of the pie?) The tools, technology and models had to be accompanied by clear principles for ensuring positive experiences and outcomes. Inherent in this philosophy is positioning experimentation, or dabbling, as a good thing. Skills and knowledge are not tied to jobs or specific career paths, and different ways of doing things and new combinations of perspectives can help the collective achieve more. Novartis was fuelling a self-propelling talent engine which, with the right support and nudging, could get people and teams ready for anything.

Other organisations have dabbled with new models for fundamentals such as organisational design and leadership. The weight of executive leadership roles in many companies is immense. Is it time for a new model to share the load? There are many benefits to having two heads and perspectives – including balancing the workload, having greater coverage and reach and being able to make better-informed decisions, as well as providing advantages for individuals in terms of well-being and sustainability.

This is a model I experienced first-hand as joint managing director for a UK commercial function. In general, it really worked. We had good alignment on key priorities, complementary skills, and having a partner to tackle challenges, formulate strategy and build energy across the team was a massive attribute. Most days I was very grateful for a co-pilot and felt more durable and impactful because of it. But it did require more effort – conversations to build alignment and explore contradictions in style, together feeling our way through how this would work and trying to set things up for success. A strong relationship and appreciation for your co-leader, combined with the ability to hold transparent and constructive discussions, is key to making this a success.

An appetite to try new things, experiment and discover what different could look like is a great source of fuel for an agile organisation.

## MULTIPLYING NETWORKS

Imagine looking at your company from above – a bird's-eye view. If you see deep-cut layers and distinct groups or functions, clear definition between forest, buildings and sea, you might find you're not ready for our fluid world. Seeing your organisation lit up with connections – ever moving, changing, expanding – looking like a bustling city at night could, however, be a sign of a well-connected organisation.

Move closer, and you'll see a buzzing community. Organisational network analysis (ONA) would show multiple relationships spanning people, teams, functions and geographies, with new relationships emerging constantly. Knowledge sharing is infectious – questions posed in Slack channels spread to other connections, feeding ideas, innovations and solutions. The networks fire up learning, in everyday scenarios: 'have you done this?', 'what happens when?', 'is this a good approach to take?' spill across teams, and the communities help steer and guide each other through the known rabbit holes, bunkers, traps and obstacles. The organisational mind, wired up to an MRI, lit up with positive emotions.

More formally, this might be supported through mentoring programmes and strong community groups across the workplace ecosystem. Schemes enabling individuals to self-select and match to potential mentors can be a great way to encourage engagement and cross-pollination. This isn't just top-down mentoring but reverse-mentoring, too, building awareness and understanding across generations and perspectives. Having regular sessions to get to know a team, or explore a prototype, can ignite networks, allowing people to share innovations and ideas. Opportunities to engage with different colleagues on important topics, some work related, some not, all help to stimulate connection and learning so the collective can do more, together. DEIB (diversity, equity, inclusion and belonging) groups can be catalysts for cross-team connection – building awareness and understanding and creating safe spaces to ask questions and talk. Many organisations do this exceptionally well and have strong relationships with external partners to keep their own learnings fresh and relevant. Universal topics such as building cultural awareness, how to have good conversations or even exploring company ways of working, models or policies in a discussive manner can create strong links across a community.

Great innovators and disruptors extend their networks

beyond their own organisation. Professor Linda Hill attributes, in part, the growth transformation at Mastercard to its prioritisation of external networks. When Ajay Banga took over as CEO of Mastercard in 2010, he knew he had work to do. The business had been struggling to keep pace, growth was faltering and the payments industry was about to undergo complete upheaval. Rather than jump straight into disrupting back and attempting to lead through innovation, he set about rearchitecting the organisation and the culture required for transformation. He built a plan for long-term growth through diversifying and building capabilities, fundamentally believing that this needed to be driven through purpose. Mastercard's purpose, Banga believed, is to influence financial inclusion – to make this accessible to groups previously excluded. This was a key social mission and presented great opportunity for Mastercard to diversify its customer base and offering. Banga and his team knew this would take new skills and perspectives and, critically, a longer-term mission for growth.

A catalyst was the introduction of Mastercard Labs, since it enabled the whole company to contribute to the 'art of the possible'. Research and development teams regularly embarked on roadshows, sharing ideas, inviting conversation and co-creating solutions together. This helped build a new culture – one where good ideas could come from anywhere, people can dare to dream and failing smart is part of the journey. However, as well as changing mindsets and behaviours internally, Mastercard knew it simply wouldn't have all the capabilities, potential and experiences within the organisation to deliver such change. Mastercard grew its ecosystem to include a diverse range of organisations – many start-ups in the technology sector which had specialist skills and experiences that could benefit Mastercard during this period. Recognising the need to extend and build networks, to fuel progress, learning and innovation was a pivotal step in Mastercard's journey. It recognised that it needed new skills and inputs to help it see what it hadn't seen before. Change took multiple years, but growth came, and Mastercard successfully transformed into a global technology payment provider.

There are many similarities in this story with the well-established philosophy of 'kaizen', credited in part for Toyota's position as one of the world's leading car manufacturers. By focusing on small changes to drive continuous improvement, the philosophy is adopted by everyone, whatever their role or level. It is reported that this approach enables Toyota to implement 1 million new ideas every year, many of which come from those working on assembly lines. The ideas might be small, but they make a big difference. Like Brailsford's marginal gains in the British cycling team, they enable constant evolution and shared feelings of progress. Other companies implement idea or innovation jams, sometimes offering rewards for ideas that are implemented, and the concept of a hackathon (a social gathering of software coders to improve on or develop new products) is a key feature in many technology-focused organisations.

## TURN DATA INTO INTELLIGENCE

The final component is capturing data (people, customer, systems, business) and turning it into intelligence, to spot acceleration opportunities and manage risks.

Every company has data coming out of its ears. Few know what to do with it.

Transformation in organisations today is no longer a big two- to three-year event; it's continuous. The aim of the game is to be nimble and agile, constantly moving, reshaping and anticipating to get your proposition and people in the place of greatest potential. To facilitate this reinvention, companies leading the way are making the most of their data to inform their next move. However, according to analyst Josh Bersin's research, only 7 per cent of companies are fully 'dynamic' organisations – ready for constant evolution (perhaps those adopting the kaizen philosophy are already way ahead in their focus on collective constant evolution). Dynamic organisations have many of the attributes we have explored (they flatter, focus on building skills everywhere and empower people across the whole organisation to come up with fresh ideas). In short, they know that they need the whole machine to be firing to deliver long-term value.

The most dynamic organisations can pinpoint *where* to

invest and can identify *who* has the capability to turn this into growth.

For example, picture a leading technology engineering business which, having grown through acquisitions, has employees scattered across multiple sites. The company needs to know where to hire more engineers to optimise talent availability and cost. Using data on the talent market – including supply, demand and the skills available in combination with salary information – it is able to identify the optimal location for hiring and focus efforts on this area, saving money, time and effort by using insight to focus its approach.

Similarly, imagine that a large European energy organisation had identified an opportunity to diversify its offering and needed someone to lead the set-up of this division. There's a moment in time to act, before competitors establish themselves in this field, and so finding someone who knows and understands the company's business will be key. This is a brand-new area so those internally are unlikely to have done anything like this before. Rather than pick up the phone to a headhunter, the boss turns to their people analytics team and poses the question, who might have capability and potential within our company to take this on? Together they determine the key profile – essential experiences, behavioural capabilities and indicators of potential likely to determine success. Using this recipe, the analytics team crunch existing assessment data on individuals meeting the core criteria, revealing a list of potentials for the job. Most are names which the leadership team hadn't even considered. The list is diverse, too – across all groups – and enables them to place an existing employee into this critical role and identify high potentials to join the team. It's easy to see how this data-led approach can enable a solution meeting everyone's needs, in an agile and effective way and with a focus on the longer-term, communicating to employees that this is an organisation where effort and potential is rewarded.

Spotify has a well-established approach to combining people and business data to fuel transformation. It describes its different data sets as locks in a canal:

> Data sets that are kept isolated within their own silo/lock are nice to have but their use is very limited. The trick is to open the gateways between the locks, combine the data sets and allow the analysis to flow freely, just like water in the canal. That way your data can really take you from one place to another, to a higher level.

Spotify uses this insight to guide cultural and business transformation. For example, using people analytics, its learning and development team found that managers who spend at least sixteen minutes having one-on-one discussions with each direct report per week had 30 per cent higher engagement than managers who don't. Spotify used this insight to promote behavioural change through storytelling and enabling others to implement what works. It is easy to see how this information (if not extracted) could be overlooked and the impact missed – 'we've hit a hard spell, so we need to reduce cost in management layers'. Other applications include management dashboards combining timesheet and project data, flagging when individuals are overutilised and at risk of burnout. This informs capacity planning and can improve on-boarding and development interventions at specific stages. Again, without this insight, our organisational minds would likely tell us to keep pushing everyone harder, to achieve the outcomes we need, and this would result in bigger challenges through burnout and attrition.

As Spotify says: 'It's about mastering the organisational muscle of using data to make better decisions; to hypothesize, discover, measure and adapt.'

Many businesses have gone up in flames. BlackBerry, according to the latest movie, was too distracted by its own genius inventions to realise that Apple had completely reinvented the market. Blockbuster had a similar story of burying its head in the sand before it woke, surrounded by piles of videos collecting nothing but dust. We only hear what we want to hear. There are a plethora of start-ups with great ideas which fail to incorporate the right minds to turn a concept into sustainable growth. And the giants, too – big enough to weather a storm – are experiencing barren years and brand-damaging poor decisions. IBM's supercomputer

Watson has promised to revolutionise, well, everything, but it is still shrouded in mystery. Disney recently celebrated its 100th anniversary but faces ongoing challenges to make its streaming services profitable. Shares are down and unlike other competitors such as Warner Bros., Disney struggles to find an answer to alternative digital streaming services like YouTube and TikTok. It also faces a ticking clock for *the* key succession decision to replace Bob Iger, who came out of retirement to lead the firm until 2026. Time will tell whether Disney has the talent insight to inform a business-critical decision to set it up for a transformative second century.

Organisations that stand the test of time inherently understand that it all starts with people.

*All* of their people.

Systems, processes and tools must be designed to embrace the power of the collective, and these must be underpinned by a clear understanding of everyone's value to society. Such value is strengthened by allowing intelligent experimentation and using predictive analytics, which together combine to spark human and business growth against a molten landscape.

Just like the human mind, when fear, stress or excitement overwhelm groups of people, the neural pathways or networks we establish in organisations can narrow. We tend to make sense of things by closing down options and making assumptions. Yet to see the best possible path forwards, we need to broaden our perspective and understanding.

# A GUIDE TO REWIRING YOUR ORGANISATION'S MIND

## EVALUATE ORGANISATIONAL READINESS

Rate where your organisation is on the following continuums, and use this to inform targeted action:

### REWIRE THE ORGANISATIONAL MIND

| Job roles are static and career paths locked | 1 2 3 4 5 | Skills and experiences fuel talent marketplaces |
|---|---|---|
| Talent processes focus only on the top | 1 2 3 4 5 | Everyone has potential |
| Managers supervise tasks and gatekeep | 1 2 3 4 5 | Managers are empowered to enable people growth |
| Culture just happens | 1 2 3 4 5 | Culture is proactively managed as an asset |
| Rules are at the core | 1 2 3 4 5 | Guiding principles enable us to align, differently |
| Metrics help us track the past | 1 2 3 4 5 | Talent intelligence drives the future |

## PUT YOURSELF IN THE PLACE OF MOST POTENTIAL

Move from roles to skills:

- Moving to a framework of skills will instantly create greater agility in your organisation
- Many frameworks exist. You can, if you wish, pick one up and simply get started, or choose to design your own
- Start by mapping skills required for success in your most critical roles (these might be those most difficult to hire for, with greatest impact or most in demand)
- This will quickly help you to capture the top skills in your company and begin to introduce a model for HR, leaders and employees to talk about development and mobility within the organisation
- You might decide to fire this up through technology platforms and linking to learning systems (to fuel skill capability), but this can come later...

Measure and connect potential:

- Incorporating views on potential alongside skill capability will flood your organisation's mind with possibilities...
- If you don't use objective measures of personality and motivation, then find a provider you like and include this in your core approaches
- If you already use these, are you taking full advantage of their power by using the insight to inform hiring, on-boarding, development and succession planning?
- You can map these tools to your skills model, instantly identifying who could have potential to develop critical new skills and move into new roles, projects and teams (if you wish, you can make this simple and intuitive by technology platforms and solutions)
- Make sure to feed back the insight collated to the individuals themselves – this can be an incredibly rewarding and enlightening experience, spreading feelings of value, inclusion and engagement

## NURTURE A CULTURE OF LEARNING, LABS AND DISCOVERY

Create an insatiable appetite for learning and new discoveries will emerge! Getting comfortable sharing feedback can be a game-changer and embedding objective assessment tools (as outlined above) can be a great starting point for building a feedback culture.

- Develop and support daily learning habits:
  - o Choose a model for giving feedback (e.g. like Netflix's 4As model)
  - o Provide people with simple training and support to bring this to life
  - o Get people managers on board and using this as part of the everyday culture
  - o Embed tools and technology to support this in a manageable way (e.g. AI-generated hints and tips embedded in the flow of work or learning content platforms) – alongside time to use these
  - o Get comfortable talking about failure as an opportunity to learn. Setting up your own formats for doing this (e.g. lessons learned, failure case stories or senior leaders sharing their own experiences to set the tone) can help these to become a core part of the company's DNA
  - o Check your model delivers what you need!
- When you have developed strong learning habits across the business, you could consider embedding broader initiatives to encourage organisational-wide discovery and innovation:
  - o See the earlier example of Mastercard Labs' initiative, kaizen philosophy, innovation jams and hackathons
  - o Facilitate sharing and connection across teams and functions and equip people with the psychological safety as well as the tools and skills to contribute constructively, and this could lead to discovery of the next big thing!

# CHAPTER 8

# HEART AND SOUL: SPARK PERSONAL MEANING AND GROWTH

Ask anyone about their happiest, most memorable experiences at work and the answer will likely include a time when someone really understood them. These moments stand out to us. They're times when you're willing to put your heart and soul into your work because you feel trusted, appreciated and valued. This makes you feel stronger and able to tackle anything, safe in the knowledge that someone's got your back.

The heart and soul of any workplace is its people. Finding ways to create meaningful and engaging work in fair, kind and rewarding cultures can help ensure that the blood pumps effortlessly around the organisation.

The relationship between employee and manager can make or break overall experiences at work. Several years ago, in an employee engagement study, Gallup revealed that managers account for up to 70 per cent of variance in engagement levels. Seventy per cent is huge. The old saying that 'people don't leave jobs, they leave managers' resonates and it's easy to see why.

Looking back, I cherish the periods I was fortunate to work with gifted managers. Individuals who invested time in empathising with me as a person. Understanding my ways of working, appreciating my ambitions and goals and acknowledging my anxieties and fears. They knew when to push me and when to step in and offer support. I felt confident they would vouch for me if things went wrong. They helped me build connections, both inside and outside the organisation, were generous with their time and skilled in providing advice and feedback. They were committed to helping me develop and succeed and always ensured I was given credit for my work and achievements. They helped curate a happy work experience; and it became something I wanted to put my heart and soul into.

Not every experience is like this. I can also recall the soul-destroying manager relationships. Individuals in it simply for the status, who spent their time managing senior stakeholders and crushing those beneath them. The unachievable demands, the false niceties in front of others and that sinking feeling, realising that if you mess up, you will quietly disappear under the bus approaching at speed. The missed interesting project, overlooked mentoring rela-tionships and lost development opportunities because your manager quickly snaffled them up for themselves haunt your existence. Often, these are the individuals provoking the culture cracks in organisations (see Chapter 3), their management responsibilities expanding their negative impact. Being stuck with a poor manager can be bruising, at times humiliating, anxiety-inducing and snuff out positivity.

## THE BEATING HEART

When a company is well managed, something magical happens, rippling throughout teams and departments, fuelling engagement, invigorating innovation and stimulating collaboration. This is the beating heart of human workplaces. The secret to happy, healthy and growing organisations is to identify and nurture people with an aptitude for understanding others into manager roles. I believe this is the most impactful move any company can make.

This is where the key ingredients of a human organisation come together:

- It starts with the body, with solid organisational foundations (explored in Chapter 6)
- The second step is to fuel the organisational mind with objective tools, data and systems to guide better decisions and connections (explored in Chapter 7)
- This next step focuses on the heart and soul – the relationship between managers and individuals. Get this right, and the blood pumps effortlessly around the company, creating a network of trust, bringing warmth and fostering belief

## EMPOWER MANAGERS

Businesses often overlook their management population, focusing instead on those with rapidly evolving technical skills or on senior leaders. This is a massive missed opportunity and exposes the risk of hiring or promoting the wrong person into a management role, which can result in organ rejection within the company.

Managers today need to rely on human skills more than ever, to build genuine understanding of their team members, forge candid connections and show empathy but also provide constructive feedback in a kind and supportive way, without glossing over the reality. They must translate strategic objectives from the top, read into market conditions to anticipate what might be required next, and constantly share inspiring and motivating (tailored for everyone) stories that make people feel valued and part of the onward journey. These skills are difficult to develop and even harder to sustain. Investing in objectively identifying and developing people managers with these capabilities will help build long-term company value and durability.

When the connection between managers and individuals is strong, you can feel it across the whole organisation. Learning and ideas flow. Communication and opportunities pulse around teams. There's a distinct, reassuring, rhythm keeping people in synch and moving in the right direction. That's when the hard work starts – to maintain the beat. New people join, obstacles emerge, thoughts and feelings are modified constantly. The dynamic can shift in an instance, and the manager needs to constantly learn, try new things, dig deep and keep focused on understanding, engaging and motivating their people through changing conditions. Management is distinct from leadership, yet dependent upon it, too. As we will explore in Chapter 10, leaders need to create the climate for human growth by setting direction, building safe and fair cultures, providing guidance on what 'good' looks and feels like and, critically, stepping back, trusting and empowering managers to make this a reality. With this in place, managers can focus on understanding people and facilitating experiences to bring out the best for employees and the organisation.

## UNDER PRESSURE AND BURNING OUT

This vision sounds wonderful. But for so many, it is just that, an image far from reality. In many organisations, managers are overburdened and burning out. They're stuck in the middle and squashed from all directions. The pressure can feel immense – task lists grow, teams get bigger and more dispersed than ever, shareholders and leaders expect more and more. Employees are shouting louder, particularly as work bleeds into life and expectations for meaningful, purpose-driven jobs become the standard. Managers find themselves spinning many plates: dashing from meeting to meeting; discussing the latest performance metrics with leaders and committing to delivering better, faster; engaging with stakeholders when things go wrong, mopping-up issues, smoothing over relationships; trying to help and support their team when they need it – from issues inherently linked to their job (how should I approach the presentation with this new stakeholder?) to big, prickly, emotional topics as people feel overwhelmed by the mounting pressures of work and life.

Being a manager has never felt more challenging.

Over the past thirty years, management has changed considerably. In the 1990s, the focus was on applying expertise to improve processes. Managers had access to information and knowledge before others; they controlled the cascade and were gatekeepers to career development opportunities. This provided power and control, and many were attracted to the position for these reasons. These are the managers who would instantly give you their business card, always sign-off emails with their full title and spend every penny of the higher-level car allowance (taking care to ensure their expensive car is parked in full sight).

In the 2000s, digitisation began, followed swiftly by agile ways of working. This initiated a loss of control as information and people became much more freely available. Employees no longer relied on their managers sharing updates or imparting knowledge – they could access this for themselves through company intranets and instant messaging. Building networks and sharing information up and down an organisation became much more acceptable, and employees could open their own doors to career development.

Historically, companies nurtured managers with expertise. They had mastered their profession, were the go-to people on tricky topics and difficult-to-solve issues and could command a room through projecting authority. Individuals aspired to climb the ladder, seeking to reach key milestones, unlock new layers of knowledge, gain expertise and 'look the part'. Managers talked and others listened. Work was mainly nine to five, in a workplace, with tasks delegated and supervised. Manuals and playbooks were developed to follow processes and navigate predictable scenarios. Human resources (HR) worked in partnership with managers on performance management, remuneration and succession planning for critical roles.

It was exactly that, human *resources*.

## DO WE EVEN NEED MANAGERS?

More recently, a school of thought has been growing that perhaps organisations no longer need managers. Some go as far as to suggest that people and businesses would be better off without them. The brand associated with managing others has become tarnished. Managers are stuck in the middle, the pressure valve between the top and the bottom, cushioning constant requests, pushing tasks down, attending endless meetings, reporting figures and promising to do more with less. It's no wonder that terms such as 'management bloat' and the 'frozen core' have emerged, and people frequently switch to hushed tones to share how awful their manager is with anyone willing to listen.

One company which has chosen to scrap manager roles is Jellyfish, a digital agency network. Instead, people have a support network – a capability partner, a people partner and a mentor. They help employees navigate the company, tackle challenges and develop skills. Much like a talent marketplace, they match skills and passions to tasks, naturally encouraging people to take accountability because they don't have a manager who bails them out or takes credit for their work. Jellyfish claims it works well for the 'right' type of people: those who want to take accountability, to learn and grow and to contribute to the company's success. For those motivated by power – status, title, money – who relish the opportunity that management can bring to claim rewards for other people's work, who get a kick massaging their egos by broadcasting how many people they manage, it holds less appeal.

Corporate Rebels – a company established to make work more fun – also promote 'bossless' organisations. It builds on the work of Koldo Saratxaga, a former-CEO of a Basque manufacturing company who captured a new philosophy for work called *nuevo estilo de relaciones* (new style of relationships). This radical way of working centres on the belief that people are responsible, sensible and motivated by nature. This is characterised through several principles, including committing to radical transparency (educating the whole company in how financial performance is measured and sharing regular updates – not hiding or altering information), giving all employees a share in the profits of the company and organising around networks of teams rather than traditional hierarchies (linking people who need to work together and asking them to self-appoint a leader every six months). Saratxaga has seen impressive results across several companies using this approach and now Corporate Rebels have created a private equity firm (Krisos) to put these ideas into practice and build progressive firms.

Others are considering whether managers could be replaced by AI. Could we capture the formula for success and train AI to manage people more effectively and efficiently than humans?

Let's imagine...

## MY MANAGER IS AN AI BOT

Every morning I wake up and ask 'Blake' what's on my task list for the day. She appears in avatar form, and very politely shares a list of activities and interactions. She shares her view on the priorities – creating a to-do list by scanning various messaging, email and shared sites.

Blake can effortlessly remind me of the company's goals this quarter, and relay performance data for previous periods, including how my work has contributed (or not) to its mission. She shares the interdependencies between my work and that of others; highlighting who's waiting for my input and the impact this has on broader outcomes – their engagement, the response to the client or the revenue lost. Her management style is somewhat matter of fact, but, hey, sometimes we need that push in the right direction. She even makes suggestions on key learnings useful to others, offers insights on my style during meetings (how much time I spent talking vs others, my overuse of certain words etc.) and can be very direct in delivering feedback on things to improve! The volume of data points she can process is hugely impressive.

Blake has a team assistant, Mel, whose job is to whip up team morale and spark collaboration. Mel sends us nudges to speak to each other (with helpful personalisation e.g. Dani is celebrating her fifth work anniversary, why don't you congratulate her?) and makes suggestions on who might be in the office and when to encourage in-person meetings. He also prompts us to socialise as a team: 'Thursday night drinks after our team meeting, who's in?'

It took some adjusting to Mel and his chief cheerleader role, but my colleagues and I can see the perks. It takes the pressure off us taking the initiative – Mel can even make a reservation and book the time in our calendars to meet! In a world of synchronous projects and tasks, perhaps we do need reminders to be human, to interact, to laugh and to learn together.

But interactions with Blake can feel uncomfortable if they involve cynicism (saying something I don't really mean), if I share negative emotions (appear upset, stressed or confused) and if I ask for support with something novel or for tailored suggestions on developing my career.

You can see the algorithm strain. Blake searches through preloaded scenarios, shares standard advice for dealing with difficult people or managing stress, but undoubtedly it falls short. She asks limited questions to understand more. There are no reassuringly supportive words, change in tone, eye contact or advice offered from her own experiences. She offers no kind check-in a few days later to see how I'm feeling or if there's anything else she can help with.

And there ends the reign of the AI manager.

This is a scenario I hope we never encounter. Certainly, technology and AI can make things easier, faster, more efficient and even provide in-the-moment insights and suggestions, but I fear a world where people are solely managed by robots.

These examples acknowledge the need for something different. Today, managers are in the business of optimising human experiences to enable growth, and this requires an entirely different profile for success. If we get it right, I believe great managers can bring to life the heart and soul in human organisations.

## HUMAN MANAGERS
## – NURTURING NETWORKS OF TRUST

The shift in tasks and impact has crept up on us, and therefore the skills required for success and the tool kits we provide are often out of date and ineffective. We need to remodel and redefine what human management looks like.

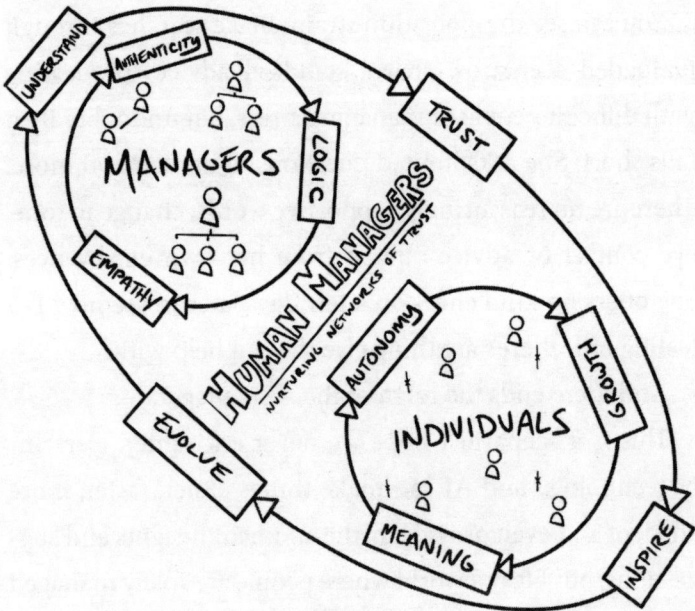

sketchnote by
KACY MAXWELL

What do today's brilliant managers do differently?

They enable their team to evolve and grow (even if it means becoming more accomplished than themselves), and they keep people feeling inspired and optimistic about the future. They recognise that their work is never done and are motivated by achieving through others. IBM's former chief HR officer Diane Gherson and Professor Lynda Gratton talk about this in their *Harvard Business Review* article 'Managers Can't Do It All', and highlight a move from manager to 'people leader' – empowering, enabling and coaching to nurture capabilities for future success.

At the core, brilliant managers skilfully and consistently build trust. Bestselling authors Anne Morriss and Frances Frei describe trust as a triangle. People trust you based on three aspects:

1. Authenticity – people need to feel they are interacting with the real you
2. Logic – people need to have faith in your judgement and capability
3. Empathy – people need to believe you care about them

Building on this trust, the following are the elements that great managers embed through their actions every day:

## THEY'RE IN THE MIX OF THE DAY TO DAY AND THEY LOVE IT

They do this job because they care about people and measure success through making things more fulfilling. Spending time with their team across multiple scenarios and settings is their priority. Many establish a clear rhythm for when they meet with employees, providing much sought-after clarity in times of great disruption. They're clear about the purpose of these meetings, with one-to-one meetings to review progress, discuss challenges and offer support in the day to day being clearly separated from sessions focused on career aspirations and development, or weekly team huddles, to share experiences, celebrate successes and facilitate support and learning for the week ahead: 'Sushma has a project using some new software, can anyone help her get up to speed with it?' They consider the time available, helping focus conversations and ensure a good share of airtime between participants. Marie Popp, a manager I worked with, created a shared digital dashboard providing a snapshot of the things her team is working on, each week. The team keep it updated, enabling individuals to share knowledge and access support in the moment.

Allocating time to meet in person for longer periods is a valuable investment, too. A good goal to aim for is to do this once a quarter, ideally offsite, away from the day to day to improve connections. This is something I regularly organised for the teams I led. This time was used to look back, gather feedback and learnings from the group and plan ahead for what's coming next. I incorporated opportunities for individuals to take the stage and share their own stories and moments of pride, and I also invited external speakers – colleagues from other teams or outside – with broader topics to explore and discuss. I finished it off with a chance to socialise informally – perhaps dinner and an activity to enable laughter and bonding. Eating a meal together is a great leveller for a diverse team. Rank, status and experience, in many respects, go out the window and different conversations can flow. Simply inviting people to eat lunch or go for dinner can help build psychological safety and stronger connections.

## THEY CONSTANTLY WORK TO REBALANCE
## THE POWER DYNAMIC

Great managers are eminently comfortable in the knowledge that people in their team will know more and have better skills than themselves. In fact, that's a marker of success. Researcher and executive advisor Liz Wiseman talks about 'multipliers' – managers who see their role as fostering a culture of intelligence (as opposed to 'diminishers', who drain it – stamping out ideas, grabbing credit and stifling development). An important trait that Wiseman identifies is managers seeing themselves as coaches and teachers, enabling others to operate independently by letting people own their results and rewarding employees' successes. These managers often share their own mistakes and encourage constant learning. But they don't spend too much time talking – using skills in asking open questions to facilitate conversation, jumping in to move things on when needed, add reflections and involve others. Bert Simonis, a manager I worked with, did this brilliantly. Stepping in when people got stuck and needed support and listening to their challenges and objectives. He energetically offered advice and suggestions, co-creating a path forwards, making sure to subsequently enable the individual to take the reins again. It was their project, their idea, their delivery, and this meant they owned it.

Ross Brawn, considered one of the most successful technical directors and team principals in Formula One, turned a failing team (which hadn't won a championship since

1979) at Ferrari into multichampionship winners. Many would have come into a failing team and made swift changes, brought in people they'd worked with before and rebuilt from scratch. Brawn chose not to do that. Instead, he invested time in learning about the team he had inherited, getting to know them and understanding their strengths and experiences rather than making rapid decisions based on early impressions. This reinforced to the team that they were just as capable of winning as the other teams and set the basis for a culture characterised by trust, humility, learning, relationships and structure. Brawn chose not to use his power to overhaul what was there but to understand and optimise it.

## STRONG MANAGERS LEAD WITH EMPATHY

They do this because they possess an innate desire to truly understand and support people to thrive. They show compassion. They read when an individual needs support. They're in tune and in the right places. These managers aren't hiding away in offices or swerving virtual calls; they're there and visible when their teams need them. They spread their senses wide, talking to a varied network, noticing patterns or changes in behaviour ('Jo seems to be working later than usual, I wonder what's going on there') and initiating conversations to check in and offer support, catching problems before they escalate. They care for and support the whole person: coaching behaviours, developing skills and enabling connections. Offering support when challenges emerge – e.g. sick children, caring for elderly relatives, experiences of discrimination or harassment, disagreements or managing mental health issues. The patchwork of topics is vast, as our work and home lives become one and complexity soars.

It's certainly not for managers to solve all these problems; they have impact by being prepared to listen, offering support where they can and making suggestions on accessing specialist advice. Ed Rivlin, a manager I worked with, did this skilfully. Listening to his team's challenges, empathising but with a pragmatic, action-focused approach. He makes suggestions on who might be able to help, encouraging the individual to take control in moving to the next step. The research and consulting firm Gartner highlights the strengths of 'connector' managers: humble in their approach, they draw upon the strengths of those around them to provide the best support and advice for their team.

## A COMPASSIONATE APPROACH DOESN'T NEGATE DELIVERING HIGH PERFORMANCE

Gifted managers know that a thriving team delivers growth for the business, and this requires regular and timely conversations about performance gaps and development needs. They fundamentally believe that optimal performance depends upon the whole of the team and fostering an environment for growth built on trust is paramount. This might look like helping teams understand business decisions such as hiring freezes or not backfilling key roles, by sharing broader business performance information and outlining the drivers for this decision. Being kind isn't about telling people what they want to hear, or cushioning development feedback so that it gets lost in a sea of compliments. They are adept at picking up on areas for improvement, getting on the front foot and sharing experiences and suggestions for maximising impact. They know when someone has hit cruise control and could do more to develop and grow their careers, sensing when it's time to push the accelerator and provide opportunities to make this a reality. They have a laser focus on facilitating human growth.

You will often find great managers surveying the horizon before purposefully diving down into the weeds. They'll be joining project meetings or customer calls and co-presenting with team members because this provides the opportunity to coach and share standout examples with the broader team. They don't let things fester. Feedback held back and shared in a quarterly review is rendered useless if the behaviour and impact could have been changed sooner. Lilly Ashton-Smith, a manager I worked with, did this effortlessly. I would frequently overhear conversations she was having with her team, discussing their recent experiences. She would throw in sentences such as 'what did you learn?' and 'what would you do differently next time?' encouraging them to reflect and bottle learnings. Her supportive and pragmatic approach helped ensure that this wasn't a big deal, setting a safe tone for continuous improvement.

## GREAT MANAGERS CAREFULLY MANAGE GREAT EXPECTATIONS

They revisit psychological contracts regularly. The assumptions we all hold about what will happen, when. 'I will get promoted when I deliver X results for this project.' These need to be unpicked and discussed regularly, especially as things move and change so quickly around us. Great managers discuss aspirations and reality continuously. Managing expectations fairly and honestly ensuring psychological contracts don't go up in flames – e.g. 'I understand that promotion by the end of the year is your goal, and I support you with that and will do all I can to try to make this a reality. However, the business is facing a tougher period and so I believe there is a possibility that promotions will be delayed. I commit to keeping you updated on any news I hear on this.'

## BEING FAIR AND UPHOLDING ETHICAL STANDARDS IS FRONT AND CENTRE

Knowing that a manager expects high standards and will challenge unethical behaviour or unsustainable ways of working provides a solid and secure base for people to invest in their work. They steer and create culture in a positive mould, protecting employees from the cracks that emerge. This might mean resisting temptation to cut corners in hiring or promotion processes (even if the individual is a known entity) to ensure that everyone has fair opportunity to progress, and calling out poor behaviour even when it drives strong results (e.g. credit-grabbing behaviour or pulling long hours at the last minute to make up for not putting in the preparation ahead of time). They deal swiftly and confidently with any aggressive behaviour, or early signs that things might escalate. If colleagues lock horns in a meeting or misunderstand each other, skilled managers carefully and politely nudge the conversation in a new direction, settling the dynamic in the here and now, and picking up separately with individuals involved to identify support needed to move things forwards.

They proactively seek to nurture diverse teams, identifying gaps and opportunities for improving collective intelligence and going out of their way to hire in new perspectives and experiences. They keep an eye on the future path, gathering feedback across the team and stakeholders, understanding that what's gone before might not provide the recipe for success in what's yet to come.

## THEY HAVE A STRONG SENSE OF PERSPECTIVE AND SPRINKLING OF HUMOUR

Building work environments that enable the harmonising of people, purpose and profitable businesses, to guide healthy, sustainable and growing organisations, is a life's work for those managing teams. Whilst this is serious, heavy stuff, many great managers balance this with a good sense of perspective and a sprinkling of humour to help people make light of what can feel intense and daunting. The welcoming smile and warmth or chats about what happened over the weekend or a new TV series provide constant reminders of the outside world and that life goes on.

This is quite the list!

It's certainly not exhaustive, nor a tick list. Not every people manager is made the same. Human managers are fundamentally focused on building and sustaining trusted relationships. They share their real selves; their actions support their words. They have faith in the capabilities of others, and they care about bringing out the best in, and for, their people. The way they do this takes different forms. But just a few of these attributes can enable trust to flow around the organisation, bringing work to life for people every day.

## SPARKING MEANING AND GROWTH

Despite difference in style, there is one feature that today's brilliant managers all share. Examine the conversations, coaching and insight they reveal in the flow of work and you'll see there is a formula for success. Great managers help people find personal meaning and growth. The optimal combination of autonomy, meaning and growth can make for happy experiences of work, throughout scenarios, ages and life stages.

### THREE LITTLE WORDS WITH INCREDIBLE POWER AND IMPACT

This isn't as straightforward as it sounds, because as humans, we often think we need something else. We confuse fulfilment with the things we have, the accolades we receive or the status we achieve. This might make us feel good for a while, maybe even satisfy us for the short term. But soon we'll yearn for something else, something more durable:

- Autonomy (feeling empowered, trusted and able to make individual choices)
- Meaning (being fuelled by purpose in what we do and experiencing strong social relationships such that we feel a sense of belonging and inclusion)
- Growth (developing, learning and growing through interesting and varied career opportunities)

Brilliant human managers curate this recipe for their teams all the time. However, it can be hard to differentiate a brilliant manager from one who is squashing this in everyone around them. At a surface level, the actions both these managers take can appear quite similar; yet the motivation behind their behaviour and exacting experience they create can crush or elevate.

Here are a few 'under the hood' explorations of typical scenarios, outlining the difference in impact between a manager of old vs a human manager:

SCENARIO 1: AN OPPORTUNITY TO ORGANISE AN EVENT
A few times a year, there are big events to organise – a team kick-off meeting, maybe a client event or an awards evening

to celebrate success. These are the things we enjoy when we get there but can dread in the run-up, particularly if it falls on us to arrange it. Often this is the type of activity managers choose to delegate...

A manager of old would likely call the chosen one (the first name that springs to mind) into a meeting, announcing that they have a great opportunity for them. They have probably chosen a reliable star performer; someone who works hard and gets stuff done. After all, their own reputation is on the line. They 'brief' the individual on the task – involving sharing vague information and forwarding an email from their boss about what's required. Of course, they will be available to discuss and help shape things as it progresses – their door is always open. Job done. Off the employee goes, a mix of excitement and trepidation flooding their brain. What follows is a flurry of calls, information-seeking and comparing of notes for the individual taking this on. They piece together the requirements, trying to find the best path through, calling in favours from colleagues to cobble a plan together. Several times they attempt to share updates and seek input from their manager on how the plan is progressing, but they can't access time in their diary. There are a few moments where content appears to clash or presenters misalign on the topics they want to speak on. The manager parachutes in, taking the reins and apologising for their team member's lack of skill in this area – it is the first time they've done this. The event is now just a few days away, and their manager *now* wants to see what's going on. The individual takes them through the various conversations with stakeholders, explaining the rationale, balancing of time, space available and participant needs. But the manager has other ideas – this must be spectacular! Have *they* got enough airtime to impress? They're not convinced about the visual design. The individual's stress levels soar. There are only a few days before kick-off, but they pull all-nighters to get it done and meet the whimsical needs of their manager. The event is a glowing success. The manager basks in the glory, sending a cursory thank-you note and voucher to the individual several days later. The employee, chosen for this once-in-a-lifetime opportunity, is exhausted, deflated, angry that their hard work has barely been acknowledged and certain they don't want to take anything like that on again.

Conversely, a human manager carefully considers who could take this on. Perhaps not the usual suspects, but someone ready for a stretching assignment and who will really value the networking and skill development opportunity. They collate all the information they have, providing a clear brief and checking first whether the individual has capacity and motivation to get involved. They let them take charge, asking when and where they need them throughout the process. They organise regular catch-ups and agree they'll both join sessions with key stakeholders to ensure expectations and parameters (budget, time etc.) are carefully managed. The manager holds time in their own diary to review anything on which the individual needs their input. There are some challenges encountered; late switches in the agenda, clashes with messaging that require ironing out. The individual comes up with suggestions for solving these, talking them through with their manager when they need to. The manager encourages the employee to take on a visible role on the day itself, and whilst this feels like a stretch – in capacity and capability – they agree to it, and their manager coaches them through preparation for the day. The event goes without a hitch. Everyone is impressed and the individual takes centre stage, enjoying the moment and benefitting from the praise. They feel empowered, supported, able to grow and energised by the event. This is a place where they feel trusted and able to develop their career.

## SCENARIO 2: WHEN TARGETS FEEL UNACHIEVABLE

The end of year approaches and management layers are heads down in budgeting. They have spent several weeks working through scenarios and models, and then targets for individuals and teams pop out the other side. This year's goals look really challenging – there's a 10 per cent uplift on last year and market conditions have been tough. Teams feel this could be too stretching and worry this will limit their ability to earn a bonus.

The manager of old keeps their head down. They've heard some rumblings about discontent over targets, but this tends to happen this time of year; individuals always feel they've been hard done by and then things turn out OK.

They'll wait and see if anyone raises it. A couple do – in one to ones. The manager brings out the old pep talk: 'I know things are tough, but this is our moment to shine. The company desperately needs a good year, and I'm hopeful for promotion, so we needed to take on something ambitious. But look at the last few months' performance. You and the team have shown some promising progress, and I know you're very talented, I think this is totally within our reach, don't you? You worry too much; have faith in our capabilities, it will all be OK!' The individual leaves feeling a little better but still not clear how this has been worked out. What's behind the numbers? How will the strategy support this growth? And is this a place where I can continue to perform and get rewarded? I'm not sure.

The human manager tackles this differently. Their approach to budget setting has already involved several conversations with the team, sharing broader business goals and strategy. They've asked for their input on what might be possible, given different types of investment – new products in development, possibly new team members and software to make work more efficient. Now this starts to pay dividends. There are a few murmurings about the targets feeling stretchy, but people in the team are already equipped with the rationale for growth. They can reason amongst themselves because they understand how this is possible and why it's important. To ensure clarity, the manager uses a weekly team call to talk this through again. They're open and honest, sharing the information they can and describing the opportunities they see for the team to have a successful year. They turn the moment of doubt into confidence and motivation. The path ahead is for the whole team, everyone is in it and everyone will benefit from their shared successes.

The small everyday actions of talented human managers create environments where people flourish.

Great managers understand the power of autonomy, meaning and growth and they are the conduits for this in their team. They enable autonomy by share guiding principles, not rules, talking through broader goals and trusting others to determine the path forwards. They extract and elevate meaning through identifying the impact of the work they deliver. They understand that jobs are not simply created and set for life – they require constant review and recrafting to ensure individuals feel motivated to keep delivering value for the company. They proactively build growth mindsets, fundamentally believing that people have the capability to learn, reskill and evolve.

They recognise that it isn't about themselves. Success for them comes through understanding, empowering, coaching and seeing others grow.

## GET THE BLOOD PUMPING

Managers today must help buffer the ambiguity and clarify the complexity. They can personalise and bring meaning because they have a deep understanding of individuals and the environment in which they're working. Skilled managers effectively navigate the grey – balancing tensions between purpose and profit, fairness and equity, performance and sustainability. They show kindness and compassion but also provide honest and constructive feedback. They lead with empathy, asking questions to understand more, facilitating learning from mistakes (their own included) and they anticipate the future whilst dealing with the now. They build the trusting relationships upon which work can be delivered, challenges overcome, change successfully navigated and the future imagined.

They are, if enabled to be, the heart, pumping blood throughout organisations. However, they need our help and support to optimise and sustain their impact:

## IDENTIFY A NEW BREED OF HUMAN MANAGERS

To build a human work era, we must firstly value human management. This requires identifying people with the right skills and potential to excel in delivering against this new blueprint. We need a new profile of manager for success. Someone motivated by delivering results through others, who has the humility to get out of the way and nurture the talents of their team, who can cope with constant and varied requests and challenges and is skilled in building trust, understanding and personalising support and development. Someone who understands that this isn't about themselves but about their team and the results they can nurture through them. For many companies, this requires ripping up existing job descriptions, hiring processes and tools and assumptions about who would make a good manager. We need to rely on objective measures to reveal those who can bring vigour to manager and employee relationships. We must step away from the hunches and judgements formed about people in our organisations, to explore properly the potential each person could bring.

## INVEST IN AND VALUE MANAGEMENT SKILLS

Across many organisations, management is viewed as a necessary stepping stone, a tick box to achieve to breakthrough to leadership or become a technical authority. This can mean that people who have no aspiration, skill or potential to manage others end up in these crucial positions; and it can also mean that those who could be brilliant are overlooked. In many companies I have worked with, management is tacked on to existing responsibilities – a talented individual contributor is asked to oversee a team because they're good at what they do. But no one stops to consider whether they *can* or even *want* to manage. This does significant damage to everyone. We need to provide people with multiple and varied tracks to progress their careers (technical and managerial focused), so they don't feel they have to earn the badge of management and move on. In addition, we need to rework the people manager 'brand': how managers are perceived, positioned, rewarded and even talked about in the organisation could bring significant return. Managing others well demands a specialist set of skills, and when we get it right, the impact on others is significant.

The range of skills that managers need to develop and hone is huge – asking good questions, listening to understand, establishing rhythms for connection, empowering and motivating others, having constructive feedback conversations and navigating complex and emotionally charged scenarios. A mix of on-demand and in-person training to provide safe spaces to practise and receive personalised feedback is essential. Regular injections of support and channels to access guidance will quickly provide return on investment.

Managers can amplify and diffuse trust, energy, engagement, productivity, ideas and retention. This is the lifeblood in any organisation. We need to design the role, identify who is best suited to fill it, support them to excel and reward them with this impact in mind. Make management feel aspirational, a highly skilled profession and key to business success, because it absolutely is.

## EMBED TECHNOLOGY TO FOCUS HUMAN IMPACT

If carefully chosen and embedded, AI can help by freeing up time for managers to focus on using their uniquely human skills. Generative AI tools can wade through mountains of information, identify themes, draft priorities and formulate communications. AI can provide prompts about a lack of or over communication to improve frequency and type of messages shared. It can also provide insights on teams, such as behavioural strengths and gaps, well-being red flags and working habits to inform targeted coaching and support. Automated AI feedback from psychometrics and behavioural assessments can also be useful. I can see a role for Mel, and his collaboration and engagement nudges, particularly as teams become increasingly diverse and dispersed. VR and avatar-based tools could also help managers prepare for challenging scenarios, to practise messaging and deal with questions and concerns ahead of interacting live.

Well-placed, well-designed and well-maintained AI should feature in a human manager's toolkit. This can enable managers to focus where they have greatest impact: building human connection, personalising roles to bring meaning, sharing wisdom and advice and telling stories to inspire, motivate and bring teams together to have fun, learn and grow.

## CREATE COMMUNITIES TO GUIDE AND SUPPORT

It would be a travesty to leave this vital group out on their own, surrounded by a large team and yet feeling isolated and lonely. To be successful, we need to bring together communities of people managers who can lean on each other, share experiences, access live support and suggestions and join a safe space to vent when things feel overwhelming. The pace of change is intensifying, the complexity of our world and lives increasing and the variety of scenarios we face expanding. Getting the recipe right for autonomy, meaning and growth for individuals across cultures, roles, time zones, life stages and demographic groups takes significant skill, effort and continuous learning.

This compassionate and dedicated group deserve equipping with skills, support and reward.

The reward for us all is clear – organisations with heart and soul.

---

### THE BEATING HEART: ACTIONS TO EMPOWER HUMAN MANAGERS

Define, identify and value *human* managers:

- Review existing definitions of management and revise these to describe the people-oriented motivators, attributes and skills that make the difference today
- Use this new recipe to objectively identify the best people to take on this pivotal role. There will likely be great people managers in your business today whom you can find and support to thrive. Take care not to be deceived by surface-level actions. Examine motivations, behaviour and impact carefully – it could mark the difference between crushing and elevating your people
- Make managing attractive! Reward and showcase those doing it well. Demonstrate that it's a key value driver in your business

Help managers prioritise activity with their people:

- Review where managers spend their time today. What percentage is spent interacting with their teams? What's taking up too much energy? What could be simplified?
- Identify opportunities for technology to take on more of the burden, in the right places. Use tools, processes, apps and AI to enable faster processing of information and easier access, to embed feedback tips to help hone management style and impact

Build a community of human managers:

- Managing can feel lonely. In this new era of work, we need to provide live support systems and communities to help managers tackle new and complex scenarios. Being part of a community where knowledge, learning and advice can be easily accessed will bring support and improve productivity and engagement
- Look for opportunities to develop skills that transcend functions, regions and phases of growth. Tools and modules that strengthen giving constructive feedback, facilitating conversations, listening and coaching will always prove worthwhile investments

---

# CHAPTER 9

# GET BETTER AT BEING HUMAN

Dear human,

This is about you *and* those around you.

*You* have an opportunity to get better at being human and, in doing so, to build something more fulfilling for us all.

First, let me take you back to just before the turn of the century. A time when we didn't know what would happen when the year flipped over to 2000. Would life as we know it end? Would clocks, planes, cars and computers all melt down? Would an alien invasion wipe out humankind?

Thankfully, none of that happened. We sailed into the twenty-first century with Robbie Williams's 'Millennium' ringing in our ears. In fact, songwriters, film directors and artists were all grappling with the same big questions we do today – who am I? What is life all about? What does it mean to be human?

Listen closely to the words of the 1990s hit song 'Everybody's Free (To Wear Sunscreen)' and you will find that

Baz Luhrmann imparts some sage advice, which can be summarised as:

- Don't be too hard on yourself
- Keep learning and growing
- Be kind to others (and don't tolerate unkindness)
- Focus on what you can do, not what others are doing
- Be energised by the positive, don't dwell on the negative
- Invest time in relationships
- It's OK to change your mind and not know the answer
- Keep yourself and your ego balanced
- Value those closest to you
- Look after your body – you only get one!

Collectively, we can embed these features front and centre into our experiences of work – and life. We have choices to make. We have opportunity to learn and improve. We can take steps to get better at being human.

So, toggle in, choose a new journey and start developing better human habits!

Yours,

A hopeful human

PS Do have a read of the lyrics to 'Everybody's Free (To Wear Sunscreen)' by Baz Luhrmann – there really are some gems that might just make you stop and rethink everything!

## AN EMOTIONAL BANK ACCOUNT

Being human can feel hard and, in many ways, we're wired to make it harder.

It's widely believed people have between 50,000 and 70,000 thoughts per day. Things we mustn't forget, which way to drive, song lyrics, emotions (happy and sad in relation to the days' events or memories unsuspectedly triggered), what to write next, what to have for dinner, feeling cold/hot, willing a long-awaited message to flash on your phone, the things we wished we had said to the irritating person on the train, what we hope will happen next, our dreams, anxieties, fears. In this rapidly flowing river, psychologists suggest that as much as 75 per cent of our thoughts are negative. The 'I can't do that', 'what happens if', 'what will they think of me?', 'I'm too scared' and 'I'm not as good as them' outweigh the positive self-talk in most people. Perhaps it is no wonder we often collectively create hurtful, isolating and risk-averse work environments.

Yet, as Baz Luhrmann suggests, we can choose to interrupt and forge a different path. This is something we *all* have a part to play in, and our actions will affect us and those around us. It starts with getting better at being human, and collectively, our commitment to this will enable us to build a world where we can flourish as humans. This is our mission.

Psychologist John Gottman uses his research to try to help people build better relationships with their partners. He talks about the emotional bank account, how positive and negative exchanges between partners can leave individuals feeling in credit or in debt, listened to or not. Importantly, he identifies that it is possible for couples to improve their bank account position, by focusing on a 20:1 ratio of positive to negative exchanges during each day (and 5:1 during moments of conflict).

There are many aspects of Gottman's advice that resonate in relationships between friends, colleagues, family members as well as partners. These include being an active listener (listening to understand, not simply to respond – asking questions, summarising and making eye contact), offering to help (particularly when someone else is feeling stressed, even if it isn't your area of responsibility), showing others that you're thinking of them (dropping them a message, sharing something funny or bringing in treats to share), showing validation (using phrases to show support and understanding such as 'that makes sense' or 'I understand why you feel that way'), being responsive to requests for connection (when someone attempts conversation, letting them in and building the discussion with them) and practising empathy (particularly in moments of conflict – seeking to understand and appreciate, rather than judge and dismiss). Couples who invest time and commitment in making these small changes, rebalancing their emotional bank accounts, reaped the rewards. But they had to put in the work.

Many of these elements are things that we know we should do, but in reality, life gets in the way. Pressures mount, time passes and it feels easier to revert to type. We should eat healthily, get some exercise and brush our teeth twice a day. We should wear sunscreen but sometimes it's a hassle, so we risk it, running out to the sea, trying to stick to the 'shadier parts'. The next morning, we wake up sore, crisp and remorseful! We learn the hard way that the effort upfront is seriously worth it. It's the same deal with life and, in particular, the relationships we value and nurture.

We can choose to make things better in three steps:

1. Toggle in
2. Choose a new journey
3. Develop better human habits

## FIRST, TOGGLE IN

- Someone else will do that → I'm accountable
- Me → We
- Trust is given → Trust is earned
- I can't do that → I can't do that, yet
- What will make me look good? → How could this help others?

We often find ourselves waiting and observing. Seeing if someone else will step in and solve a problem. Hoping a new door and opportunity will open to rescue us from the dreariness of our current space. Assuming someone else has more experience, better skills, even though the job described sounds incredible. Waiting for *the* perfect moment to ask a crucial question.

The first step to a more fulfilling, more human experience is to toggle in to life. To move from being a spectator to being in the mix of the action. To start creating and making things happen.

## SECOND, CHOOSE A NEW JOURNEY

To change the destination, we need to embark on a new journey.

A journey where we choose to put ourselves amongst it. To 'take responsibility for the circumstances that we are in', as professor and organisational psychologist John Amaechi says, and decide that we can personally influence change.

On this journey, there are three tools you'll need to bring with you and develop along the way:

1. An accountability ladder
2. A growth mindset
3. Emotional intelligence

### I. AN ACCOUNTABILITY LADDER

We need to ascend the accountability ladder to truly understand the situation and take responsibility for the impact of our behaviour. This is a well-established model, but it's very effective and versatile. It can be used at work and home settings, with individuals, managers and leaders, even children and teenagers!

It was made popular in 2007 by Bruce Gordon, the then president of the National Association for the Advancement of Colored People (NAACP), an American civil rights organisation. He explained that people on Levels 1 to 4 of the eight-rung accountability ladder typically believe things happen to them and behave as the victim, whereas those on Levels 5 to 8 believe things happen because of them and behave in ways that are proactive and truly accountable. Critically, those on the higher rungs are able to identify and acknowledge the role they play in all scenarios. They avoid placing blame and take personal responsibility for rectifying or changing things, choosing to look at what they can personally do to make things better.

You'll recognise each of the levels – likely in yourself and in others:

- Level 1 – being unaware: 'I didn't know that report was due in today' or 'No one told me we had visitors coming in for that meeting'
- Level 2 – blaming others: 'You weren't very clear about exactly what you wanted me to write'
- Level 3 – making excuses: there's a level of awareness but an excuse ready – 'We always meet in that room, so I didn't check the invite'
- Level 4 – waiting and hoping: 'If I simply don't mention that we've failed to hit target this month, maybe no one will notice?'
- Level 5 – acknowledging reality: this is when things start to tilt. This is the person who acknowledges something should have been done about the problem but is unlikely

to actually do anything – 'Maybe I should have done something different there, but it's done now'

- Level 6 – owning it: 'Rest assured I will make sure that doesn't happen again'
- Level 7 – finding solutions: the individual takes it a step further, owning resolution and being specific about finding a solution – 'I understand the problem and here's what I am going to do about it'
- Level 8 – making it happen: the individual takes Levels 6 and 7 and adds action – 'I appreciate that wasn't ideal, I understand where we went wrong and here's what I've done to make it better'

Of course, you can't be accountable for everything, and there are absolutely times to step back and let others lead or allow time to heal. However, in most situations, pushing yourself up the ladder of accountability is no bad thing. Get a copy and print it out. When tough scenarios strike, look at where you are on the accountability ladder. Are you blaming others for failure to deliver the project on time? Or are you discussing with the team what went wrong, what you can learn and agreeing what you will personally do next to resolve things?

Turn commonly encountered scenarios such as working for a poor manager into being accountable for delivering good work. That, you can own. Or turn feeling undervalued in a role to taking accountability for showing other people (maybe different colleagues or external stakeholders) your true value. And turn failing to deliver on a commitment into accountability for learning how you can meet it next time. It even extends to situations where you observe others behaving poorly. Perhaps they're being rude, using inappropriate language or making someone feel excluded or uncomfortable. It can feel challenging to be the person who says something – calls them out on their behaviour, asks a question to draw in the individual who has been isolated or talks to the perpetrator after the exchange. But these interventions, when you feel safe to make them, can hold real significance for the people involved and influence future behaviour and dynamics.

## FROM ACCOUNTABILITY TO PSYCHOLOGICAL OWNERSHIP

David Marquet, an ex-US Navy captain, advocates for 'turning the ship around'. In a military setting, heavily influenced by hierarchy and power, he observed that people followed him no matter what he said. On the submarine the *Santa Fe*, officers sought his permission for almost every task, yet the submarine wasn't performing well. Against his 'leadership instincts', Marquet started to turn this dynamic on its head, replacing the captain authorising actions with conversations of 'intent'. Instead, he asked his team, 'What are we trying to accomplish?' They would share the desired outcome. And Marquet would simply ask, 'What's the best way to approach this task to achieve that outcome?'

Marquet pinpoints two pillars for making this possible – having technical competence (skill and knowledge) and organisational clarity (an understanding of whether this is the right thing to do). In the existing model, the officers were dependent upon him, as captain, for organisational clarity, and yet, if he could equip them with this (as well as good training and knowledge), he instinctively felt it would be better to push the authority to where the in-depth knowledge was (in the ranks, not in the commander).

In doing so, Marquet says he created psychological ownership. In time, he had '135 thinking, active, passionate, creative, proactive, taking-initiative people'. And that, Marquet said, is 'a tidal wave – you don't stand a chance!'

The crew became completely engaged, contributing their full intellectual capacity every day. The *Santa Fe* set records for performance, morale and retention. And over the next decade, a highly disproportionate number of *Santa Fe* officers were selected to become submarine commanders. Marquet hadn't just created the best-performing US Navy submarine in history; he had created the conditions for human growth, through giving ownership and creating leaders.

Workplace culture and teamwork consultant Gustavo Razzetti says that accountability is the path to psychological ownership but that accountability and ownership are different things: 'Ownership inspires people to go above and beyond. It's a state of mind in which you feel in charge. Not only do you have the motivation, agency and willingness to step up – you will also do whatever it takes to achieve the goals.' David Marquet certainly built a culture of ownership aboard the *Santa Fe* and reached the top of the accountability ladder.

A lack of accountability might make for entertaining reality TV – with *Big Brother* housemates strenuously denying being the one leaving a trail of washing up around the house, or *Apprentice* contestants ferociously blaming each other for failing to see the massive flaw in their product idea – but this rarely makes for a fulfilling life. There's strong psychological evidence that when we feel more in control of our own destiny, our feelings of well-being improve and so too do our levels of performance. It's far more damaging to bury our heads in the sand, pass the buck and pretend it never happened than to stand up, take ownership and build a plan for action.

Climb the accountability ladder and see how this changes your view and ability to toggle in to taking ownership for shaping your experiences of work and life.

## 2. A GROWTH MINDSET

Having a growth mindset is proven to deliver higher levels of performance for individuals and organisations. The even better news is that mindsets can be changed. Through building self-awareness and focusing effort, a growth mindset can be nurtured.

Professor Carol Dweck – who coined the term 'growth mindset' – says we all have a blend of fixed and growth mindsets and therefore people and teams can increase their propensity for growth. Seeking feedback, sharing mistakes, discussing learnings, collaborating and innovating are all attributes of a company with a growth mindset culture.

*The Last Dance*, the Netflix story of the Chicago Bulls throughout the 1980s and '90s, shares a great example of a team which developed a growth mindset. Having led the field and won three consecutive championships in 1991–93, the Bulls are attempting to do this again with Michael Jordan returning from retirement to lead the charge. They face multiple challenges, setbacks and obstacles (including Dennis Rodman going missing in Las Vegas), but a commitment to hard work and training to learn from mistakes shines through. They put improvement first, practise positive self-talk, have team rituals and try new things – watching hours of games, analysing plays and competitors, getting ready to be the best they can be. The Chicago Bulls went on to achieve the three-peat, winning three consecutive series in 1996–98.

Matthew Syed, a Commonwealth champion table-tennis player and now a world leader in the field of individual and organisational high performance, is a strong advocate for growth mindsets: 'The great institutions and successful individuals are adaptive for a simple reason: they realise that in a complex world, they don't already have the answers. They are therefore not threatened by information about their weaknesses. Indeed, they actively look for it.' Having been an elite athlete, surrounded by others at the top of their game, and worked with highly successful business leaders, Syed and his team have identified nine core

behavioural traits that underpin a growth mindset in individuals. These are: growth, attitude to feedback, attitude to
failure, attitude to complexity, humility, perception of potential, curiosity, collaboration and agility. Understanding
and developing these can turn a fixed mindset into growth,
and on mass, build cultures where agility, adaptability, innovation and continuous improvement are key features. In
our complex and changing world, these factors are essential
to our survival.

People with fixed mindsets see new information or alternative views as a threat. They hide their gaps in knowledge,
glossing over topics, hoping they won't get caught out. They
believe the talents and skills they have are set in stone and
unchangeable. They need to work with what they've got.
When they receive feedback, they can get defensive and
blame others – clinging to the lower rungs of the accountability ladder.

Those with a growth mindset, on the other hand, believe
their talents can be developed through hard work and support from others. They worry less about looking smart and
put more energy into learning.

Syed talks about the difference in culture between organisations where growth mindsets are deliberately nurtured
and where they're not. In a Ted Talk, he compares the
aviation industry with healthcare. In aviation, a focus on
learning, looking at trends, anticipating issues and reviewing mistakes is innate. Black boxes record all information
in planes, and pilots, crew and engineers are all well versed

in discussing what went wrong and how they can improve. Notably, at the beginning of the last century, travelling by air was the riskiest form of travel. Now, plane crashes are very rare. The focus on learning and growth has propelled an industry into new dimensions.

Conversely, healthcare organisations often hold the view that talent is enough. Those at the top – the best surgeons, anaesthetists and hospital directors – are infallible. They're the best of the best; what they don't know isn't worth knowing. This is a culture where failure is seen as a threat. Issues are covered up and cues missed. If something goes wrong, typically those lower down the chain are blamed. Of course, it's a heavily litigated industry and the stakes are high. We still live in a time where preventable medical errors kill huge volumes of patients every year. But progress is definitely being made. Atul Gawande, an American surgeon and writer, has developed pre-operation checklists, inspired by the aviation industry, and these are now used across many healthcare organisations. They help surgeons catch basic mistakes before they happen and improve bonding within the team (one of Gawande's checks is ensuring that everyone in the operating room knows each other's name, which has resulted in people feeling more confident to speak out if something goes wrong).

Developing your growth mindset is a fantastic investment for you and those around you. Moving your thinking from 'I can't do that' to 'I haven't learned to do that, yet' could open new doors and chapters for your work and life. Today, there are so many options available for on-demand skill development – support that can be accessed from colleagues, mentors and managers but also from external networks – allowing people to take time to learn, ask for feedback and share with others, which can provide considerable breakthroughs (and enjoyment).

The next time you think 'I don't know that' or 'I can't do that', pause.

Think – *how could I learn?*

## 3. EMOTIONAL INTELLIGENCE

The final tool to pack for this new journey is emotional intelligence (EI). This holds the key to understanding others and nurturing strong relationships. Many of the practices psychologist John Gottman describes for improving the ratio of positive to negative interactions relate to this. Whilst some people might naturally have more than others, this is also something you can develop and improve.

Contrary to popular belief, having strong EI isn't about being nice. Daniel Goleman, a leading thinker on EI, has a well-established model covering four elements:

1. Self-awareness
2. Self-management
3. Social awareness
4. Relationship management

## SELF-AWARENESS

Self-awareness is about being consciously aware of your own thoughts and feelings and the impact this plays. Being aware of your own feelings puts you in charge, not your emotions. Your values and sense of purpose help set your course of action. This is the core to building emotional intelligence. This part is explored in more detail in the final section of this chapter.

## SELF-MANAGEMENT

Self-management is about your capability to regulate and redirect impulsive emotions. Goleman describes this as the battle between the 'bad boss' (the amygdala in our brains – responsible for raising the alarm if threat is detected) and the 'good boss' (the prefrontal cortex – the control centre in our brains. It handles complex planning tasks and is the space where we work out tough problems in our heads. Importantly, it also helps moderate emotions detected by the amygdala).

The amygdala is a bit like a toddler – driven mostly through innate urges and detection of threat (I might not get the snack I want or I sense my parent is about to leave me) – and the prefrontal cortex is the adult, trying to reason and reassure, sharing examples of overcoming this scenario previously and being aware of the need to bring balance and control.

This discussion happens within our brains all the time. Seeing an email flash up with the heading 'Organisational

Announcement', the amygdala signals our stress response; this is it – we're all losing our jobs. Then, the prefrontal cortex steps in and says, 'Hang on. We've seen this before and it wasn't as bad as we thought. Take a deep breath. We've got this.'

You have also likely witnessed, or experienced yourself, an 'amygdala hijack'. Think a toddler melting down in the middle of a supermarket. Arms and legs flying everywhere. Tears rolling down their face. Desperate sobs. You assume something horrendous has just happened, but you move a little closer and realise it's a complete and utter loss of control over wanting a specific snack. Of course, in work, this might look more like someone unable to speak on stage. Suddenly frozen, their heart races, palms are sweaty and their mouth is dry. The carefully prepared speech in their head has been hijacked by their amygdala. This is an automatic response – your body acts without any conscious input from you. Your brain is telling you this is a threat – get out of this situation to save your life!

Ryan Reynolds, the actor and investor, has described the anxiety he feels before appearing on live talk shows, highlighting the battle between his amygdala and prefrontal cortex: 'I remember I'd be standing backstage before the curtain would open, and I would think to myself, "I'm gonna die. I'm literally gonna die here. The curtain's gonna open and I'm just gonna be, I'm just gonna be a symphony of vomit," just, like, something horrible's gonna happen!'

Reynolds noted that 'as soon as that curtain opens' before

he goes on stage, 'this little guy takes over', ultimately helping him manage his anxiety: 'And he's like, "I got this. You're
cool." I feel, like, my heart rate drop, and my breathing calm,
and I just sort of go out and I'm this different person. And
I leave that interview going, "God, I'd love to be that guy!"'

This fight-or-flight response is something everyone experiences and sometimes it can take us by surprise. I've taken
many flights and never really felt scared. Yet more recently,
even mild turbulence can trigger a stress reaction. The good
news is that it is something we can all work on to improve.
Even simple things such as relabelling the emotion – e.g.
in a public-speaking scenario, going from 'I am speaking
in front of hundreds of people, that's terrifying' to 'isn't it
exciting, I'm speaking in front of hundreds of people' – can
help you rechannel emotions. In addition, practising feeling and managing the emotions will help (e.g. practising
with smaller audiences, seeing how you feel and respond
when you step out onto a stage or even acknowledging the
feelings can help you manage them). Mindfulness is also
proven to provide a mechanism for strengthening the prefrontal cortex.

It doesn't matter who you are. These human moments
affect us all.

## SOCIAL AWARENESS

Social awareness is about understanding and reading
others. Goleman describes two main competencies in
this area – empathy and organisational awareness. In

organisations, we need to understand others as individu-als and also appreciate the dynamic of the setting around them (e.g. hierarchy, power in relationships and the forces at work in shaping how people interact). Empathy is a key theme running throughout this book – since it is the con-nection between us and other people. This is the unique skill we have as humans. Those high on empathy can sense others' feelings and appreciate their perspective. They are actively interested in people and seek to understand their concerns. They even sense the unsaid – picking up on cues, such as body language and changes in tone, and knowing something isn't quite right. Their motivation isn't about power or influence; it's simply about understanding how best to collaborate with other people.

In work environments, it can feel difficult to talk about emotions. There are many in organisations today who grew up learning to leave emotions at home. The hard, often cold, businesses evolved from this position. And leadership twenty, thirty years ago was perhaps shaped by this expec-tation. Thankfully, things are changing, and there is clear acknowledgement (in most companies) that emotions are an everyday part of work (because we're human).

Being empathetic isn't, however, just about showing sympathy. Professor and author Brené Brown defines empathy as fuelling connection, whilst sympathy drives disconnection. She describes the difference using nursing scholar Theresa Wiseman's model of empathy, involving four elements:

- Ability to take the perspective of another person
- Staying out of judgement
- Recognising and acknowledging emotion in other people
- Feeling with people

Brown describes empathy as a 'sacred space': when someone's in a deep hole, feeling stuck and overwhelmed, empathy is you climbing down to join them, saying that you know what it's like to be down here and that they're not alone. Sympathy is looking down at the person in the hole, saying, 'It's bad down there, right?' Brown sees empathy as a vulnerable choice. To connect with that person, the individual needs to find the emotion in themselves and share experiences. Sympathy often starts with comparison: 'At least you've still got...' Without empathy, we try to find a silver lining. It's not so bad, things will move on, pull yourself together.

Brown says, 'Rarely can a response make something better. What makes something better is connection.'

For all of us as individuals, developing our skills in empathy can open up a whole new level of impact.

## RELATIONSHIP MANAGEMENT

Goleman defines this final element of EI as 'friendliness with a purpose'. It's the ability – honed through inspiring others, managing conflict and fostering teamwork and other competencies – to move people in the direction you desire.

Trying to improve relationship management is something that many of us spend our whole lives attempting to do.

Having assessed hundreds of people across companies, industries and countries, I can share that relationship management is a common theme in development. It is difficult to master (and perhaps we never fully master it) because of the multitude of variances – people and situations, on top of our own changing mental and emotional states. These interact in many ways. Having to try to persuade someone towards a point of view is incredibly difficult when you don't believe in it yourself. A situation not panning out how we expected (e.g. an unexpected attendee in a meeting) can result in an amygdala hijack and render the already established relationship with others in the meeting lost. Emotions expert Liz Fosslien and organisational designer Mollie West Duffy have written a brilliant book, *No Hard Feelings*, in which they explore some of these emotion-filled scenarios at work. They share practical examples and tips on how to strike the best balance between feeling your emotions but not letting them run wild. This is the emotional tightrope we walk every day, and the triangulation of different people, scenarios and our own emotions mixing in new ways will always keep us on our toes.

In roles managing and leading others, behaviours such as inspiring and influencing become more important (although these are still important whatever your role – being able to adjust approaches, build rapport, establish credibility and be memorable are key in so many aspects of our lives, including when dating, interviewing for jobs and building new friendships). However, universally applicable are skills in teamwork, sharing feedback with others and managing conflict, and these feature in Goleman's EI competencies.

Switching your lens from thinking about how you contribute to how you contribute to a *team*, can help identify where you add greatest value. It might not be in the typical way you show up in other settings, as each team will have different characteristics. You will frequently find yourself in situations where you need to share feedback with others. Either formally – at the end of an engagement – or informally, the 'can I ask for your advice'-type conversations. In these scenarios, we often have a choice: to be honest or kind. However, we can confuse being 'kind' with being nice. Often being honest and constructive is the kinder thing to do. These skills can also be helpful when managing conflict, an inevitability of working with others. Starting with sentences such as 'Can I share how that made me feel?' can help create a more constructive space for sharing feedback, as it takes the emphasis away from the individual and pushes it more onto you and your feelings. Weaving in language such as 'my advice would be…' or 'I have found things like this can help' and even simply changing the word 'feedback' to 'advice' somehow feels less prickly.

So, what is the prize for developing strong emotional intelligence?

Research shows that people with higher emotional intelligence are better able to collaborate, manage conflicts, build successful relationships and make thoughtful decisions – which are ultimately the fundamentals for creating a life surrounded by humans we care about, and who care about us.

## THIRD, KEEP DEVELOPING BETTER HUMAN HABITS

Research tells us that the things we regret frequently relate to not doing what you *really* wanted; failing to genuinely understand or appreciate someone who is important to you; or missed opportunities to make real progress through harnessing the power of multiple minds and perspectives (Daniel Pink's book *The Power of Regret* is an enlightening read on this topic).

Getting the most out of life and building a more human era at work requires ongoing investment in building better human habits.

## UNDERSTANDING YOURSELF

As cheesy as it sounds, it's so true – if you don't know yourself, then how can you achieve what you want?

So often we meander through life feeling slightly disgruntled. Fed up. Hard done by. Lacking in energy and purpose. This is something *you* can change before, or even when, feelings of regret gather.

Here are five steps for building a better understanding of yourself:

## I. REGULARLY EXPLORE WHAT IS IMPORTANT TO YOU

Understanding what you value can offer a great starting point. Values can be broad, tap into greater meaning or purpose, and therefore cross the boundary of work and life. People who can connect with their purpose are repeatedly shown to live happier, healthier lives and to have a positive impact on businesses. Taking time to review and understand your own values can be rewarding and revealing. For many, it can lead to new priorities and different decisions moving forwards, and in this era, multiple versions of work are possible.

## 2. IDENTIFY WHAT ENERGISES YOU

Write down the moments, scenarios, tasks and people involved. What are the commonalities? How often (in terms of a percentage of time) do you feel like this? What would you like that percentage to be? And what steps could you take to increase this? Being in 'flow' is a wonderful feeling and key to this is achieving the right balance between challenge and skill – not too challenging that we feel overly anxious and not too easy that we get bored. Understanding the conditions that make you feel energised can help you curate a better blend for more sustained periods of your life.

## 3. GET TO KNOW YOUR STRENGTHS AND DEVELOPMENT AREAS

We all have blind spots – things we secretly know we're not so good at, or even things we think we can do but in reality don't do well. Do you have a realistic picture of your own capabilities? Building self-awareness can unlock so many things: nurturing more meaningful relationships, improved experiences and maximising the impact of what we do. Having varied skills and styles as well as the ability to develop new ones is a key part of being human. Be brave and hold up the mirror, and as your courage grows, ask others for their feedback on the work you're doing, the impact you have and their advice on how to improve.

## 4. FIND AN 'ACCOUNTABILITY PARTNER'

Telling someone else what you're doing and what you're hoping to achieve instantly makes you more likely to stick to it. In fact, regular check-ins with this person can make you 95 per cent more likely to achieve your goal. This could be a trusted mentor, coach, colleague or friend. They can help to shine a friendly spotlight on you and constructively establish what is important to you to develop, to get the results you want. Share with them what you find out, have conversations about how you will use the information, how it's helping you to reflect and what it could mean for shaping your life moving forwards.

## 5. UNDERSTANDING YOURSELF IS NEVER DONE

As humans, we constantly evolve. Our roles and responsibilities (as individuals, parents, employees, friends, business owners, leaders etc.) change and so you owe it to yourself to keep checking in and revisiting questions such as: what is important to me now? When do I feel at my best? What changes could I take to make this a more regular feature in my life? After all, you are the only person who is truly invested in making a fulfilling life your reality.

Finding routes to enable feelings of autonomy, meaning and growth will benefit you and those around you. Getting better at being, and thriving, as a human is worthy of regular review to course-correct and develop new habits that will strengthen your experiences and opportunities in life.

## UNDERSTANDING OTHERS

When people reflect on their lives, it's rarely what they've done but whom they've spent time with – the relationships they've developed, the people they have helped and the time spent laughing and learning with others. And the regrets – the moments of lost friendships, precious time missed with loved ones and feeling unable to overcome disputes and negative emotions which eat you up for years. Our ability to truly understand and value others lies at the heart of a fulfilling life.

As entrepreneur Steven Bartlett says, 'Today you're going to plant seeds in everything you do and with everyone you meet. Based on how you show up, those flowers will become flowers or weeds.'

Yet, today, this is our status quo in workplaces:

1. One of the biggest drivers of attrition is having a manager who doesn't care
2. Recent graduates don't know how to make small talk

3. People don't have friends at work

We're on a rocky path. What we want is becoming clearer, and technology could enable something brighter, but we mustn't forget what we could later regret. Being human is about understanding and appreciating others. This is our superpower and reason for existence.

You can play a part in building a world of work where our relationships with others are prioritised and valued:

### 1. CHOOSE TO SPEND TIME WITH OTHER PEOPLE

No one is going to create a schedule for you to build your own social connections. That's down to you. But it doesn't have to be onerous. Develop a rhythm of going into workspaces but don't spend all that time plugged in, on virtual calls. Use it for collaborating – in-person discussions, workshops and creative thinking – and simply for social connection: smiling, making eye contact and being open to conversation can put you in the best position to connect. Invest time in building trusted relationships. We need to remind ourselves that these elements of work are important and valuable, too. The conversation over lunch with a colleague that turns into a better appreciation of them as a person. Or realising someone is great at storytelling – perhaps they could help next time you need to prepare a presentation? Conversations often lead to new introductions and more discussions. Your network grows, and the snowball can propel you to new, exciting things.

## 2. LISTEN AND ASK QUESTIONS

We're all guilty of it. Nodding along, but we're actually waiting for a pause to share the response we had prepared several minutes ago. We stopped taking in what the other person
said at that point! The biggest cause of conflict is a lack of
understanding, and frequently that's because we simply haven't listened. Set yourself a challenge – see how long you
can keep another person talking by asking them questions.
And not just about what they did, or the technique or tools
they used, ask questions about their emotions – how did
they feel? What did they find challenging? What did they
learn? Why is that important to them? Social connection is
most often built when we're curious, we engage with emotions, we seek to understand what motivates people and we
make others feel valued.

## 3. USE EMPATHY TO DIFFUSE CONFLICT

You're in a discussion and someone says something with
which you vehemently disagree. The blood starts pumping,
you feel the prickly heat rising up the back of your neck
– an emotional outburst is about to erupt! Sometimes this
is needed. But at other times, it can create tension, misun-
derstanding or even conflict that you then carry around for
many days after. Instead of reacting, can you ask questions
to understand their perspective? E.g. that's a different way
to view things, can you help me understand a little more?
What are the outcomes you're trying to create with that

approach? Your perspectives might remain misaligned, but you will have greater insight into what's important to the other person, and demonstrating you appreciate their perspective (even if you don't agree) can help leave a relationship in a positive place. Err on the side of kindness over judgement. This can be particularly helpful when interacting with your manager – remembering they're human, too, asking for their views, trying to appreciate the context they're working within and understanding them as a person will help in building a strong relationship.

## 4. IDENTIFY WHERE YOU COULD MAKE A BIGGER DIFFERENCE TO OTHERS

Reflect honestly on when your laziness, carelessness or ego gets in the way of being a better human to others. We all have our moments. Are you contributing to a culture crack in your team or company? Are you enabling negative behaviours around you by remaining passive? How could a change in your behaviour positively affect others? Small actions can really ripple and shape cultures. Likewise, small actions can mean a lot more to others than you realise. Our tendency to overanalyse and misinterpret or catastrophise is also a common human trait – are there times when your behaviours make people feel confused, anxious or uncertain? Completing a personality questionnaire and accessing feedback can help build awareness of how your work styles manifest in different situations and enable action to enhance your impact.

## 5. SHOW GRATITUDE, APPRECIATION AND SEE THE FUNNY SIDE

It sounds simple, but saying thank you speaks volumes. Thank people for sharing their views, acknowledge when someone has shared something challenging or difficult and show appreciation when others try something new or take on board feedback. When someone does something fantastic, tell others – use it in small talk to introduce people to each other, or in team meetings, sharing standout achievements or lessons learned. Be humble – let others take the limelight, share what you've learned and be generous with your time in return. A sprinkling of good humour can also have a positive effect, for you and those around you. Laughing releases feel-good hormones in our brains (endorphins and dopamine) and reduces stress (cortisol). It is also proven to speed up social connection and can make leaders appear 27 per cent more motivational. Yet when we reach the workplace, the percentage of time we enjoy a good laugh falls off a cliff (and doesn't climb again until we reach almost eighty!). Humour can feel like a tricky thing to get right. The key, according to Stanford Professors Jennifer Aaker and Naomi Bagdonas, is shifting the focus from 'will this make me sound funny?' to 'how will this make others feel?' Feeling valued, appreciated and part of something brings out the best in people.

Like any skill – using Excel, playing an instrument or cooking – without regular practice and relearning, our ability to truly understand ourselves and others can fade. This is particularly important right now, as technology advances. Without an understanding of what's important to us, we risk being swept up and spat out somewhere we wish we'd more carefully curated.

I genuinely believe this should be at the heart of every learning agenda, across education, work and personal lives – an injection of skills to understand ourselves and appreciate others can significantly change a relationship and enhance our experiences of work and life.

We often strive for the external accolades, status, promotion or more money, thinking these are the things that will make us happy. Yet they rarely have a lasting impact. The real key to happiness lies within us: having choice (autonomy), the ability to engage in purposeful work and build strong, trusted relationships (meaning) and defaulting to kindness first and accessing opportunities to learn and develop as we go (growth).

But don't just take my word for it.

Maria Branyas, who is 117 and the world's oldest living person, is in the best spot to impart her wisdom. Her advice: 'exercise optimism and empathy, delay gratification, seek out the funny side of life, keep learning'.

Branyas definitely still has her wits about her and regularly shares her advice for living a long and happy life on X (formerly Twitter): 'Order, tranquillity, good connection with family and friends, contact with nature, emotional stability, no worries, no regrets, lots of positivity and staying away from toxic people.'

To make it human, we need to understand, embrace and get better at being human.

Your actions truly make a difference. Thank you for helping build a happier, more human future for us all.

# CHAPTER 10

# HOW TO LEAD A HUMAN WORKPLACE

Dear human leader,

This isn't about you.

It's about us.

And our mission to build workplaces for human growth.

You can make this shift, for yourself and for those around you. They're eager to hear your thoughts. They're watching your every move. Most of all, they're hoping you can help us find a better path.

You can.

You can choose to do things differently and build an inspiring vision for our future. In doing so, you could help people in your patch of the world to see potential. To feel part of something. To develop and grow. To find undiscovered ways of working. To leave a lasting impact. For their families, and their families, and their families...

There are people and teams out there making real progress – using their leadership positions to forge something better. There are many shining lights. To create durable change, we need more, and we need to join forces.

To lead a human work era, we must first embrace what makes us human. It will feel difficult, uncomfortable and scary at times, but creating a climate where human capabilities can expand will fuel understanding and enable progress. You don't have to do this alone. Other leaders, managers, colleagues, teams and friends can and want to help in this shared mission. Draw upon the collective intelligence and potential to create new possibilities.

In a hundred years' time, work *could* be more meaningful, people healthier and happier and collectively we might have created something sustainable, fulfilling and more human.

This is how we add greatest value to the people we work with, live with and the planet we live on.

In your corner of the world, make it human.

Yours,

A hopeful human

## FROM THREAT...

In the industrial age, people were mere cogs in a machine to drive outputs. The goal: to do more with less. Leadership focused on spotting the opportunities to improve tools, enhance processes, build leaner workforces and find ways to get more from people in economically advantageous ways. This worked for a while. The concept of a five-day working week was born, jobs were generally for life (and salary increases or promotion entirely at the employer's discretion), more efficient ways of working were discovered and automation and then digitisation brought significant gains. Many leaders and businesses have since pivoted to more people-focused missions. HR morphed from personnel into a multidisciplinary, strategic function. There is talk in boardrooms, in strategy and on websites of building both engaged workforces and profitable businesses. There is certainly ambition for a model that benefits both humans and business.

However, over the past fifteen years, global productivity has flatlined. Collectively, we've reached the levels we can, with the tools, techniques and capabilities we have. Work is now fundamentally about what we know and what we can do with the knowledge we have. It is no longer primarily about the physical tasks we perform – e.g. lifting, digging, stacking and assembling – but how we think, the ideas we create and the emotions we manage and engage with to elevate our impact.

Yet the things we measure and label as 'success' are often stuck in a bygone era.

Many employees today feel under threat. In some organisations, conflict between employer and employee is raging (what should work in a hybrid and knowledge-based era look like?); economic challenges have leaders reaching for the throttle (and damaging the carefully engineered culture and design of their companies and teams in doing so);

constant restructure and lay-offs create an always-on anxiety of job loss; and the rapid emergence of generative AI and other technologies into our everyday lives, whilst offering excitement and promise, brings fear of irrelevance. Before technology determines the next phase, we must draw breath and purposefully consider what we wish human work to look and feel like.

In a time shaped by uncertainty and fragility and with an overwhelming sense of responsibility to do better, we are battling and beating our stressed-out people, forgetting what it is that we, collectively, really need to thrive.

## ...TO SAFETY

Just after the Covid pandemic, a team of psychologists and I researched the impact that our collective experience had had on our personality preferences and motivators. We found that the prolonged period of stress and uncertainty had pushed us back to our core. Having previously been focused on growth, fulfilment, progression and earning more money, the trauma had pushed us down the rungs of Maslow's hierarchy to seek less demanding and more achievable tasks, job security, a reliable salary and the ability to balance the demands of home and work life and access support. Through this experience, many paused to reflect on what is important in their lives. The slower pace of life and limited options for socialising and connection provided an opportunity to make more conscious decisions about who and what is a priority. In addition, we found that women in a post-pandemic world are more likely than men to be demotivated by work with excess challenge and demanding hours. Rebuilding the foundations for humans to thrive and taking deliberate steps to ensure fair and equitable approaches to work division and progression have never been more important.

MIT Sloan research published in 2021 explored the key drivers of highest-rated cultures on the company review site Glassdoor. Through natural language processing, they discovered the top ten common things behind the ratings of 1.4 million employee reviews. The results might be surprising but are much in line with what we unearthed following the shock of the pandemic.

The best company cultures in the world have:

- Respect
- Support
- Security
- Values

Maybe you thought it would be friendly colleagues, inspiring visions or growth opportunities? They're there, and they're important, but there's a baseline every strong culture must achieve first before these can be layered on top. Even then, the core things employees are judging you on are:

- Being respected (am I listened to? Can I shape ideas?)
- Having supportive leaders (is there someone looking out for me? Is my boss kind, caring and considerate?)

- A sense of job security (do I feel safe? Can I continue to add value here?)
- People behaving in a values-aligned way (do you do what you say? Is it consistent with the company's values? Do you quash toxic and unethical behaviour?)

This is where being a good leader firmly aligns with being a good human. Except your actions as a good human leader can have a multiplying effect on others – positive or negative. The culture cracks we see permeating so many companies often start with leaders. There are daily pressures to dehumanise our behaviour. Those in charge will keep asking 'how can you do more with less?', making you reach to take control, reverting to carrot-and-stick techniques, to threat and cost-cutting – simply because you can. This might work for a brief spell but certainly not long. And when your boss comes back in one, two months' time, with the same question, what then?

Your opportunity is to reframe and modernise this question for our hybrid, knowledge-worker era – to consider how we can make this better.

The challenge and opportunity for a human leader today isn't to watch the output dial and poke and prod to ensure the steam gushes out, the dial bouncing up and down over maximum. It's to create the conditions for knowledge to flow, environments where ideas can be formulated, technology advanced and augmented and new possibilities (we haven't yet imagined) envisioned. The teams in organisations today are poised to create new medicines and find cures to human diseases. They might invent sustainable energy solutions or redesign education and social services to serve a diverse and ageing population. Perhaps they will come up with a compelling vision for high streets, finding inventive ways to bring people and communities together. Their success won't be measured on production rates but creativity, impact and durability. Creating a climate for human growth requires a new type of leader.

## YOU CAN'T PREDICT A HUMAN

In the book (and TV series) *Lessons in Chemistry*, Elizabeth Zott is exasperated when her newborn baby fails to respond in the same way each day to the routine she establishes. Being a scientist, she expects a set routine and controlled stimuli to elicit a predictable response. Her neighbour, a mother of two, empathetically shares that you can't treat a baby as you would a science experiment; each day, and each baby, will vary!

Historically, we have relied upon attempting to control and predict organisations: projecting quarterly revenue positions and holding managers to these forecasts, even when the context completely turns upside down; filling intranets and shared workspaces with how-to guides and playbooks; trying to find ways to steer and align how workforces respond to everyday challenges. These can help, to some extent. But they can also constrain – blinker our vision, limit thinking to the way things have always been done, resulting in overlooked new and exciting opportunities. As David Marquet found, a new era of work demands a new approach to leadership. He literally turned core concepts – control, authority and power – on their head, empowering his team, in pressurised environments, to become leaders themselves. He moved from a position of power through knowledge, control and authority into guiding, coaching and enabling. This equipped him to develop the best-performing naval submarine the US had ever seen. Having the eyes, ears, minds and hearts of 135 officers engaged and feeling ownership for navigating what came their way, put them in the best position to thrive.

## A NEW MISSION: THIS AND THAT

The days of distant, autocratic and all-knowing leaders are fast becoming the past, and a new era has already begun.

To make work human, we need to find fulfilling and sustainable opportunities. In this quest, we are increasingly encountering dichotomies where we need to achieve both outcomes:

- Create space for individual *and* collaborative work
- Enable individual choice *and* inclusion and belonging
- Provide global consistency *and* cultural relevance
- Cultivate continuous growth *and* bring balance and sustainability
- Build shared understanding of expectations *and* manage ambiguity

- Build comfort with the unknown *and* confidence about the path ahead
- Remain relevant and profitable *and* shape clear purpose and ethics

Leaders, navigating these paradoxes and leading businesses through novel and changing times, need new priorities. They need to feel comfortable stepping away from controlling and into empowering. Creating the conditions where people feel confident in making decisions and solving challenges themselves, because they understand the priorities and the behaviours that will enable them to be successful. With these in place, leaders step back, enabling managers to carefully orchestrate the experiences that shape positive outcomes for people and the organisation.

Leadership models for decades focused on developing a specific style to be successful (e.g. transaction, transformational or situational). PwC's 'Six paradoxes of leadership' brochure sums up the need to balance both, often opposed, sides of a paradox to succeed (e.g. being both a 'Humble Hero' and a 'Strategic Executor'). PwC says: 'To truly differentiate yourself as a leader, learning how to comfortably inhabit both elements of each paradox will be critical to your success.'

Similarly, a *Harvard Business Review* article by Jennifer Jordan, Michael Wade and Elizabeth Teracino outlines seven 'tensions' that leaders need to navigate – and the key skill is knowing when to deploy which approach to tackle particular tensions. Other recent models emphasise the criticality of human traits, in particular empathy, emotional intelligence and the ability to understand when a particular approach or style is required. Gartner's 'human leader' model highlights the need for authenticity (role modelling safe self-expression at work), empathy (addressing broader life needs of people) and adaptivity (curating individualised experiences and opportunities). The company's research goes on to show that those demonstrating good human leadership drive greater levels of retention, engagement and well-being. Despite this benefit, Gartner suggests only 29 per cent of employees feel their leaders model these behaviours. There's clearly work to do.

Liz Rider, an organisational psychologist and LinkedIn Top Voice in Leadership, vouches for 'human-centric leadership'. She suggests we need to move from business-centric models focusing on growing and optimising the business, fitting people into the system, to human-centric ones – prioritising listening, understanding, developing, coaching and unlocking the potential of employees. This is an approach the Top Employers Institute also advocates for, putting the belief that employees are motivated individuals who want to do a good job, and building environments where trust and empowerment are at the centre of organisational design. The early signs, from companies such as Best Buy, suggest that a human-centric model could help us deliver *both* human and business growth.

## AUTHENTICALLY HUMAN

As a leader, it can feel daunting. Suddenly, the focus is on being you, authentically: creating an inspiring, purpose-led vision pulling together diverse groups to focus on a bigger cause; consistently and proactively communicating (even when things are unknown); facilitating psychologically safe cultures where people feel able to express themselves and innovate whilst driving consistent performance; never settling – being on the front foot looking at the next risk or opportunity to drive transformation; and nurturing a climate for trusting and caring relationships – role-modelling this from the top with teams and partners, recognising that success is about the team and organisational legacy you create.

Yet being authentically human is to embrace constant learning and growth. This is something Herminia Ibarra, a professor at London Business School, talks about frequently:

> The only way we grow as leaders is by stretching the limits of who we are – doing new things that make us uncomfortable but that teach us through direct experience who we want to become. Such growth doesn't require a radical personality makeover. Small changes – in the way we carry ourselves, the way we communicate, the way we interact – often make a world of difference in how effectively we lead.

This is why introverts can be brilliant leaders, and extroverts excellent coaches. Being 'authentic' doesn't mean painting our profile and rigidly sticking to it; rather it's embracing the opportunities to develop and grow, and in doing so, to learn more about who we are. This is something I learned to embrace as I stepped into leading others. Being more introverted in preference, I thought I needed to impress with academic insights, remember facts and figures to project credibility with teams and clients. I spent hours preparing for meetings and presentations, writing and rewriting notes, meticulously rehearsing my message. When it came to the live event, I rarely had the impact I was striving for. In fact, a more common sight was bored, confused faces! Sometimes, I felt so frozen by the weight of what I needed to relay, the words simply wouldn't come out. I had to rethink. I realised, through observing others skilled in engaging audiences, I was approaching it with the wrong objective in mind. The focus was on me, recalling the facts, impressing with my knowledge and advice. When I needed it to be about them – the people I was meeting with. What would make the content engaging and interesting to them? The answer – something far more entertaining! I embarked on learning skills and styles in telling stories, stepping away from all the facts, evoking emotion and sparking connection. It's still a work in progress, but the proportion of bored, confused, sleepy faces has declined, so I think I'm moving in the right direction! Importantly, I am developing in a way that still holds true to me, and growing with who I am.

Human leaders have a strong sense of self-awareness and

understanding that they will never be the finished article. Management consultant Daniel Ofman talks about 'core qualities'. These are the strong points individuals have – often the characteristic that immediately springs to mind when describing someone. Used well, they can form clear strengths, and even infuse less-prominent qualities. However, if these qualities become overdeveloped or overdominant, they can become pitfalls. For example, someone with a core quality of helpfulness can trip into interfering; someone very flexible can be perceived as inconsistent or unreliable; and someone who is decisive risks becoming pushy. Workplace performance company Hogan's 'derailers' model explores the dark side of personality, measuring eleven scales including traits such as 'sceptical', 'mischievous' and 'cautious'. These are the aspects of personality that can emerge in moments of stress. Leaders need to develop strong self-awareness to sense when they could be overplaying their core qualities or becoming derailed and learn how to balance these with the areas likely to be less instinctive to them (e.g. to develop skills in becoming both decisive and patient at the same time). Choosing to learn from instances where relationships become strained, trying out different approaches and being open to and seeking feedback can help leaders in their constant quest to learn and grow.

A leader able to flourish in today's environment is supremely aware of their own emotions and how this affects their behaviour, decisions and, critically, the environment and atmosphere they create for teams around them. The sheer volume of emotions felt, even in just one day, can be huge. From feelings of pride when a milestone is achieved and excitement at the signs of progress and the journey ahead to apprehension and self-doubt about the weight of significant decisions. When reflecting on his role as CEO at DS Smith, a multinational packaging business, Miles Roberts highlighted this capability as critical for success:

> You need to make it easy for the people who work for you. You need to be consistent so people know what they will get with you. If they are worried if you are in a good or bad mood – it makes it all about you and that's not right – it's a waste of everyone's time.

How could you possibly know it all?

We are certainly looking for a very different leader to that described in 1840 in Thomas Carlyle's 'great man' theory – one of the earliest known theories of leadership suggesting that great leaders are simply born, and chosen when they are needed most. Of course, we have since learned that leadership is much more complex, hard earned and certainly not limited by gender. Leaders of the past got there based on what they knew. Their expertise was, seemingly, more advanced than those around them. Leadership focused on control – seeing information first, making decisions on behalf of others, approving requests, setting direction and telling people what to do. The path was set, the environment known and the leader in charge of steering the group towards the best results possible. If things went wrong, it wasn't *their* fault. Someone else down the chain would get the blame; talented people used and abused for their capabilities and then cast aside.

This approach is, fortunately, running out of road. Even the concept that one person could 'know it all' nowadays feels absurd. The complexity, ambiguity and level of change and uncertainty in our world today requires something different. We need to create safe places where people can think, share ideas and collectively innovate to come up with new solutions. However, there are still places where this style is the default, and times when old habits creep in. Under pressure (and there's a lot of that), we return to old methods; trying something new feels too challenging and risky.

There is another way, and those bold enough are beginning to shape the path forwards for human leadership.

## ALL SEEING, ALL KNOWING... ALL SENSING

In today's complex and molten world, I see another layer of skill in leaders who make a lasting impact – leadership 'senses'. Standout leaders use their senses to guide every action. They pause if things don't feel quite right, ask for support and are prepared to backtrack on initial ideas as the situation changes or new information comes to light. They're acutely aware of how their own emotions interact and affect the climate and they adapt and moderate these accordingly (e.g. interrupting and redirecting senior leader or board-level meetings if group politics are undermining conversations or shaping negative experiences for other attendees). These leaders can be seen listening, consulting, rethinking, discussing and openly sharing their feelings and senses, almost turning 'leadership' into a team effort; yet they're prepared to make clear decisions and carve the future path, when the moment feels right. Their antennae are always twitching; looking for signs of the impact they and others are having and course-correcting to optimise outcomes. Creating and preserving a culture for human growth is their primary objective.

## LEADERSHIP SENSES ARE A MULTIPLIER

Behavioural capabilities, market knowledge and wisdom through experience can be multiplied when a leader is able to pull upon their senses to intuitively read a situation and context and nimbly shift gear to align their approach:

- Fairness (ultimately believing everyone plays a role and deserves to contribute)
- Purpose (constantly being guided by a bigger cause and inspiring others to join this)
- Future focus (looking several steps ahead to curate continuous evolution)
- Empathy (automatically tuning into others' needs and showing genuine care)
- Humility (championing a growth mindset, consulting with, and learning from, others, focused on building a lasting legacy)

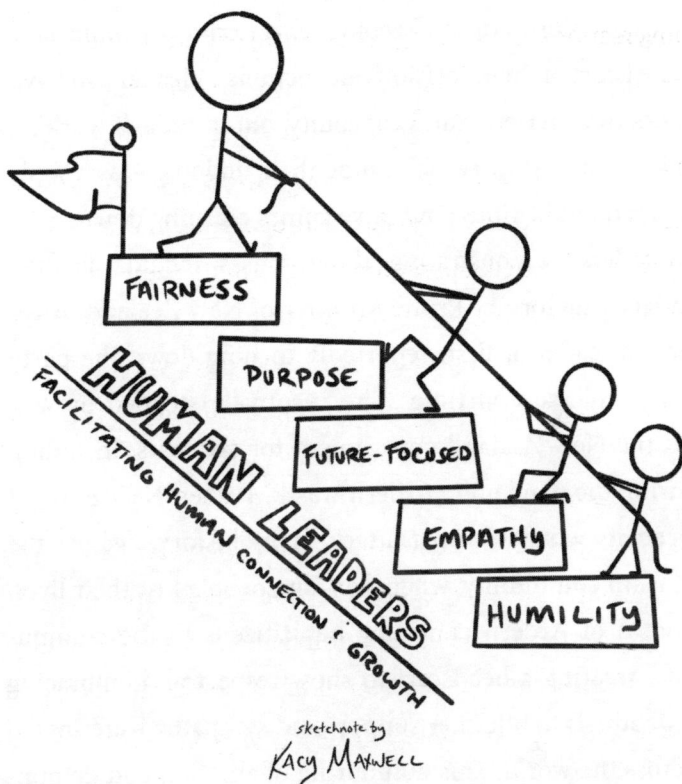

sketchnote by
KACY MAXWELL

Drawing upon these five senses, a leader can anticipate where challenges might emerge, what's most important right now (e.g. we are about to embark on a period of change, so we really need to tune in and listen to our people to understand their feelings so that it lands well) and when plans should be revised (recognising how significant events in society change the landscape – e.g. societal events cutting to topics of equity and inclusion or economic changes affecting people's lives). Their leadership senses help them to feel their way through ambiguous and complex information – keeping what's critically important at the heart of their decisions and actions. A leader can have stacks of experience and capability, but in today's world, a lack of leadership 'sense' can be their undoing – as a well-planned but ill-timed initiative comes crashing down.

Leaders demonstrating these senses include Jacinda Ardern, the former Prime Minister of New Zealand. A reluctant leader at first, reportedly turning down the party leader role several times, she eventually stepped up and led the New Zealand government for six years, including during the pandemic. Ardern was PM when New Zealand faced its worst terrorist attack in its history, against the Muslim community, when fifty-one people lost their lives. Photos of Ardern consoling her citizens in the community, wearing a headscarf to show respect and embracing individuals to offer her support and sympathy were shared across the world. This outpouring of emotion and demonstration of empathy was far from the stoic-faced, distant leader we have so often seen in moments of crisis. Ardern led with empathy, strongly believing that leaders could be both empathetic and strong and sensing what needed to be prioritised in that moment:

If there's anything that people need right now, it's that they just need to see human beings doing their best as leaders. And that means that from time to time you'll stumble, and you should be honest about that; it means that people will see your failings and we should be honest about that too.

In 2023, Ardern made the decision to resign, recognising she no longer had 'enough in the tank' to do what the job requires:

> I know there'll be much discussion in the aftermath of this decision as to what the so-called 'real reason' was. I can tell you that what I'm sharing today is the only interesting angle that you will find – that after going on six years of some big challenges, I am human. I know what this job takes, and I know that I no longer have enough in the tank to do it justice. It's that simple.

Self-awareness and a laser focus on her purpose and responsibility perhaps enabled her to make the call others might not have. To step aside, and enable someone who, at this moment, can do what it takes to deliver success for the country.

Language analysis of CEOs by S&P Global revealed that since the pandemic, female CEOs steadily increased their use of words linked to diversity, empathy, adaptability and transformation. Through analysing the communications of almost 7,000 leaders, the study found that women used proportionally more expressions of joy, trust and anticipation, versus men who used more anger, sadness and surprise.

The way male and female leaders responded to the Covid crisis was quite different.

In outcomes, this mattered. Countries led by women achieved better Covid-19 outcomes, because many made decisions to lock down earlier and suffered half as many deaths on average as those led by men.

The early successes during the pandemic of leaders such as Germany's Angela Merkel, New Zealand's Jacinda Ardern, Denmark's Mette Frederiksen, Taiwan's Tsai Ing-wen and Finland's Sanna Marin held similarities in approach and attracted interest.

The Centre for Economic Policy Research analysed 194 countries and concluded that the difference by gender is real. 'Our results clearly indicate that women leaders reacted more quickly and decisively in the face of potential fatalities,' said Supriya Garikipati, a developmental economist at Liverpool University, co-author with Reading University's Uma Kambhampati. Garikipati said female leaders 'were risk averse with regard to lives', choosing to lock down their countries significantly earlier than male leaders, suggesting they were 'more willing to take risks in the domain of the economy'.

A strong sense of 'what's right' in the moment and skill in executing on this priority marked out country leaders who were able to protect the lives of their people. Inherently, they were leaning on their instincts as human leaders.

Leadership senses are also visible in many leaders of big

corporations. Satya Nadella, CEO of Microsoft, integrated empathy into the heart of his transformation strategy for the company when he took over as CEO in 2014. Nadella believed that without empathy, Microsoft would never succeed in understanding customer needs and delivering solutions to meet those needs: 'Empathy makes you a better innovator. If I look at the most successful products we [at Microsoft] have created, it comes with that ability to meet the unmet, unarticulated needs of customers.'

Creating a customer-centric organisation, founded on empathy with a strong culture of collaboration, space for innovation, experimentation and the ability to learn and move on from failures are some of the features attributed to Nadella's successful transformation of Microsoft.

Another critical leadership sense is knowing when to wade in and make clear decisions or provide direction. There will always be times when this is necessary – in emergencies, if there's risk to life and even when bad, toxic behaviour starts to simmer. Today, it is just as important to swiftly manage behaviour that disrupts the culture as it is to espouse the positive. This is something that one of the most successful entrepreneurs and business leaders in recent history, Richard Branson, reflects upon: 'The hardest thing I had to learn was to fire people. You must do it to protect the integrity of the company and the culture of the team.'

Hubert Joly, the former CEO of Best Buy, talks about the secret to success coming through creating environments for 'human magic'. He describes this as a state when employees instinctively work to do what's right for customers and colleagues, without being told what to do.

At Best Buy, Joly was facing emerging competition from digital providers. He automatically knew a different approach to leading the company was needed to enable new paths and possibilities:

> Admitting you don't have all the answers is a sign of strong leadership, and putting meaningful purpose at the heart of business is the only way for companies to move forward in hard times. Humans are not a resource; they are the creative engine of innovation and change that companies urgently need.

Having experienced leadership in an era of 'superhero' CEOs (think GE's Jack Welch), Joly realised this was initially the type of leader he gravitated towards. Later in his career, he made a conscious decision to change that. When he became CEO of Best Buy, he insisted on always flying commercial, setting up guardrails to keep him and his ego firmly on the ground. He even said, 'I am not the CEO of Best Buy' – meaning this wasn't his full identity and acknowledging that he was individually dispensable. He targeted creating ways of working that didn't require him to be there and facilitated him to operate in the background, empowering the collective, driven through strong purpose, to do more.

We aren't always, however, instinctively drawn to the 'sensing' leaders. Looking around organisations and governments, it is clear that those with leadership senses aren't consistently being hired or rising to the top. The narcissistic, Machiavellian and sociopathic leaders keep emerging, particularly in times of crisis, with the trail of destruction taking decades to repair.

It takes courage and conscious effort to choose a different approach to leading others.

A new generation of leadership is under construction, but it needs help to be identified and encouragement to grow. These leaders are not always immediately visible. They might be lurking in the background, encouraging others forward into the limelight. They are humble in describing their own talents, focusing instead on the capabilities of others; getting out of the way for talented managers to tailor positive experiences and for specialists to develop innovations. Look more closely, and they're the people who have built a strong team culture, drawn on emotional intelligence to build relationships and optimise their impact, realising their legacy is more important than their ego. They nurture psychologically safe spaces for people to share ideas and problems, identify potential within their teams to do more and mobilise people into the optimal place to maximise their impact. Jennifer Holmgren, the CEO of Disruptor 50 (listed in 2020) company LanzaTech, which uses a microbe to turn pollution into a fuel, is an introvert who prefers to listen rather than speak. This might initially seem a disadvantage when it comes to convincing factories and fuel buyers to embrace her technology, but Holmgren has turned this into a superpower, using listening to figure out what her counterparts wanted during negotiations and empathy to craft a compromise that could work for everyone.

Most significantly, this new breed of leaders is vehemently focused on building a climate for human growth in everything they do. As Miles Roberts, CEO at DS Smith, identifies, this is inextricably linked to what makes us human: 'As CEO you have to do what's right for the business, what's right for the people who work for you. That requires understanding the emotional aspect and recognising that in yourself and others ... If you didn't do that you wouldn't be human.'

## HABITS OF HUMAN LEADERS

As we seek to shape a new era in work and leadership, it's important to deliberately consider the habits that will enable us to develop and strengthen these new muscles. Here are the things human leaders do, every day, to nurture human growth cultures:

### LEADERSHIP IS A TEAM SPORT

Human leaders spend a lot of time watching and listening. They soak up what's going on around them. The dynamics, the conversations, what's said (what isn't), the decisions made and the actions taken. They're a big part of the company, but they're not *the* star. The star is the impact that the whole company has – it's purpose, mission and reason for being. It's not all about the leader. You'll often find this leader walking the floor, engaging in chance conversations, joining team meetings simply to hear what people are working on, what they're learning and where they need help. They proactively want to learn and understand. In return, they help connect the dots, facilitate learning and opportunities across different parts of the business. This is a priority because it makes the climate tangible. Great leaders capture the big things they learn, turn these into commitments they share with their teams, following up with progress updates – 'You told me it is difficult to access information between departments. I agree, and here's what we're doing to address this.' They also share when they *can't* deliver on a commitment; explaining why and what will happen next, rather than brushing it under the carpet. They're part of the team, moving in the same direction and build grown-up, empowering relationships across the business. Some organisations are taking this a step further by creating dual or even team-based top leadership roles. Oris, the watchmaker, has co-CEOs in place, as have global invest-ment firm Vontobel and Netflix. Consulting firm Palladium has four CEOs in place and has found that the model has helped breakdown silos, increase diversity of thought and improve decision-making. In a time when leadership carries considerable weight, it feels sensible to consider shared re-sponsibilities. This does, however, rely upon leaders' willing-ness to share their vulnerabilities, skills in communication and commitment to leadership as a team sport.

## UNDERSTANDING AND LEARNING IS <u>ALWAYS</u> A PRIORITY

Jeff Bezos used to bring an empty chair to meetings to ensure the customer's viewpoint was actively considered. Hamdi Ulukaya, CEO of yogurt company Chobani, regularly stands outside his store to listen to his customers. Airbnb CEO, Brian Chesky, spent six months staying in his company's rental homes, whilst Laxman Narasimhan, CEO of Starbucks, spent several months working as a barista. These habits help ensure focus on why a company exists, understanding its true value and magnifying broader impact. This applies to employees, partners, shareholders and other stakeholders, too. Regularly spending time with the groups you need to understand and influence to be successful in your journey is critical. But this can't simply be a 'show and tell'-style conversation. It needs to focus on understanding and learning: asking questions, exploring why and facilitating learning through mistakes. Getting on the front line and experiencing interactions first-hand can prove invaluable. In the 1980s, IBM took a 'tell' approach to conversations with its customers. Experts would share the products coming down the pipe, telling customers how this would meet their needs. It is thought, by some, that this led it to miss key opportunities to innovate. Many of its customers had partnerships with other providers or in-house technology expertise. Employees could see new possibilities but weren't given the opportunity to share and collaborate on future developments. IBM famously lost much of its computing business to competitors such as Dell and was forced to broaden its portfolio to consulting services to deliver growth. This was far from the 'infinite game' that Simon Sinek suggests is required for success in today's business world. In organisations, there isn't a final whistle or score line; work carries on, to-do lists gain items and different ways to innovate are identified. Sinek highlights Apple as an infinite player: it maintains focus on its cause rather than going tit for tat against competitors. It seeks to truly understand its customers' needs and keep advancing solutions to meet them. The game never ends. When Microsoft released the 'Zune' to compete with the iPod, Apple wasn't ruffled. It was already working hard on the next thing, and a year later, the iPhone was released, redefining the whole smartphone category and rendering both the Zune and iPod obsolete. Steve Jobs was famous for anticipating customer needs, before they even knew what they wanted, and he nurtured a culture around this ethos: 'A lot of times, people don't know what they want until you show it to them.'

Practices enabling understanding of needs, learning and curiosity across stakeholder groups can provide sustenance to fuel genuine innovation and progress, rather than simply keeping up.

## PROACTIVELY SEEK DIVERSE PERSPECTIVES
Human leaders proactively seek to bring in and listen to different and conflicting perspectives. They know they don't have all the answers, and in our complex environment, new possibilities and perspectives need to be considered. They

install mechanisms for bringing in diverse thoughts and ideas. This might involve partnerships with organisations in different markets (e.g. Mastercard established relationships with much smaller, start-up organisations to access their insights and knowledge on technology transformation, as well as practices to attract, hire and nurture diverse talent within the organisation). In 2023, Compass Group, a global food and hospitality company, announced a career hub to support candidates from a range of backgrounds who are facing barriers to entry into the job market, including ex-offenders, care leavers, long-term unemployed individuals and people with disabilities. Establishing partnerships with organisations assisting people who have been unemployed for the long term can provide a brilliant mechanism for increasing diversity, since so often this segment includes under-represented groups, as well as providing people with the break they need to restart their career. Other organisations, such as Timpson (a UK-based key-cutting and household items repair service), established similar schemes for employing ex-offenders, and UK hardware store B&Q focuses recruitment on older generations in response to customer feedback that they wanted to access expertise from those carrying out DIY tasks in their own homes. In a world where talent is scarce, tapping into diverse and available populations also brings benefits of faster hiring and valuable skills, such as motivation to learn, wisdom through varied life experiences and practised customer-service skills.

It takes concerted effort to build and sustain a diverse community, and good practices must be layered into the culture enabling two-way dialogue if the collective potential of a diverse organisation is to be realised. Human leaders proactively seek advice from others. They value their connections and invest in building and managing a network to feed a flow of varied thoughts, wisdom and counsel. Of course, the viewpoints must also be listened to and skilfully managed, even if they don't offer what you want to hear. This was something NASA tragically discovered during the Challenger disaster in 1986. Despite warnings from engineers before the launch of the spaceship that the O-ring seals would fail in the cold temperatures forecast for launch day, NASA executives chose not to delay the launch. Seventy-three seconds into its flight, the space shuttle disintegrated, killing all seven crew members on board. Consulting and deferring to expertise, asking the right questions and knowing when to jump in, make decisions, backtrack on commitments, to do what's right (even if it risks a bruised ego) is front and centre in a human leader's toolkit.

## THE GOAL IS A DURABLE BUSINESS

An unrelenting focus on building something that lasts, beyond the short-term cycle of a financial year or investment cycle, is at the core of all businesses. Human leaders know this is about the long game, and deliberately work towards becoming dispensable through developing the capabilities of their teams. They take a holistic approach to measuring success (see the new world of work method in Chapter 6), understanding that when their people grow, the business will too. They keep things simple and impactful when sharing objectives with the company, avoiding over-complicating and confusing messages to build alignment and momentum. They share guidelines and principles and spend time discussing what this could look like in practice – enabling individuals to weigh up information and make decisions themselves. A key shift is enabling power and authority to reach the people with the practical knowledge to make the best decisions. Human leaders empower, enable and equip their people managers to build trust-based relationships and make good decisions (see Chapter 8). They step back and give them space to create understanding, helping their teams to find autonomy, meaning and growth in the work they do. Instinctively, they know that facilitating an environment where there is a shared understanding of the mission, guidelines on what's important and skilled and empowered managers to personalise experiences and provide support will fuel a self-propelled durable organisation. Timpson provides its store managers with autonomy over a budget to make sure they can deliver great service experiences to their customers. Executives know that their managers, on the front line, are best placed to know what will help ensure customers leave feeling satisfied. Actions like this, in turn, create space for leaders to use their senses to identify where new explorations, investment or support can further optimise the conditions for growth.

## COMMITTED TO CULTIVATING CULTURE

Culture is often the justification provided for a significant failure or overwhelming success. Yet great human leaders know this isn't simply by chance. Culture doesn't just happen, and when it does, it often goes spectacularly wrong. Human leaders work hard to manage culture, appreciating that it can be the biggest driver of success for people and business. They set up the purpose, values and ways of working to nurture an environment where people can grow. At a time when ideas, innovations, collaborative breakthroughs and the ability to transform determines durability, creating conditions for humans to thrive is the biggest and best investment any leader can make. It isn't enough to simply capture these and stick them on the walls; great leaders know the real work happens in co-creating culture in the day to day. Some companies adopt practices such as culture workshops, discussing tensions and disconnects between the culture they wish to nurture and the daily realities challenging this. For example, pressure around productivity, cost, profit and revenue will always emerge and there will inevitably come opportunity to achieve these results in a way that renders the cultural values redundant. This is where strong human leaders differentiate. They hold strong and commit to the long-term behaviours they know will yield better workplaces and broader impact.

Personally, they role-model what they say, ensuring this is visible to others: embedding transparent, fair and objective processes for people joining and progressing their careers, providing access to development opportunities and ensuring achievements and contributions are accurately attributed. They're prepared to make tough decisions to intervene and potentially move people on if behaviour threatens their culture. An individual might deliver results, but if the way they achieve this compromises culture, the toxicity could rot the whole apple cart. They recognise this must be stamped out, and fast. Human leaders also take a systematic approach to monitoring and continuously improving their culture, just as they would any organisational asset. Exploring data points to understand strengths and threats, identifying where culture cracks could be simmering and taking action to strengthen these areas, they protect and improve the company culture since this is the real legacy they will leave. Culture is a regular conversation point with teams, sharing updates, asking for input and ideas. They create a strong sense of psychological ownership; understanding everyone has a role to play in the culture we create. It is the culmination of our collective actions, big and small, that make the most impact.

## PRIORITISE HUMAN CONNECTION AND MEANINGFUL GROWTH

Finally, take a glance at a human leader's diary and you will see a mass of time spent with people. They know that creating a climate for human growth requires a constant stream of dialogue with people across the business. Turning briefings into two-way discussions is a good example. David Marquet talks about moving from briefing to certification during his time leading the *Santa Fe*. Traditionally, if there is a significant operation to undertake, the captain gathers their team and runs through their responsibilities, checking understanding before moving to execute. The problem is this is passive; the only person really involved is the leader, and this is a common scenario across sectors. Instead, Marquet shifts to a certification. This involves the team members talking through their responsibilities and key decisions that they feel they will need to make. They feel empowered. This helps the leader and team determine any risks and whether they are ready to initiate the plan. The sense of ownership becomes shared and can help reduce mistakes. The constant dialogue, sharing, asking questions and listening are defining features of the human leader.

Another proven ingredient for building connection is an ability to tell stories. Stories can unite us; they help us feel emotions, decipher meaning and make information memorable. Storytelling has even been proven to increase our tolerance to uncertainty. Through structuring our experiences in a coherent story, or even hearing others' stories, we can feel better equipped to deal with uncertainty, a constant ingredient in our lives. Being able to tolerate uncertainty can help us uncover new possibilities and paths.

Barack Obama, the former US President, amongst many attributes, is a very talented storyteller and has demonstrated this skill on multiple occasions. Notably, at a speech during a campaign for Hillary Clinton, he told the story of attempting to win the endorsement of a state representative in South Carolina. She offers her support, if he travels to her hometown to meet with her. A month later, exhausted from the campaign trail, he describes waking up early, dragging himself out of bed, fighting a cold, facing a miserable rainy day, but knowing he has made a promise to meet her. He makes it relatable, shares the daily motivational battles we all have, the annoyance with the rain, feeling grumpy. When he reaches the meeting, Obama describes hearing a lady shout from the back of the room: 'Fired up!' The crowd respond: 'Ready to go!' This continues for several minutes, back and forth. He later discovers the representative is a well-known character in the community and this is her thing! Then Obama shares that he started to feel fired up himself and joined in the chant. This element later becomes a key feature in his campaign. The way he tells this story is a masterclass in building connection through humanising. His audience can feel the emotions. His story, despite being told by one of the most powerful people in the world, is relatable. Everyone's right there with him, feeling his challenges, and he makes them laugh, too. Importantly, he has a key message to share, and it's grounded in his motivation for leading the country:

> One voice can change a room. And if it can change a room, it can change a city. And if it can change a city, it can change a state. And if it can change a state, it can change a nation. And if it can change a nation, it can change the world.

In that moment, he is one of them, they are all part of the community and everyone is aligned on their mission. We won't all be Obama-level speechmakers and storytellers, but we can bring messages to life through telling stories, carefully choosing words to evoke emotion and build meaningful connection and impact for our people. These are the moments people remember and this can inspire them to join, stay and give more to your organisation and community.

Being a leader is hard. It is also a privilege and an incredible opportunity to make a difference.

There is no playbook to follow for every scenario. The stakes are high as pressure mounts to achieve the right balance of profitable and sustainable; aligned and diverse; empowering and consistently growing. You have an opportunity to make this possible. Taking steps to build and maintain a climate for human growth will put you and your teams on the path to something brighter, for humans and businesses.

# CHAPTER 11

# A CLIMATE FOR HUMAN GROWTH

The workplace we are trying to reach exists within a climate for human growth.

The good news is that it's within our reach. It's not a mythical beast we can only imagine. The even better news is that you can see many of these signs across multiple companies today.

Human growth is being nurtured. It is out there. But it can be pushed down the list of priorities. Short-term financial goals march in and demand our attention. We drop what we're doing, abandon the 'nice to have' longer-term stuff and rally round finding ways to make more money, now.

Too often this comes at the cost of ourselves, our families, teams and planet.

We look frazzled and beaten. We're lonely and lost. We don't even weigh up finishing work on time to be with our family vs working late to get the next item on the list done. We zombie-march on autopilot to finish the job.

Then, one day, we wake up and life has passed us by. Our

bodies are exhausted. Muscles wasting away. Minds full of doubts, regrets and opportunities lost.

I got it wrong. It's about human growth, first.

For you, for us, for my daughter and for generations to come who are yet to experience any form of work, it's not too late. Technology offers great opportunity to automate, scale and increase the value we provide. But this must encapsulate the best of both human and machine. How we truly arrive at a destination where the collective is greater than the sum of the parts, and which enables us to fuel human growth, is our shared mission. The choices we make today can shape a better future.

There are good foundations on which to build. I'm sure, like me, you have experienced many memorable, happy moments at work. Having spent over twenty-years of my life working, the times when I have been able to balance and experience seemingly juxtaposed elements stand out:

- Working hard *and* having fun
- Being career focused *and* making friends
- Blending creativity and emotion *with* logic and reason
- Contributing my best at both work *and* home

It is across these paradoxes that we learn new things, engage in different projects, work with a variety of people and achieve new levels within an organisation. But also, and perhaps more memorably, it is where we experience moments of great camaraderie – working long days (and nights) to complete assignments as a team; being able to turn to a colleague for advice when you aren't sure how to tackle a tricky scenario; instances of infectious hilarity when a group of people with strong levels of trust and psychological safety know exactly how to make each other laugh; and many friendships outlasting the duration of your tenure across various roles.

Like most of you, I hope, I have worked in some brilliant teams and cultures. I have also experienced the darker moments, the unkind, unfair and unhuman features we can breed in work communities. Seeing and experiencing both sides is what drives me to want to help people nurture and sustain climates for human growth that help us all to experience happier and healthier lives.

Here's what a climate for human growth (see the accompanying model 'a climate for human growth' via the QR code on page 316) looks and sounds like when you make it human.

## WORKPLACE

This is a place where people can thrive.

It sounds like this:

- 'How can I help?'
- 'Let's speak tomorrow, we both need to switch off and spend time at home'
- 'You look tired. That piece of work can definitely wait a few days'
- 'How could we make this more inclusive?'

- 'What can I help with whilst you're on holiday?'
- 'I think I'll work from home'
- 'Shall we go for a walk and talk it through?'
- 'I changed my mind, what about this?'
- 'I'm sick, so I'll be offline today'
- 'What timeframe would feel achievable?'
- 'How can we make best use of our time together?'
- 'I was disappointed not to get promoted, but the process was fair'
- 'I am looking forward to discussing the feedback with my manager'

# ACCOUNTABILITY

In a human-focused workplace, people understand expectations and how to contribute:

- 'I understand the impact of my work'
- 'How do you feel things are going?'
- 'Are we meeting your expectations?'
- 'Can you help me understand the priority?'
- 'I'd like to explore doing something different'
- 'I feel proud of the work I do'
- 'I understand what I need to deliver and *how* to approach it'
- 'I think there's a risk that we need to discuss'
- 'I find it easy to describe what we do'
- 'What is our role in this?'
- 'I've got an idea!'
- 'I don't know. But let's try and find out'

- 'I'm worried that didn't go well. I'm going to discuss it with my manager'
- 'I understand why we didn't hire that person; they might have compromised our values'
- 'I'm concerned something isn't right. I'm going to raise it'
- 'Thank you for your contributions, they make a big difference'

## COMMUNITY

We feel that we're in this together and equally valued:

- 'Let's meet and brainstorm ideas'
- 'My manager cares about me'
- 'The team asked lots of questions'
- 'Can you help me?'
- 'I feel included and valued'
- 'Congratulations to everyone involved!'
- 'Did you have a good weekend?'
- 'Thanks for your support'
- 'I'm listening'
- 'We have a laugh together'
- 'Is it aligned with our values?'
- 'I can be myself at work'
- 'I have friends here'
- 'That's really interesting, can you share a little more?'
- 'We value your skills and perspective'
- 'I'm here if you need me'
- 'Everyone can excel here'

## EMPOWERMENT

Being trusted to do the right thing is key:

- 'I trust your judgement'
- 'What do you think?'
- 'I understand what good looks like'
- 'We're making great progress'
- 'Has anyone done this before? I'd love your advice'
- 'Oops. I made a mistake'
- 'My work is energising'
- 'Let's give it a go'
- 'We're exploring options and welcome your suggestions'
- 'I'm sorry I messed up, here's what I'll do to make it better'
- 'I'm sharing this feedback because I have high expectations and I know you can reach them'
- 'Thank you for your hard work'
- 'What a brilliant idea!'
- 'What might this look like in two years' time?'
- 'Where do you see opportunities for us to improve?'
- 'Let's experiment and see what happens'

## GROWTH

People feel supported and inspired to develop and grow:

- 'What are your goals?'
- 'I've learned a new skill'

- 'Perhaps a mentor could help?'
- 'Let's book time for a dry run'
- 'This is a great opportunity, who could take it?'
- 'I can grow my career here'
- 'I trust my manager'
- 'I feel supported and able to develop my potential'
- 'That's brilliant, let's share it'
- 'What might be possible?'
- 'What do our customers need?'
- 'What have you learned?'
- 'I feel ready'
- 'You can learn that'
- 'I can help you'

Building a climate for human growth takes hard work and commitment. Maintaining one can prove even harder as global contexts, competing demands, emotions, motivations and human and technological capabilities advance. Having a clear vision for the workplace we wish to nurture, combined with devotion to continuously strengthen the tools and habits we develop as people and communities, can determine who gets to this destination.

As people, society and the planet constantly evolve and transform, it is inevitable that cracks will emerge. It takes all of us, individually and as a collective, to nurture lasting conditions for human growth to ensure we move forwards from the state many encounter today:

## I. REGULARLY REVIEW DATA TO IDENTIFY ANY CRACKS TO CONTINUOUSLY IMPROVE YOUR CULTURE

Enable and encourage people to identify these and make them known, so together you can target action to repair and strengthen the five elements for happy, healthy, human workplaces (workplace, accountability, community, empowerment and growth). Complete the culture cracks diagnostic to access high-level indications on where these might be lingering (using the QR code shared on page 316). Just as we need to as individuals, in workplaces we must keep reviewing and investing in the body (an organisation's purpose, mission, values and its human leaders who create a climate for growth), mind (fuel with tools, systems and skills to enable fair people decisions and reveal unseen possibilities) and heart and soul (the relationship between individuals and human managers, facilitating experiences of autonomy, meaning and growth) to keep the whole company strong, agile and ready for the next phase.

## 2. DEVELOP UNDERSTANDING OF YOUR OWN HUMAN HABITS AND KEEP AN EYE ON THEM

Recognise when these could be detracting from human growth. This is when our brain's shortcuts, biases, impulses and instincts to keep us safe, and desire to feed our egos, creep in, hijacking the way we behave. This might look like assumptions clouding our judgements (e.g. 'that person was late to the call, they don't have what it takes for the project') or playing it safe and subconsciously restricting voices at the table to those we know will endorse our thinking. Or perhaps ignoring the negative yet constructive and helpful feedback, because it hurts our egos, or isolating someone from a social group because they once offended us. Sometimes our skills gaps in preparing and planning can limit opportunities for others – sharing information last minute or heaping pressure on others to finish work in an even tighter deadline. As humans, changing our default thought process from 'what will make me look good?' to 'how could this help others?' could be the operating system upgrade we need.

## 3. MAKE IT HUMAN

Here are the top five actions, regardless of background, organisation, role, level, personality or motivations, we can each embed in our daily actions to help shape happier, healthier, more human experiences of work:

Choose to spend time with **Humans**

Seek to **Understand**

Make your work **Meaningful**

**Add** a little exploration

**Never** stop learning

A culture of human growth is in our hands. It takes commitment and skill to develop, nurture and maintain, but the prize of happier, healthier, more human organisations is more than just reward for our efforts.

Together, let's make it human.

# RESOURCES

## MAKE IT HUMAN IN YOUR TEAM AND WORKPLACE: JOIN THE MAKE IT HUMAN CLUB

Join a growing community of leaders, managers and individuals passionate about building better, brighter workplaces and receive FREE insights, stories, tools and exclusive offers to help make it human where you are.

Subscribe to receive free insights straight to your inbox, every two weeks (you can unsubscribe at any time):

## MAKE IT HUMAN MODELS

The make it human models referenced throughout the book are:

- Ten signs of culture cracks (including a short diagnostic)
- The messy middle

- New measures of success
- A climate for human growth

You can view these in full via this QR code:

Sketch illustrations by Kacy Maxwell:

sketchnote by
KACY MAXWELL

For further information and consulting support, head to:
https://make-it-human.com/

# REFERENCES

## CHAPTER 1

Young, S. (2023), 'Tech Leaders Warn of AI Dangers', Leaders, https://leaders.com/news/leadership/top-tech-leaders-warn-of-a-i-dangers/

Clifton, J. (2023), 'The Global Rise of Unhappiness', Gallup, https://news.gallup.com/opinion/gallup/401216/global-rise-unhappiness.aspx

Gratton, L. and Scott, A. (no date), 'The 100-Year Life', The 100-Year Life, https://www.100yearlife.com/

Tupper, H. and Ellis, S. (2023), 'The Squiggly Career', Amazing If, https://www.amazingif.com/books/

Patel, A. and Plowman, S. (2022), 'The Increasing Importance of a Best Friend at Work', Gallup, https://www.gallup.com/workplace/397058/increasing-importance-best-friend-work.aspx

Hart, J. and McDade, A. (2023), 'Your co-workers don't know what to say to you at work – so they're googling it', Business Insider, https://www.businessinsider.com/people-returning-work-no-one-knows-what-to-talk-about-2023-5?r=US&IR=T

Klinghoffer, D. and Kirkpatrick-Husk, K. (2023), 'With Burnout on the Rise, What Can Companies Do About It?', *MIT Sloan Management Review*, https://sloanreview.mit.edu/article/with-burnout-on-the-rise-what-can-companies-do-about-it/

Klinghoffer, D. and Kirkpatrick-Husk, K. (2023), 'More Than 50% of Managers Feel Burned Out', *Harvard Business Review*, https://hbr.org/2023/05/more-than-50-of-managers-feel-burned-out

Dhingra, N. et al. (2020), 'Igniting individual purpose in times of crisis', McKinsey & Company, https://www.mckinsey.com/capabilities/people-and-organizational-performance/our-insights/igniting-individual-purpose-in-times-of-crisis

Grant, A. (2021), 'There's a Name for the Blah You're Feeling: It's Called Languishing', *New York Times*, https://www.nytimes.com/2021/04/19/well/mind/covid-mental-health-languishing.html

Murphy Jr, B. (2023), 'An 80-Year Harvard Study Found the Secret to a Happy Life. These 9 Simple Habits Make It Possible', *Inc.*, https://www.inc.com/bill-murphy-jr/an-80-year-harvard-study-found-secret-to-a-happy-life-these-9-simple-habits-will-improve-yours.html

## CHAPTER 2

Scorsese, M. (2013), *The Wolf of Wall Street*, IMDb, https://www.imdb.com/title/tt0993846/

Doyle, M. et al. (2013), 'Culture in banking: Under the

microscope', Deloitte, https://www2.deloitte.com/content/dam/Deloitte/uk/Documents/financial-services/deloitte-uk-culture-in-banking.pdf

Franklin, J., Quinio, A. and Morris, S. (2023), 'What women employees say about Goldman Sachs' culture', *Financial Times*, https://www.ft.com/content/54bc83e3-aeaf-46a2-b004-e2deb0785022

Bloom, N., Ahir, H. and Furceri, D. (2022), 'Visualizing the Rise of Global Economic Uncertainty', *Harvard Business Review*, https://hbr.org/2022/09/visualizing-the-rise-of-global-economic-uncertainty?ab=hero-main-text

Syal, R. (2019), '"A celebrity, not a leader": how Vote Leave harnessed the Johnson effect', *The Guardian*, https://www.theguardian.com/politics/2019/jul/17/celebrity-leader-how-vote-leave-harnessed-boris-johnson-effect

Finnis, A. (2021), 'Why did Dominic Cummings go to Barnard Castle?', *i*, https://inews.co.uk/news/politics/dominic-cummings-barnard-castle-why-trip-durham-boris-johnson-row-covid-rules-explained-1018479

Kottasová, I. and Subramaniam, T. (2022), 'Boris Johnson's tenure has been defined by scandal. Here are some of the biggest ones', CNN, https://edition.cnn.com/2022/07/06/uk/boris-johnson-scandals-intl/index.html

Quinn, B. (2023), 'Boris Johnson inquiry: what is former UK PM accused of?', *The Guardian*, https://www.theguardian.com/politics/2023/mar/22/boris-johnson-inquiry-what-is-former-uk-pm-accused-of

Clarke, V. and de Ferrer, M. (2023), 'Ruth Perry: Ofsted inspection "contributed" to head teacher's death', BBC News, https://www.bbc.co.uk/news/education-67639942

Croom, S. (2021), '12% of corporate leaders are psychopaths. It's time to take this problem seriously', *Fortune*, https://fortune.com/2021/06/06/corporate-psychopaths-business-leadership-csr/

Babiak, P. and Hare, R. (2019), *Snakes in Suits: When Psychopaths Go to Work*, HarperCollins Publishers.

'Psychopathy' (no date), *Psychology Today*, https://www.psychologytoday.com/gb/basics/psychopathy

Chamorro-Premuzic, T. (2013), 'Why Do So Many Incompetent Men Become Leaders?', *Harvard Business Review*, https://hbr.org/2013/08/why-do-so-many-incompetent-men

Shue, K. (2021), 'Women Aren't Promoted Because Managers Underestimate Their Potential', Yale Insights, https://insights.som.yale.edu/insights/women-arent-promoted-because-managers-underestimate-their-potential

Henley, J. (2020), 'Female-led countries handled coronavirus better, study suggests', *The Guardian*, https://www.theguardian.com/world/2020/aug/18/female-led-countries-handled-coronavirus-better-study-jacinda-ardern-angela-merkel

Ash, S. (2021), '10 Major Leadership Theories and Why You Need to Know Them', Medium, https://betterhumans.pub/10-major-leadership-theories-and-why-you-need-to-know-them-198aa170df7e

Kets de Vries, M. F. R. (2022), 'Why the World Is Attracted

to Neo-Authoritarian Leaders', INSEAD Knowledge, https://knowledge.insead.edu/leadership-organisations/why-world-attracted-neo-authoritarian-leaders

## CHAPTER 3

Davidson, H. (2014), '"Jedi Council" sex ring: 171 Australian Defence Force staff disciplined', *The Guardian*, https://www.theguardian.com/world/2014/aug/07/jedi-council-sex-ring-171-australian-defence-force-staff-disciplined

Sull, D., Sull, C. and Zweig, B. (2022), 'Toxic Culture Is Driving the Great Resignation', *MIT Sloan Management Review*, https://sloanreview.mit.edu/article/toxic-culture-is-driving-the-great-resignation/

LinkedIn (2023), 'Global Talent Trends', LinkedIn Talent Solutions, https://business.linkedin.com/talent-solutions/global-talent-trends

Sull, D. and Sull, C. (2022), 'How to Fix a Toxic Culture', *MIT Sloan Management Review*, https://sloanreview.mit.edu/article/how-to-fix-a-toxic-culture/

Milanesi, C. (2022), 'Microsoft's Latest Work Trend Index Urges to End Productivity Paranoia', *Forbes*, https://www.forbes.com/sites/carolinamilanesi/2022/09/23/microsofts-latest-work-trend-index-urges-to-end-productivity-paranoia/?sh=1ab9301a3bae

'Partygate: Boris Johnson facing questions after photos emerge' (2022), BBC News, https://www.bbc.co.uk/news/uk-politics-61560535

Bird, J. and Gornall, S. (2019), 'How to spot a hidden blame culture', *People Management*, https://www.peoplemanagement. co.uk/article/1741883/how-spot-hidden-blame-culture#gref

Edmondson, A. C. (2023), 'Psychological Safety', Amy C. Edmondson, https://amycedmondson.com/psychological-safety/

Ross, A. (2023), 'Dan Wootton fired by MailOnline after GB News Laurence Fox scandal', *The Independent*, https://www. independent.co.uk/news/uk/home-news/dan-wootton-laurence-fox-mail-online-b2420301.html

Ettore, M. (2020), 'Why Most New Executives Fail – And Four Things Companies Can Do About It', *Forbes*, https://www. forbes.com/sites/forbescoachescouncil/2020/03/13/why-most-new-executives-fail-and-four-things-companies-can-do-about-it/?sh=11d588e76730

'The psychological contract' (2023), CIPD, https://www.cipd. org/uk/knowledge/factsheets/psychological-factsheet/#gref

Chamorro-Premuzic, T. (2013), 'Why Do So Many Incompetent Men Become Leaders?', *Harvard Business Review*, https:// hbr.org/2013/08/why-do-so-many-incompetent-men

Carucci, R. (2021), 'Does Your Company Lurch from Crisis to Crisis?', *Harvard Business Review*, https://hbr.org/2021/03/ does-your-company-lurch-from-crisis-to-crisis

Maddox, F. (2023), 'Your Team Doesn't Need You to Be the Hero', Kellogg Insight, https://insight.kellogg.northwestern. edu/article/army-leadership-awareness

Schaedig, D. (2023), 'Groupthink: Definition, Signs, Examples and How to Avoid It', Simply Psychology, https://www.simplypsychology.org/groupthink.html

'How JFK Inspired the Term "Groupthink"' (2022), NeuroLeadership Institute, https://neuroleadership.com/your-brain-at-work/jfk-inspired-term-groupthink/

Hermann, A. and Rammal, H. G. (2010), 'The grounding of the "flying bank"', *Management Decision*, https://www.emerald.com/insight/content/doi/10.1108/00251741011068761/full/html

Ritson, M. (2021), 'Jeff Bezos's success at Amazon is down to one thing: focusing on the customer', Marketing Week, https://www.marketingweek.com/mark-ritson-jeff-bezos-success-focusing-on-customer/

Key, A. (2020), '"Barnes & Noble? It's a big mess": Waterstones boss James Daunt on bestsellers and plans in the US', *i*, https://inews.co.uk/news/business/waterstones-james-daunt-barnes-noble-395187

Gioia, T. (2022), 'What Can We Learn from Barnes & Noble's Surprising Turnaround?', Honest Broker, https://www.honest-broker.com/p/what-can-we-learn-from-barnes-and

Sinek, S. (2011), *Start With Why*, Penguin.

Del Valle, S. Y. et al. (2007), 'Mixing patterns between age groups in social networks', *Social Networks*.

Gratton, L. and Scott, A. (2020), *The 100-Year Life: Living and Working in an Age of Longevity*, Bloomsbury Publishing.

De Smet, A. et al. (2022), 'The Great Attrition is making hiring harder. Are you searching the right talent pools?', McKinsey & Company, https://www.mckinsey.com/capabilities/people-

and-organizational-performance/our-insights/the-great-attrition-is-making-hiring-harder-are-you-searching-the-right-talent-pools

Sinek, S. (2020), *The Infinite Game*, Portfolio Penguin.

Beddington, E. (2022), '"If you work hard and succeed, you're a loser": can you really wing it to the top?', *The Guardian*, https://amp.theguardian.com/science/2022/jun/16/wing-it-to-the-top-leaders-boris-johnson-elon-musk

Ibrahim, M. (2019), 'Men Apply for a Job When They Meet Only 60% of the Qualifications, But Women Apply Only If They Meet 100% of Them. Here's Why', LinkedIn, https://www.linkedin.com/pulse/men-apply-job-when-meet-only-60-qualifications-women-100-mei-ibrahim/

Sull, D. and Sull, C. (2023), 'The Toxic Culture Gap Shows Companies Are Failing Women, *MIT Sloan Management Review*, https://sloanreview.mit.edu/article/the-toxic-culture-gap-shows-companies-are-failing-women/

'New Research Shows Women Are Better at Using Soft Skills Crucial for Effective Leadership and Superior Business Performance, Finds Korn Ferry' (2016), Korn Ferry, https://www.kornferry.com/about-us/press/new-research-shows-women-are-better-at-using-soft-skills-crucial-for-effective-leadership

# CHAPTER 4

Perry, T. (2023), 'Under French Law, Businesses Can't Email Employees After Work Hours', GOOD, https://www.good.is/Culture/france-lets-you-disconnect-rp

Main, P. (2023), 'The Stanley Milgram Experiment: Understanding Obedience', Structural Learning, https://www.structural-learning.com/post/stanley-milgram-experiment

Bandura, A., Ross, D. and Ross, S. (1961), 'Transmission of Aggression Through Imitation of Aggressive Models', Classics in the History of Psychology, https://psychclassics.yorku.ca/Bandura/bobo.htm

'ICE Blogs', ICE, https://www.ice.org.uk/news-insight/news-and-blogs/ice-blogs

Johny, R. M. (2023), 'Twitter employee, whose pic of sleeping in office went viral, laid off: Report', *Hindustan Times*, https://www.hindustantimes.com/business/twitter-employee-whose-pic-of-sleeping-in-office-went-viral-laid-off-report-101677476903754.html

Satell, G. (2014), 'A Look Back at Why Blockbuster Really Failed and Why It Didn't Have To, *Forbes*, https://www.forbes.com/sites/gregsatell/2014/09/05/a-look-back-at-why-blockbuster-really-failed-and-why-it-didnt-have-to/?sh=5ecbc8d51d64

'Why Employees Quit (And How to Keep Them)' (2022), Wellable, https://www.wellable.co/blog/why-employees-quit-and-how-to-keep-them/

Gelles, D. (2022), 'Billionaire No More: Patagonia Founder Gives Away the Company', *New York Times*, https://www.nytimes.com/2022/09/14/climate/patagonia-climate-philanthropy-chouinard.html

O'Brien, D. et al. (2019), 'Purpose is everything', Deloitte Insights, https://www2.deloitte.com/us/en/insights/topics/

marketing-and-sales-operations/global-marketing-trends/2020/purpose-driven-companies.html

KPMG US Careers (2014), 'KPMG We Shape History', YouTube, https://www.youtube.com/watch?v=JZmZoURcmXI

'The psychological contract' (2023), CIPD, https://www.cipd.org/uk/knowledge/factsheets/psychological-factsheet/#gref

'About Huel' (2015), Huel, https://uk.huel.com/pages/about-us

Mcleod, S. (2023), 'Stanford Prison Experiment: Zimbardo's Famous Study', Simply Psychology, https://www.simplypsychology.org/zimbardo.html

Barry, D., McIntire, M. and Rosenberg, M. (2021), '"Our President Wants Us Here": The Mob That Stormed the Capitol', *New York Times*, https://www.nytimes.com/2021/01/09/us/capitol-rioters.html

Samuelson, K. (2021), 'How the 2011 London riots unfolded', *The Week*, https://theweek.com/news/society/953705/how-the-2011-london-riots-unfolded

Tech, V. (2018), 'Employee incentives can lead to unethical behavior in the workplace', ScienceDaily, https://www.sciencedaily.com/releases/2018/12/181211122456.htm

Nanji, N., Conway, Z. and Layhe, E. (2023), 'McDonald's workers speak out over sexual abuse claims', BBC News, https://www.bbc.co.uk/news/business-65388445

Isaac, A. (2023), 'Revealed: new claims of sexual misconduct and "toxic culture" at CBI', *The Guardian*, https://www.theguardian.com/business/2023/apr/03/revealed-new-claims-of-sexual-misconduct-and-toxic-culture-at-cbi

# CHAPTER 5

'Attachment Theory' (2015), Psychologist World, https://www.psychologistworld.com/developmental/attachment-theory

'Understanding the stress response' (2020), Harvard Health, https://www.health.harvard.edu/staying-healthy/understanding-the-stress-response

Cherry, K. (2023), 'How the Hawthorne Effect Works', Verywell Mind, https://www.verywellmind.com/what-is-the-hawthorne-effect-2795234

Wooll, M. (2022), 'Your workforce is lonely. It's hurting your business', BetterUp, https://www.betterup.com/blog/connection-crisis-impact-on-work

Gratton, L. (2022), 'Cut the meetings, make more friends', *Financial Times*, https://www.ft.com/content/c95da4e0-ecd3-4f4d-9faa-ac2a3dc4fc15

Beilock, S. (2019), 'How Diverse Teams Produce Better Outcomes', *Forbes*, https://www.forbes.com/sites/sianbeilock/2019/04/04/how-diversity-leads-to-better-outcomes/?sh=884e7af65ced

Edmondson, A. C. (2023), 'Psychological Safety', Amy C. Edmondson, https://amycedmondson.com/psychological-safety/

Elberse, A. (2013), 'Ferguson's Formula', *Harvard Business Review*, https://hbr.org/2013/10/fergusons-formula

Scaletta, K. (2013), 'Breaking Down Gregg Popovich's Extremely Successful San Antonio Spurs System', Bleacher Report, https://bleacherreport.com/articles/1870815-breaking-down-gregg-popovichs-extremely-successful-san-antonio-spurs-

Mcleod, S. (2023), 'Social Identity Theory in Psychology (Tajfel & Turner, 1979)', Simply Psychology, https://www.simplypsychology.org/social-identity-theory.html

Oppland, M. (2016), '8 Traits of Flow According to Mihaly Csikszentmihalyi', PositivePsychology, https://positivepsychology.com/mihaly-csikszentmihalyi-father-of-flow/#how-to-achieve-state

Guthridge, L. (2021), 'Why Autonomy Matters and How You Can Use It to Your Advantage', Forbes, https://www.forbes.com/sites/forbescoachescouncil/2021/06/21/why-autonomy-matters-and-how-you-can-use-it-to-your-advantage

Gonzalez-Mulé, E. and Cockburn, B. S. (2021), 'This job is (literally) killing me: A moderated-mediated model linking work characteristics to mortality', Journal of Applied Psychology, https://psycnet.apa.org/record/2020-23637-001

Ackerman, C. E. (2023), 'Learned Helplessness: Seligman's Theory of Depression', PositivePsychology, https://positivepsychology.com/learned-helplessness-seligman-theory-depression-cure/

Bryant, A. (2016), 'Tobi Lütke of Shopify: Powering a Team With a "Trust Battery"', New York Times, https://www.nytimes.com/2016/04/24/business/tobi-lutke-of-shopify-powering-a-team-with-a-trust-battery.html

'Kaizen' (2009), The Economist, https://www.economist.com/news/2009/04/14/kaizen

Harrell, E. (2015), 'How 1% Performance Improvements Led to Olympic Gold', Harvard Business Review, https://hbr.org/2015/10/how-1-performance-improvements-led-to-olympic-gold

Hastings, R. and Meyer, E. (2020), *No Rules Rules: Netflix and the Culture of Reinvention*, Virgin Books.

Patience, S. (2020), 'David Epstein on kind and wicked learning environments', Driverless Crocodile, https://www.driverlesscrocodile.com/books-and-recommendations/david-epstein-on-kind-and-wicked-learning-environments/

Dweck, C. (2016), 'What Having a "Growth Mindset" Actually Means', *Harvard Business Review*, https://hbr.org/2016/01/what-having-a-growth-mindset-actually-means

## CHAPTER 6

'Discover Glassdoor's Best Places to Work in the UK 2024' (2024), Glassdoor, https://www.glassdoor.co.uk/Award/Best-Places-to-Work-UK-LST_KQ0,22.htm

Dhingra, N. et al. (2020), 'Igniting individual purpose in times of crisis', McKinsey & Company, https://www.mckinsey.com/capabilities/people-and-organizational-performance/our-insights/igniting-individual-purpose-in-times-of-crisis

De Smet, A. et al. (2022), 'Gone for now, or gone for good? How to play the new talent game and win back workers', McKinsey & Company, https://www.mckinsey.com/capabilities/people-and-organizational-performance/our-insights/gone-for-now-or-gone-for-good-how-to-play-the-new-talent-game-and-win-back-workers

Lamano, G. (2021), 'Three Tips for Boosting Business Profits: How Investing in Diversity Increases Profitability', *Forbes*, https://www.forbes.com/sites/theyec/2021/12/20/

three-tips-for-boosting-business-profits-how-investing-in-diversity-increases-profitability

'Workplace Learning Report 2024' (2024), LinkedIn Learning, https://learning.linkedin.com/resources/workplace-learning-report

Patel, A. and Plowman, S. (2022), 'The Increasing Importance of a Best Friend at Work', Gallup, https://www.gallup.com/workplace/397058/increasing-importance-best-friend-work.aspx

Jiménez, J. (2022), 'Why psychological safety matters and how to create it', BetterUp, https://www.betterup.com/blog/why-psychological-safety-at-work-matters

Fraser-Thill, R. (2022), 'The Missing, Essential Ingredient for Meaningful Work', *Forbes*, https://www.forbes.com/sites/rebeccafraserthill/2022/12/30/the-missing-essential-ingredient-for-meaningful-work/?sh=e23124b43ce0

Dhingra, N. et al. (2020), 'Igniting individual purpose in times of crisis', McKinsey & Company, https://www.mckinsey.com/capabilities/people-and-organizational-performance/our-insights/igniting-individual-purpose-in-times-of-crisis

'Mastercard Chairman Ajay Banga Defines Decency in Business' (2021), Duke's Fuqua School of Business, https://www.fuqua.duke.edu/duke-fuqua-insights/distinguished-speakers-series-mastercard-chairman-ajay-banga-defines-decency

Bodan, M. and Horn, H. (2016), 'Organizational Network Analysis: Gain insight, drive smart', Deloitte, https://

www2.deloitte.com/us/en/pages/human-capital/articles/
organizational-network-analysis.html

'About B Corp Certification: Measuring a company's entire
social and environmental impact' (no date), B Lab, https://
www.bcorporation.net/en-us/certification/

Gelles, D. (2022), 'Billionaire No More: Patagonia Founder
Gives Away the Company', *New York Times*, https://www.
nytimes.com/2022/09/14/climate/patagonia-climate-
philanthropy-chouinard.html

Sweney, M. and Davies, R. (2022), 'BrewDog loses its ethical
B Corp certificate', *The Guardian*, https://www.theguardian.com/
business/2022/dec/01/brewdog-loses-its-ethical-b-corp-
certificate

Pink, D. H. (2018), 'Pinkcast 1.18: A 5-minute exercise for
discovering your purpose', Daniel H. Pink, https://www.
danpink.com/pinkcast/pinkcast-1-18-a-5-minute-exercise-
for-discovering-your-purpose/

Pink, D. H. (2018), 'Pinkcast 1.20: Discover your purpose (in
one minute) with the napkin test', Daniel H. Pink, https://
www.danpink.com/pinkcast/pinkcast-1-20-discover-your-
purpose-in-one-minute-with-the-napkin-test/

Pfau, B. N. (2015), 'How an Accounting Firm Convinced Its
Employees They Could Change the World', *Harvard Business
Review*, https://hbr.org/2015/10/how-an-accounting-firm-
convinced-its-employees-they-could-change-the-world

De Smet, A. et al. (2022), 'The Great Attrition is making hiring
harder. Are you searching the right talent pools?', McKinsey

& Company, https://www.mckinsey.com/capabilities/people-and-organizational-performance/our-insights/the-great-attrition-is-making-hiring-harder-are-you-searching-the-right-talent-pools

Sinek, S. (2011), *Start With Why*, Penguin.

Sinek, S. (2020), *The Infinite Game*, Portfolio Penguin.

## CHAPTER 7

Sridharan, M. (2021), 'BANI', Think Insights, https://thinkinsights.net/leadership/bani/

Kitto, K. (2022), 'New Global Talent Trends: Even as Hiring Cools, People Want More Out of Work', LinkedIn Talent Blog, https://www.linkedin.com/business/talent/blog/talent-strategy/new-global-talent-trends-even-as-hiring-cools-people-want-more-out-of-work

Franzino, M. et al. (2021), 'The $8.5 Trillion Talent Shortage', Korn Ferry, https://www.kornferry.com/insights/this-week-in-leadership/talent-crunch-future-of-work

Bersin, J. (2022), 'Cultivate'22 Day 2 Opening Keynote: Industry Convergence and Transformation by Josh Bersin', YouTube, https://www.youtube.com/watch?v=I5K5rTMUFwo

Roslansky, R. (2022), 'Here's why the world of work urgently needs to put skills first', World Economic Forum, https://www.weforum.org/agenda/2022/03/work-skills-first

Sull, D., Sull, C. and Zweig, B. (2022), 'Toxic Culture Is Driving the Great Resignation', *MIT Sloan Management Review*, https://sloanreview.mit.edu/article/toxic-culture-is-driving-the-great-resignation/

McLellan, S. et al. (2022), 'Five Steps Your Organization Can Take to Make Hybrid Work', SHL, https://www.shl.com/resources/by-type/whitepapers-and-reports/five-steps-your-organization-can-take-to-make-hybrid-work/

Somers, M. (2022), 'Women are less likely than men to be promoted. Here's one reason why', MIT Sloan, https://mitsloan.mit.edu/ideas-made-to-matter/women-are-less-likely-men-to-be-promoted-heres-one-reason-why

Zenger, J. and Folkman, J. (2019), 'Research: Women Score Higher Than Men in Most Leadership Skills', *Harvard Business Review*, https://hbr.org/2019/06/research-women-score-higher-than-men-in-most-leadership-skills

'Today at Work: Quarterly Workforce Research Report – The Hidden Truth About Promotions' (2023), ADP, https://www.adpri.org/wp-content/uploads/2023/10/TaW_Q32023v2.pdf

McLellan, S. et al. (2023), 'The New Era in People Management', SHL, https://www.shl.com/resources/by-type/whitepapers-and-reports/the-new-era-in-people-management/

Burgess, W. (2016), 'Why Companies Overlook Great Internal Candidates', *Harvard Business Review*, https://hbr.org/2016/10/why-companies-overlook-great-internal-candidates

'How Standard Chartered Bank prepares for the future of work' (2023), Gloat, https://resources.gloat.com/resources/standard-chartered-bank-customer-success-story/

McLellan, S. (2022), 'Self-Insight: The Gift That Keeps Giving', SHL, https://www.shl.com/resources/by-type/blog/2022/self-insight-the-gift-that-keeps-giving/

'New Study providing updated validity estimates' (2023), Master International, https://www.master-hr.com/insights/new-study-providing-updated-validity-estimates/

Sackett, P. R. et al. (2022), 'Revisiting meta-analytic estimates of validity in personnel selection: Addressing systematic overcorrection for restriction of range', *Journal of Applied Psychology*.

Mikhailov, N. and Yankov, G. (2024), *Personality: A User's Guide*, Robinson.

Edmondson, A. (2023), 'It's OK to Fail, But You Have to Do It Right', *Harvard Business Review*, https://hbr.org/2023/07/its-ok-to-fail-but-you-have-to-do-it-right

'Novartis: Using Science to Unlock Insights & Unleash the Power of People' (2023), UNLEASH World, https://www.unleash.ai/unleashworld/session/using-science-to-unlock-insights-unleash-the-power-of-people/

Hill, L. A. et al. (2022), 'What Makes a Great Leader?', *Harvard Business Review*, https://hbr.org/2022/09/what-makes-a-great-leader

Bersin, J. (2023), 'Why Are Some Companies More Dynamic Than Others?', Josh Bersin, https://joshbersin.com/2023/10/why-are-some-companies-more-dynamic-than-others/

Berg, K. (2019), 'How We Do People Analytics', Spotify HR Blog, https://hrblog.spotify.com/2019/03/21/how-we-do-people-analytics/

## CHAPTER 8

Beck, R. and Harter, J. (2023), 'Managers Account for 70% of

Variance in Employee Engagement', Gallup, https://news.gallup.com/businessjournal/182792/managers-account-variance-employee-engagement.aspx

Brower, T. (2023), 'Middle Managers Have It Bad: 5 Things They Need Most, *Forbes*, https://www.forbes.com/sites/tracybrower/2023/03/26/middle-managers-have-it-bad-5-things-they-need-most/?sh=15e89d6b617d

Corporate Rebels (2021), 'Successful Self-Management – Video Animation,' YouTube, https://www.youtube.com/watch?v=vMjJdmW1gHs

de Morree, P. (2023), 'Becoming Bossless: An Update on the Radical Transformation of Our First Acquisition', Corporate Rebels, https://www.corporate-rebels.com/blog/indaero-transformation

Gherson, D. and Gratton, L. (2022), 'Managers Can't Do It All', *Harvard Business Review*, https://hbr.org/2022/03/managers-cant-do-it-all

Frei, F. X. and Morriss, A. (2020), 'Begin with Trust', *Harvard Business Review*, https://hbr.org/2020/05/begin-with-trust

Wiseman, L. and McKeown, G. (2010), 'Managing Yourself: Bringing Out the Best in Your People', *Harvard Business Review*, https://hbr.org/2010/05/managing-yourself-bringing-out-the-best-in-your-people

Roca, J. and Wilde, S. (2019), *The Connector Manager: Why Some Leaders Build Exceptional Talent – and Others Don't*, Portfolio

# CHAPTER 9

Rusnak, K. (2023), 'The Magic Ratio: The Key to Relationship

Satisfaction', Gottman Institute, https://www.gottman.com/blog/the-magic-ratio-the-key-to-relationship-satisfaction/

Yapp, R. (2019), 'Where are you on the "Ladder of Accountability"', Leadership Capital, https://leadershipcapital.com/where-are-you-on-the-ladder-of-accountability/

Marquet, D. (2014), 'What is leadership? – with David Marquet', YouTube, https://www.youtube.com/watch?v=pYKH2uSax8U

Marquet, L. D. (2015), *Turn the Ship Around!: A True Story of Building Leaders by Breaking the Rules*, Penguin.

Dweck, C. (2016), 'What Having a "Growth Mindset" Actually Means', *Harvard Business Review*, https://hbr.org/2016/01/what-having-a-growth-mindset-actually-means

'Top Moments: With one shot, Michael Jordan says farewell and ushers in last title' (2021), NBA, https://www.nba.com/news/history-top-moments-michael-jordan-final-shot-1998

Syed, M. (2016), 'Why you should have your own black box – Matthew Syed – TEDxLondonBusinessSchool, YouTube, https://www.youtube.com/watch?v=MmVCYqs3mko

Syed, M. (2015), *Black Box Thinking: Why Most People Never Learn from their Mistakes – But Some Do*, Portfolio Penguin.

Brown, B. (2013), 'Brené Brown on Empathy', YouTube, https://www.youtube.com/watch?v=1Evwgu369Jw

Menatian, T. (2014), 'What makes a leader: Why emotional intelligence matters', Key Step Media, https://wwwkeystepmedia.com/makes-leader-emotional-intelligence-matters/

Pink, D. H. (2022), *The Power of Regret: How Looking Backward Moves Us Forward*, Canongate Books.

Dhingra, N. et al. (2020), 'Igniting individual purpose in times of crisis', McKinsey & Company, https://www.mckinsey.com/capabilities/people-and-organizational-performance/our-insights/igniting-individual-purpose-in-times-of-crisis

Oppland, M. (2016), '8 Traits of Flow According to Mihaly Csikszentmihalyi', PositivePsychology, https://positivepsychology.com/mihaly-csikszentmihalyi-father-of-flow/#how-to-achieve-state

Chaudhuri, A. (2023), 'The buddy boost: how "accountability partners" make you healthy, happy and more successful', *The Guardian*, https://www.theguardian.com/lifeandstyle/2023/nov/27/the-buddy-boost-how-accountability-partners-make-you-healthy-happy-and-more-successful

De Smet, A. et al. (2022), 'The Great Attrition is making hiring harder. Are you searching the right talent pools?', McKinsey & Company, https://www.mckinsey.com/capabilities/people-and-organizational-performance/our-insights/the-great-attrition-is-making-hiring-harder-are-you-searching-the-right-talent-pools

Hart, J. and McDade, A. (2023), 'Your co-workers don't know what to say to you at work – so they're googling it', Business Insider, https://www.businessinsider.com/people-returning-work-no-one-knows-what-to-talk-about-2023-5?r=US&IR=T

Perna, M. C. (2022), 'Employees Want More Friends at Work. Why Aren't They Finding Them?', *Forbes*, https://www.forbes.com/sites/markcperna/2022/07/19/employees-want-more-friends-at-work-why-arent-they-finding-them/?sh=742d6f3c19ab

Aaker, J. and Bagdonas, N. (2021), 'Why great leaders take humor seriously', TED Talk, https://www.ted.com/talks/jennifer_aaker_and_naomi_bagdonas_why_great_leaders_take_humor_seriously

Roberts, Y. (2023), 'Want to live to 116? The secret to longevity is less complicated than you think', *The Guardian*, https://www.theguardian.com/lifeandstyle/2023/oct/28/want-to-live-to-116-the-secret-to-longevity-is-less-complicated-than-you-think

## CHAPTER 10

McLellan, S. et al. (2022), 'Using People Insight to Make Hybrid Work', SHL, https://www.shl.com/assets/premium-content/using-people-insight-to-make-hybrid-work-report-en.pdf

Sull, D. and Sull, C. (2021), '10 Things Your Corporate Culture Needs to Get Right', *MIT Sloan Management Review*, https://sloanreview.mit.edu/article/10-things-your-corporate-culture-needs-to-get-right

Ibarra, H. and Scoular, A. (2019), 'The Leader as Coach', *Harvard Business Review*, https://hbr.org/2019/11/the-leader-as-coach

'Six paradoxes of leadership' (2020), PwC, https://www.pwc.com/gx/en/issues/succeeding-in-uncertainty/six-paradoxes-of-leadership.html

Jordan, J., Wade, M. and Teracino, E. (2020), 'Every Leader Needs to Navigate These 7 Tensions', *Harvard Business Review*, https://hbr.org/2020/02/every-leader-needs-to-navigate-these-7-tensions

'Gartner HR Research Identifies Human Leadership as the Next Evolution of Leadership' (2022), Gartner, https://www.gartner.com/en/newsroom/press-releases/06-23-22-gartner-hr-research-identifies-human-leadership-as-the-next-evolution-of-leadership

van Ewijk, W. (2023), 'Putting People First: Top Employers Institute Shares Insights About Building a Human-Centric Organisation', Top Employers Institute, https://www.top-employers.com/en-GB/insights/culture/putting-people-first-top-employers-institute-shares-insights-about-building-a-human-centric-organisation/

Ibarra, H. (2015), 'The Authenticity Paradox', *Harvard Business Review*, https://hbr.org/2015/01/the-authenticity-paradox

'About us' (2023), Core Quality International, https://www.corequality.nl/?lang=en

Ash, S. (2021), '10 Major Leadership Theories and Why You Need to Know Them', Medium, https://betterhumans.pub/10-major-leadership-theories-and-why-you-need-to-know-them-198aa170df7e

Burke, R. M. (2022), 'Women CEOs: Leadership for a Diverse Future', S&P Global, https://www.spglobal.com/esg/insights/featured/special-editorial/women-ceos-leadership-for-a-diverse-future

Garikipati, S. and Kambhampati, U. (2021), 'Leading the Fight Against the Pandemic: Does Gender "Really" Matter?', SSRN, https://papers.ssrn.com/sol3/papers.cfm?abstract_id=3617953

Denning, S. (2021), 'How Microsoft's Digital Transformation

Created a Trillion Dollar Gain', *Forbes*, https://www.forbes.com/sites/stevedenning/2021/06/20/how-microsofts-digital-transformation-created-a-trillion-dollar-gain/?sh=33b9dae7625b

Kets de Vries, M. F. R. (2022), 'Why the World Is Attracted to Neo-Authoritarian Leaders', INSEAD Knowledge, https://knowledge.insead.edu/leadership-organisations/why-world-attracted-neo-authoritarian-leaders

Choy, E. (2021), 'How Storytelling Helps Us Lead During Uncertainty and Fatigue', *Forbes*, https://www.forbes.com/sites/estherchoy/2021/12/05/how-storytelling-helps-us-lead-during-uncertainty-and-fatigue/?sh=448d588db77c

Obama, B. (2016), 'Obama tells story of famed chant: Fired up, ready to go', YouTube, https://www.youtube.com/watch?v=5AhRqgoADbk

# ACKNOWLEDGEMENTS

Thank you to:

Stephen, Georgia and Oscar for their constant support in making this happen. It is also no coincidence this book is full of stories from engineering, motor racing and history, *and* I am married to a bridge engineer with a passion for these topics!

Gil Parsons who read (and reread!) every word and whose wisdom helped shape this book.

My mum, for always believing this was possible! My dad and Jan, for offering comparative notes on psychological stories. My grandparents, Jean and Philip Beauchamp, for inspiring a long, happy life, prioritising family and meaningful connection. And my sisters, Alice, Catherine and Jenny, for appreciating my creative scribbles.

Barry Connolly, Sim Riordan and Ed Trelinski for reviewing early drafts and providing invaluable feedback (many of your stories and insights are in here!). Kitty McCormick for being a sounding board, cheerleader and all-round inspiring human. Tanya Farbrother, Edina Komaromi-Racz and Julia Landon for your red-penning, advice (I took some of it!) and humour. Juan Cereceda for saving me hours writing the reference list.

The European PS management team who all helped nurture a human growth culture. The European professional services team (2020–23) who inspire stories of growth. Ornella Chinotti, Mohamed Farid, Sian Ferguson, Chris Fuller, Guy Murray, Ed Rivlin and Bert Simonis for helping prove leadership can be a team sport.

Ella Boardman, James Stephens, Mark Wallace and the team at Biteback Publishing for seeing potential and helping it grow.

Kacy Maxwell of Sketchwell for beautifully capturing the core concepts and ideas in the sketches accompanying this book.

The many researchers and thought leaders continuously advancing our understanding of people and work and the trailblazers in organisations also on a quest to create something brighter (many of whom are referenced in this book).

A community of believers and thought leaders on LinkedIn who inspire through sharing ideas, new perspectives, support and encouragement, in particular: Steven Claes, Nick Lynn, David McLean, Liz Rider and Loren Sanders.

It really does take a village! Thank you all.

# ABOUT THE AUTHOR

© Ingrid Weel

Sarah McLellan is a work psychologist and business leader who, over twenty years, has partnered with hundreds of organisations to nurture more human places to work. She is now founder and leader of Make It Human, a consulting company on a mission to build workplaces where people and business thrive, through combining psychology, learnings and research into practical steps. Her hope is that *Make It Human* will enable happy, fulfilling experiences of work to become the norm, for us and for generations to come. Sarah is a chartered occupational psychologist with the British Psychological Society. She lives in Surrey with her husband, daughter and cat.

# INDEX

3 activities to build human growth
    foundations 170–73
3 key components for human cultures
    149
4 elements of emotional intelligence
    (EI) 251–9
4As, the (Netflix) 131
5 elements for happy, heathy workplaces
    86–144
    accountability 98–112
    community 113–25
    empowerment 125–32
    growth 132–44
    workplace 90–98
5 steps to understanding yourself
    259–62
5 top actions for more human
    experiences 313
6 paradoxes of leadership 277
6 workplace shifts for human success
    178–80
9 behaviours in a growth mindset 249
10 signs of culture cracks 54–74

Aaker, Professor Jennifer 266
Abel & Cole 164–5
accountability 19, 135, 171, 212, 246,
    308–9
    culture of 130
    for happy, heathy workplaces 98–112,
      312

    ladder 242–5, 247, 249
    partner 261
adaptivity 278
Adidas 101
agile working 210
'always-on' 25, 55, 88, 272
Amaechi, John 242
analysis paralysis 160
analytics 24, 160, 199, 200, 202
Apple 28, 122, 201, 295, 300
artificial intelligence (AI) 5–9, 22, 25, 42,
    49, 160, 176, 213–15, 234–5, 272
assessing people 94
authenticity 217, 278
autonomy 5, 8, 18, 20, 21, 92, 104, 126,
    225–6, 231, 312
autonomy, meaning and growth 21, 225,
    231, 235, 262, 298, 312

Bagdonas, Professor Naomi 266
Bandura, Albert 88
Banga, Ajay 196
BANI (brittle, anxious, non-linear and
    incomprehensible) era 176
Bartlett, Steven 262
Bay of Pigs 68
B-Corp accredited companies 163–7, 169
B-Corporations 162, 163
behaviour 61–3, 184
    aggressive 88, 105, 224
    inhumane 81

behaviour *cont.*
   leadership 32
   managing 289
   poor 33, 60, 61, 105, 106, 115, 224
   unethical 223, 274
behavioural assessment 235
Belfort, Jordan 32, 47
belonging 55, 92, 98, 113, 115, 116, 122,
   124, 125, 162
   inclusion and 179, 195, 276
   sense of 19, 21, 84, 85, 91, 121, 133, 226
Bersin, Josh 198
Bezos, Jeff 69, 294
Biden, Joe 37
BlackBerry 161, 201
Blakely, Sara 190–91
Blockbuster 99, 161, 201
'body' 147–73
Boeing 107–11
Boyatzis, Professor Richard 79
Branson, Richard 289
Brawn, Ross 220
BrewDog 169
Brexit 37, 38, 176
Brown, Brené 255, 256
bureaucracy 57–9, 182
burnout 15–17, 54, 55, 66, 116, 126, 201,
   209–11
business
   data 200
   durable 135, 152, 297–8
   good 163, 167
   growth 152, 158, 202, 278
   outcomes 61, 119, 121, 133
   plans 135
'busyness' 54
bystander theory 60, 61

Carlyle, Thomas 48, 282
Chamorro-Premuzic, Dr Tomas 46
choices 17, 20, 24, 85, 154, 226, 306
Chouinard, Yvon 100
climate for human growth 307–13
codes of conduct 34
collaboration 78, 95, 157, 160, 173, 181,
   189, 249, 263
colleagues 18, 22, 24, 32, 139, 148, 195, 224

command-and-control models 117
communication 6, 13, 106, 117, 154, 189,
   234, 293
communities 19, 23, 28, 87, 94, 113, 158,
   166, 176, 194, 311
   effective 117
   importance of 114–17
   management 235–6
   strong 118–25
   supportive 165
   work 116, 307
community 92, 98, 113–25, 163, 309
   belonging 19, 113, 115, 125
   building 132, 133, 297
   diverse 297
   groups 95, 195
   impact on 120
   local 95
   projects 95
   religious 91
   sense of 120
   'we' community 30
Compass Group 296
competence 46–8, 66, 78, 245
compliance 34
Confederation of British Industry (CBI)
   105
confidence 42, 43, 45–8, 55, 78, 139, 231,
   277
confirmation bias 88, 89
conflict 124, 171, 240, 256, 258–9, 264–5,
   271
'connector' managers 221
continuous improvement 102, 129, 134,
   160, 197, 222, 249, 300
'corporate clones' 70–72
Corporate Rebels 212
cost of living 17, 176
Covid-19 12, 18, 37, 38, 47, 59, 100, 117,
   191, 272–3, 286–8
creativity 6, 13, 275, 306
Croom, Simon 41
culture 51
   abusive 105
   alignment 106, 107
   'always-on' 88
   as an asset 179–80

culture *cont.*
  blame 58
  cloud 61–3, 75
  collaborative 63, 155
  company 36, 52, 53, 76, 157, 273, 300
  continuous improvement 300
  cracks 53–74, 75–81, 83, 86, 207, 274, 300, 312, 315
  cracks model 28
  cultivating 299–300
  gender 78
  gendered experience 79
  growth 142, 156, 203, 292, 342
  growth-oriented 188
  health 156–7
  inclusive 142, 155
  intelligence 219
  leaders 95–7
  learning 191, 204
  negative experiences 80–81
  organisational 49, 52, 53, 65, 76, 77, 79, 111, 132
  people-focused 11
  safe 279
  supportive 106, 155
  sustainable 92
  toxic 27–41, 52, 78, 81, 93
  workplace 78, 179, 246
  workshops 299
Cummings, Dominic 39
curiosity 94, 98, 123, 125, 191, 249, 295
CVS 169

Danone 165–6
data 157, 158, 159
  business 200
  capturing 198
  collation 157, 176
  engagement 98, 143, 180
  exit 98
  historical 49
  massaging 155
  models 158
  objective 181
  performance 213
  points 214, 300
  project 201

  quantitative 148
  review 312
  sets 79, 200
  sharing 160
  sources 159
Daunt, James 70
decision-making 18, 20, 42, 93, 108, 284, 293
DEIB (diversity, equity, inclusion and belonging) groups 195
Deliveroo 28
democratisation of opportunities 188
Diamond, Bob 34
dichotomies 276–7
diffusing conflict 264–5
digital societies 176
digital ways of working 175
'diminishers' 219
discrimination 27, 35, 36, 49, 221
Disney 202
diverse perspectives 295–7
diversity 14, 35, 95, 157, 184, 195, 287, 293, 296
diversity of thought 14, 293
double standards 32, 39, 56–7, 75, 76
durable business 135, 152, 297–8
Dweck, Carol 138, 247
dynamic organisations 161, 198

EBITDA (earnings before interest rates, taxes, depreciation and amortisation) 30
Edmondson, Professor Amy 118, 190–91
efficiency 14
emotional bank account 239–40
emotional intelligence (EI) 8, 79, 242, 251–9, 278, 291
empathy 43, 45, 217, 240, 254, 284, 286–7, 289, 292
  diffusing conflict 264–5
  enabler 121–2, 125
  leading with 220–21, 232
  model 255–6, 278
employee
  development 183, 184
  experience 151, 180, 188
  journey 180

employee *cont.*
  surveillance 55
  vitality 156
employee/manager relationship 205–7,
  233, 271
empowerment 55, 58–9, 81, 125–32, 137,
  161, 278, 310
  management 208–9, 236
'Everybody's Free (To Wear Sunscreen)'
  238

Facebook 28, 114
failure 130–32
FatFace 166–7
Federal Aviation Administration (FAA)
  109
feedback 8, 80, 103, 104, 131
  constructive 24, 67, 81, 131, 208, 232,
    234, 236
  gathering 22, 98, 218, 224
  personalised 234
  receiving 131, 139, 144
  seeking 247, 281
  sharing 91, 104, 204, 258
Ferguson, Sir Alex 121, 122
fight-or-flight 115, 123, 254
financial metrics 73, 80, 152, 158, 160, 203
financial organisations 32–6, 75
financial success 152, 169
*Financial Times* 35
flexibility 16,24, 88, 90–91, 103, 117, 155,
  180
flow of work 159, 180, 189, 204, 225
'flow' 125, 126, 127, 260
Fosslien, Liz 257
Fox, Laurence 61
Frei, Frances 217
friends 11, 13, 91, 115, 116, 263, 306, 309
friendships 16, 119, 124, 179, 258, 307

Gartner 21, 278
gaslighting 44, 127
Gawande, Atul 250
gender 11, 35, 78, 79, 282, 288
Gherson, Diane 216
Glassdoor 154
global financial crisis 28, 34–6

Global Talent Trends report 52
Goldman Sachs 35
Goleman, Daniel 79, 251, 252, 254, 256,
  258
good business 163, 167
Goodwin, Fred 34
Gordon, Bruce 242–3
Gottman, John 239, 240, 251
government 36–40
Grant, Adam 18
Gratton, Professor Lynda 216
group dynamics 60
Groupthink 68, 69, 91
growth 21, 132–44, 225, 235, 267, 310–11
  business 152, 158, 202, 278
  commercial 108
  company 100, 142, 151, 159
  continuous 113, 276
  culture 142, 156, 203, 292, 342
  financial 73, 108, 158
  -focused 120, 180
  foundations for 147–73
  habits 138–41, 144
  human 133–6, 141, 144, 161–3, 169,
    222, 278, 284, 305–13, 316
  long-term 196
  meaningful 300–303
  mindset 138, 231, 242, 247–51, 284
  opportunities 21, 100, 273
  personal 142, 144
  sustainable 132, 156, 201

hackathon 197, 198, 204
*Harvard Business Review* 172, 216, 277
Hawthorne studies 116
'heart and soul' 149, 205–36, 312
'hero complex' 65–7, 77, 78, 79
hierarchy of needs 89, 272
Hill, Professor Linda 196
Hogarth, Robin 136
Holmgren, Jennifer 291, 292
*House of Cards* 45
HR (human resources) systems 159,
  160, 211
human
  authenticity 279
  -centric leadership 278

human *cont.*
  connection 235, 300–303
  experience 25, 147, 215, 242. 313
  growth 133–6, 141, 161–3, 278, 284,
    305–13
  habits 259, 312–13
  hunches 181–2, 188
  impact 234–5
  leader 274, 292–303
  leader model 278
  leader's toolkit 297
  manager's toolkit 235
  managers 179, 215–36, 216, 312
  organisation 98, 181, 207, 215, 313
  oversight 161
  skills 24, 183, 208, 234
  traits 148, 265, 278
  work era 232, 270
  workplace 86, 113, 147, 149, 163, 207,
    269, 307–8, 312
'human' age of work 11
humanising companies 148
humour 48, 224, 266
hybrid working 14, 16, 55, 79, 180, 271,
  274

Ibarra, Professor Herminia 279
IBM 201, 202, 216, 294
impact 119–21, 157–8, 225–6, 234–5
'in flow' 125–7, 260
inclusion 21, 27, 59, 125, 144, 179, 184,
  192, 195, 203, 226, 276, 285
Industrial Revolution 10
infinite game, the 74, 172, 295
information flow 160, 161
in-group 125
innovation jams 197
integrity 34, 35, 40, 75, 93–4, 96, 98,
  162, 170
intelligent experimentation 202
intelligent failures 190, 191

Janis, Irving 68
Jellyfish 212
Jobs, Steve 295
Johnson, Boris 37, 38, 39, 47
Joly, Hubert 289, 290

kaizen 128, 197, 198, 204
kind environments 136–8
knowledge exchange/sharing 22, 95,
  117, 194
knowledge-based 6, 14, 271

LanzaTech 291
leaders 95–7
  good 269, 271, 274, 278, 301
  habits 292–303
  human 274, 278, 292–303
  new 63, 121
  new breed of 292
leadership
  as a team sport 292–3
  behaviour 32
  dual/team-based roles 293
  human-centric 278
  models 277, 278
  paradoxes 277
  responsibility 121
  roles 41, 46, 193, 293
  senses 283, 284–6, 288, 289, 291
  team 36, 39, 61, 108, 200
learned helplessness 126, 153
learning 188–91, 194–7, 203, 204, 294–5,
  33
  development and 144, 159, 183, 200
  growing and 11, 21, 95, 157, 226, 238,
    250, 279
legacy 11, 67, 74, 279, 284, 291, 300
Lehman Brothers 34
*Lessons in Chemistry* 275
LinkedIn 52, 114, 177, 278
lockdown 38, 39
logic 88, 217, 306
loneliness 12–14
longevity 11, 40, 49, 74, 102, 158, 172
long-term performance 141
long-term value 121, 183, 198
Luhrmann, Baz 238, 239
Lütke, Tobi 127

McDonald's 105
McDonnell Douglas 107
Machiavellianism 42, 44, 45, 47
machine learning (ML) 176

McKinsey 17, 100, 157, 172
*Mad Men* 43
management 41, 52, 74, 108, 209, 210,
 234, 236
  bloat 212
  burnout 209–11
  communities 235–6
  compassion 221–2, 232
  conflict 256, 258, 259
  empathy 220–21
  empowerment 208–9
  expectations 223
  good 179
  human 216, 232
  middle 58
  need for 211–13
  performance 211
  relationship 251, 256–9
  responsibilities 207
  roles 16–17, 133, 208
  scenarios (old versus human) 226–31
  self-management 251, 252–4
  skills 233–4
  supervisory 179
  talent 131, 183, 192
  team 62, 134, 136, 140, 342
  technology and 234–5
Marquet, David 245–6, 276, 300, 301
Maslow, Abraham 89, 272
Mastercard 154, 158, 196, 197, 204, 296
meaning 25, 91, 95, 98–9, 141, 226, 231,
 235, 260, 262
  personal 83, 205–25
  searching for 17–21
measures of engagement 151
measures of success 155–9, 161, 172, 173,
 316
mentoring 195, 206
'messy middle' 92, 137, 177, 315
MeToo movement 61, 106
metrics 76, 143, 155, 161, 172, 173
  financial 73, 80, 152, 158, 160, 203
  performance 143, 209
Metropolitan Police 40
Microsoft 55, 289, 295
Microsoft Viva 160
middle management 58

Milgram, Stanley 88
'mind' 149, 162, 175–204, 207, 312
mindset 66, 138, 196
  fixed 249
  growth 138, 231, 242, 247–51, 284
  outside-in 69, 94–5, 98
misogyny 40
model of empathy 255–6
moments in time 183, 199
Morrison, Lt. General David 51
Morriss, Anne 217
motivation 19, 135, 143, 152, 180, 183, 203,
 226, 231, 255
'multipliers' 219, 284

Nadella, Satya 289
narcissism 42, 43, 44, 45, 47
natural language programming (NLP)
 157
nepotism 70–72
Nespresso 166
Netflix 131, 204, 248, 293
Neumann, Adam 32
'new style of working' 212
NHS 40
*No Hard Feelings* 257
Nordic countries 56, 87
Northern Rock 34
Novartis 191–3

Obama, Barack 301, 302, 303
obedience studies 88
objective assessment 159, 184, 185, 186,
 187, 188, 204
Ofsted 40, 41
optimism bias 89
organisational
  awareness 254–5
  clarity 246
  culture 49, 53, 65, 76, 77, 79, 132
  design 159, 193, 257, 278
  foundations 162, 170, 173, 207
  mind 162, 182, 195, 201, 203, 207
  needs 143, 177, 183
  network analysis (ONA) 157, 160, 194
  readiness 203
  strategy 101, 141

outcomes 55, 102–3, 112, 276
business 61, 119, 121, 133
out-group 124, 125
outside-in mindset 69, 94–5, 98
ownership 19, 97, 135, 245–7, 276, 300, 301

pandemic *see* Covid-19
'parent–child' relationship 64–5
partnerships 95, 165, 294, 296
'Partygate' 39, 56
Patagonia 165
Pearl Harbor 68
people
    analytics 199, 200
    as resources 15, 148
    assessing 94
    -centric 154
    decisions 94, 181, 183, 185, 188, 312
    leader 66, 67, 217
    managers 182, 204, 208, 225, 233, 235, 236, 298
    nurturing 192
    processes 94
    understanding 180, 182–7, 209
performance metrics 143, 209
Perry, Ruth 40, 76
personality 186–7
*Personality: A User's Guide* 187
Pincher, Chris 39
Pink, Daniel 171, 172, 259
positioning experimentation 193
potential 142–4, 179, 180, 182–7, 203
*Power of Regret, The* 259
predictive analytics 202
presenteeism 17, 55, 89, 156
problem-solving 13, 20
productivity 9, 27, 117, 148, 158, 180, 184, 236, 271, 299
'productivity paradox' 55
profit over purpose 72–4, 76
profitability 152, 158
psychological contract 64, 103, 112, 223
psychological ownership 245–7, 300
psychological safety 59, 75, 79, 105, 112, 118, 125, 157, 169–70, 204
psychometrics 159, 185, 234

psychopaths 41–9
psychopathy 42, 45, 46
public services 36–41, 75
purpose 95, 100, 101, 157–8, 167, 171–2, 226, 260, 277, 284
purposeful work 19, 100, 267

Raab, Dominic 39
racism 40
Rainforest Alliance 166
Razzetti, Gustavo 246
redundancy 114, 115, 130
regular reviews 172–3
regulating behaviour 15
relationship management 251, 256–9
relevance 11, 114, 173, 178, 276
remote working 9, 16, 25, 55, 59, 72
reporting 46, 160, 180, 211
resources 9, 15, 148, 153, 211, 315–116
retention 12, 18, 59, 156, 234, 246, 278
reverse-mentoring 195
reward 93, 95, 125, 141–2, 234, 236
rewiring the organisation's mind 182, 203–4
Rider, Liz 278
*Right Kind of Wrong* 190
Rite Aid 169, 170
rituals and traditions 91–2

Sackett, Professor Paul 185
Saratxaga, Koldo 212, 213
search for meaning, the 17–25
self-awareness 186, 247, 251, 252, 261, 280, 281, 287
self-importance 43
self-management 251, 252–4
sense of belonging 19, 21, 84, 85, 91, 121, 133, 226
sense of humanity 14–16
sense of identity 105
sense of purpose 17, 172, 252
shared vision 128
sharing feelings 103, 104
Shopify 127, 135
silence 59–61, 75, 76, 77, 78, 79, 80, 124
Sinek, Simon 74, 172, 295

skills 102–3, 178, 183
   assessments 159
   communication 293
   development 186, 212, 220, 236, 281
   framework 94
   gap 23, 79, 313
   human 24, 183, 208, 234
   management 233–4
   model 203
   new 74, 114, 131, 159, 176, 179, 183,
      203, 310
   people 79, 102
   sets 41
   shortage 178
   social 79
   storytelling 24, 280
   teamwork 258
smart technology 5, 118
*Snakes in Suits: When Psychopaths Go
  to Work* 42
social
   awareness 79, 251, 254–6
   belonging 115
   connections 20, 87, 91, 97–8, 115–16,
      119–21, 125, 140, 263–4, 266
   conscience 163
   expectations 56
   groups 88, 91, 313
   identity theory 124
   impact 100, 162
   media 28, 114, 176
   relationships 21, 226
   skills 79
speaking out 60, 105
Spotify 200–201
stakeholders 24, 125, 168, 206, 210, 224,
   228, 244, 294
Standard Chartered Bank 183–4
storytelling 24, 48, 183, 201, 263, 301
strengths and development areas 260–61
success 119–21, 134, 152–4
   business 80, 234, 295
   company 72, 117, 144, 154, 158, 212
   financial 152, 169
   measures 72, 155–9, 161, 172, 173, 217,
      275, 298, 316
*Succession* 44

support networks 16
sustainability 11, 74, 101, 166–7, 193, 232,
   276
sustainable 19, 73, 97, 104, 155, 270, 275,
   303
   Adidas 101
   culture 92
   growth 132, 156, 201
   living 100
   opportunities 276
   organisations 155, 224
   quality 166
Swissair 69
Syed, Matthew 248–9

talent
   crisis 177
   initiatives 182
   internal 159
   management 131, 183, 192
   market 150, 184, 188, 199, 203, 212
   pools 176, 178, 182
   retention 18
   scarcity 296
   sharing 4, 95
   systems 180
teams
   contribution 258
   diverse 4, 22, 62, 70, 95, 117, 218,
      224
   empowered 70, 113, 128–32
   healthy 118
   inclusive 22, 95
   leadership 36, 39, 61, 108, 200
   management 136
   managing 224
   motivated 73, 138
   supportive 100
   trusted 128
technical competence 245
technology 234–5
*Ted Lasso* 122–3
Timpson 296, 298
'toggle in' 241–2
Tony's Chocolonely 167
Top Employers Institute 278
toxic culture 27–41, 52, 78, 81, 93

transformational potential 159
Trump, Donald 36, 37, 39, 47
trust 55–7, 75–6, 81, 90, 129–32, 241, 278,
     310–11
   battery 127, 135, 137
   building/ building on 217, 221, 232,
     298
   networks 207, 215
   triangle 217
Twitter 28, 37, 96, 267
two-way interactions 90, 91

Uber 28, 35, 96, 289
*Undercover Boss* 96
unhappiness 12
Unilever 100
user interface (UI) 24

values 11, 34, 41, 51, 96–7, 252, 260,
     273–4, 299, 309
virtual
   call 15, 220, 263
   communication 13
   environments 15
   meetings 13, 14, 90
   reality (VR) 10, 22, 176
VR (virtual reality) 10, 22, 176

Waterstones 69, 70
'we' generation 29, 31, 32
weakness 54, 248
well-being 5, 11, 16, 18, 56, 73, 126, 150,
     193, 247
West Duffy, Molly 257
WeWork 29–32, 47, 75, 92
'when you're ready' approach 137
whistle-blowing/whistle-blower 34, 75,
     106, 108, 11, 295
Whitman, Walt 123
wicked environments 136
Wild, Mark 94, 95
Wiseman, Liz 219
Wiseman, Theresa 255
*Wolf of Wall Street, The* 32–3, 75
Wootton, Dan 61
working hours 54, 55, 56, 98, 130
work–life balance 23, 78, 87

workplace
   culture 78, 179, 246
   horrible 1–144
   human 86, 113, 147, 149, 163, 207, 269,
     307–8, 312
   warfare 27–49, 75–6
world of work 8, 263
   new 20, 155–9, 172, 298
   today 9–11

Zimbardo, Philip 105